Woodland Potters and Archaeological Ceramics of the North Carolina Coast

A Dan Josselyn Memorial Publication

Woodland Potters and Archaeological Ceramics of the North Carolina Coast

Joseph M. Herbert

The University of Alabama Press
Tuscaloosa

The University of Alabama Press
Tuscaloosa, Alabama 35487-0380

Manufactured in the United States of America

Typeface: Garamond

∞

The paper on which this book is printed meets the minimum requirements of American National Standard for Information Sciences-Permanence of Paper for Printed Library Materials, ANSI Z39.48-1984.

Library of Congress Cataloging-in-Publication Data

Herbert, Joseph Miner.
Woodland potters and archaeological ceramics of the North Carolina coast / Joseph M. Herbert.
p. cm.
Includes bibliographical references and index.
ISBN 978-0-8173-1638-9 (cloth : alk. paper) — ISBN 978-0-8173-5517-3 (paper : alk. paper) — ISBN 978-0-8173-8119-6 (electronic) 1. Woodland culture—North Carolina—Atlantic Coast. 2. Indian pottery—North Carolina—Atlantic Coast. 3. Pottery craft—North Carolina—Atlantic Coast—History. 4. Indians of North America—North Carolina—Atlantic Coast—Antiquities. 5. Excavations (Archaeology)—North Carolina—Atlantic Coast. 6. Social archaeology—North Carolina—Atlantic Coast. 7. Atlantic Coast (N.C.)—Antiquities. 8. North Carolina—Antiquities. I. Title.
E99.W84H47 2010
975.6'01—dc22

2009017654

Contents

Illustrations

Figures

Tables

Preface

This volume is an archaeological study of the ceramics of the Woodland cultures of the North Carolina coast and their relation to those of the greater Atlantic Coastal Plain. It is also an exploration of broader topics, for instance, how pottery traits reflect the evolution of technology and how pottery styles relate to ancient social networks and boundaries between ethnic groups.

The Woodland era, which begins about 2000 B.C., is set apart from the preceding span of Archaic history by several important cultural and technological achievements. People began to reside in settlements for longer periods of time wherein their attention to useful plants led them not only to harvest but also to selectively encourage and eventually domesticate some species. In this period too the remarkable technological practice of making cooking vessels of fired clay was developed. The nature and sequence of these achievements are known to us only remotely through archaeologically recoverable material remains, including those related to the practice of pottery making.

The following chapters explore the evidence for geographic differences and temporal trends in pottery traits that reflect technological practices arising from practical understandings of how to build and fire pots as well as cultural preferences for certain styles. Pottery is the focus not only because it is ubiquitously preserved on archaeological sites from this period but also because of its unique way of encoding an intimate record of the performance art of the potter, her concept of functional effectiveness, social appropriateness, and personal achievement.

The task at hand, therefore, is an exposition of the variation in the prehistoric potters' art across space and time and an exploration of how these variations reflect the social contexts in which the potters lived and worked. Many of the bridging arguments that allow us to move from the potsherds on our laboratory tables to the thoughts, behaviors, and social lives of ancient potters require explanation. At the outset I should say that the best evidence suggests that pottery making among Native people at this time was largely gender specific, essentially a woman's art, and that the time-space variation of its archaeological reflection represents differences in the information shared by women whose pots varied in accordance with the communities in which they learned and practiced their craft. Although we know this to be true from a variety of ethnohistoric accounts and ethnographic data, it is wise to allow some leeway in this interpretation, as it is also evident that women's social roles were sometimes adopted by men. Given that the structural properties of Woodland societies entailed gender roles that typically prescribed the rules of heterosexual marriage and coresidency, I follow a long archaeological tradition in assuming ceramic technology to be a reasonable measure of some aspects of social structure and social boundaries. Ethnoarchaeological case studies provide a means of assessing the mechanics of how social structure and gender roles may have affected the transmission of pottery-making techniques and how sociocultural boundaries are reflected in the distribution of ceramic traditions.

Pottery types, defined as specific sets of attributes, have long been established for various periods and areas of the Atlantic coast, but their relationships and meaning have not often been explicitly examined in regional context. Exploring these relationships, this study examines the manner in which pottery traits crosscut taxonomic types, tests the proposition that communities of practice existed at several scales, and questions the fundamental notion that ceramic types accurately serve as ethnic markers. Before such issues can reasonably be explored, however, much background information is needed to document that part of the archaeological record comprising the temporal sequence and spatial distribution of ceramic variation. While this necessary explication of archaeological minutia may be the very substance into which some professionals prefer to sink, other readers may choose to skim these sections.

The archaeological research for this volume, conducted over a period of several years, was supported by many agencies, colleagues, and friends to whom I am deeply grateful. The principal source of support was provided in the form of academic positions and grants. Vin Steponaitis, Director of the Research Laboratories of Archaeology at the University of North Carolina, Chapel Hill, played a central role in developing the direction of the research, and several other colleagues made significant contributions. Jim Feathers, University of Washington Luminescence Laboratory, performed thermoluminescence dating, and Ann Cordell, Florida Museum of Natural History, conducted the petrographic analysis of pottery. Mark Mathis, North Carolina Office of State Archaeology, provided information on many critical issues regarding the archaeology of the coastal region. To these colleagues I offer my warmest thanks for their help and friendship.

Compiling all known radiocarbon dates for the Coastal Plain of North Carolina was accomplished with the help of many colleagues including Randy Daniel, Jane Eastman, Charles Heath, Dan Higginbottom, Mark Mathis, David Phelps, Erica Sanborn, Patti and Scott Shumate, Kay Simpson, and Paul Webb. Ron Hatfield of Beta Analytic assisted in recalibrating the dates processed by his outfit, and Paula Reimer consulted on the process of recalibrating marine samples.

I am grateful to many friends and colleagues who contributed in various ways. Kate McIntyre, Laura Murphy, Chris Rodning, Bram Tucker, and Eileen Green, Alexis Ionnitiu, Trish McGuire, and Melissa Salvanish provided assistance in excavation and analysis of pottery. Wayne Boyko provided support for TL dating of pottery from the Sandhills and access to the Loftfield Collection at the Fort Bragg Cultural Resources Program curation facility. I am also grateful to Bill Haag for donating his collection of excavated and surface-collected assemblages of pottery from coastal sites to the Research Laboratories of Archaeology, UNC-Chapel Hill. It was an honor and a delight to talk with Bill about his work, which in many ways set the standard not only for his time but also for this volume. I am also indebted to Lynn Sullivan, Jim Stoltman, and Henry S. Ward for reading and commenting on the manuscript prepared for this volume.

Funding for luminescence and radiometric dating was provided by a grant awarded by the National Science Foundation. Funding for test excavations and dating was provided by a Survey and Planning Grant from the State of North Carolina, Department of Archives and History, Office of State Archaeology, and by Sigma Xi.

Introduction

This study begins with a brief history of the Woodland era in Chapter 1, which is followed by a consideration of the methodological and theoretical concepts used to bridge the gap between ancient behaviors and modern artifacts (Chapter 2). The methods used in the analysis are presented in Chapter 3, and this is followed by an exposition of the stratified and dated contexts for pottery from several key sites (Chapters 4, 5, and 6). A revised ceramic sequence for eastern North Carolina is offered in Chapter 7, and the geographic patterning of types is explored in Chapter 8. Chapter 9 turns once again to the question of social causes for the archaeological patterns, and a conclusion (Chapter 10) summarizes the major findings.

The practical objectives of this study are to refine the regional ceramic taxonomy, improve the sequencing of types, and assess the geographic distribution of types. This effort is designed to provide a comprehensive model of the prehistoric pottery-making traditions of the Coastal Plain of North Carolina as a foundation for discussions of the social conditions that lay behind the observed archaeological patterns.

The geographic focus of the study is the Coastal Plain of North Carolina, from the Atlantic Ocean to the Piedmont, from South Carolina to Virginia. Three environmental zones are encompassed: (1) the Embayed Section of the coast, including the broad estuaries and tidal rivers that lie behind the Outer Banks from the Neuse River north to Virginia; (2) the Sea Island Section of the coast, encompassing the narrow sounds and tidal rivers lying behind the barrier islands south of the Neuse; and (3) the Sandhills, consisting of the westernmost portion of the southern Coastal Plain comprising a few counties in the south-central part of the state (Figure P.1).

Temporally the study focuses on the period from the inception of pottery making in the Late Archaic until the time of European contact (ca. 2200 B.C.–A.D. 1600). Representation is, of course, dependent on pottery assemblages that cannot be assumed to reflect all regions and periods equally well. Despite unavoidable

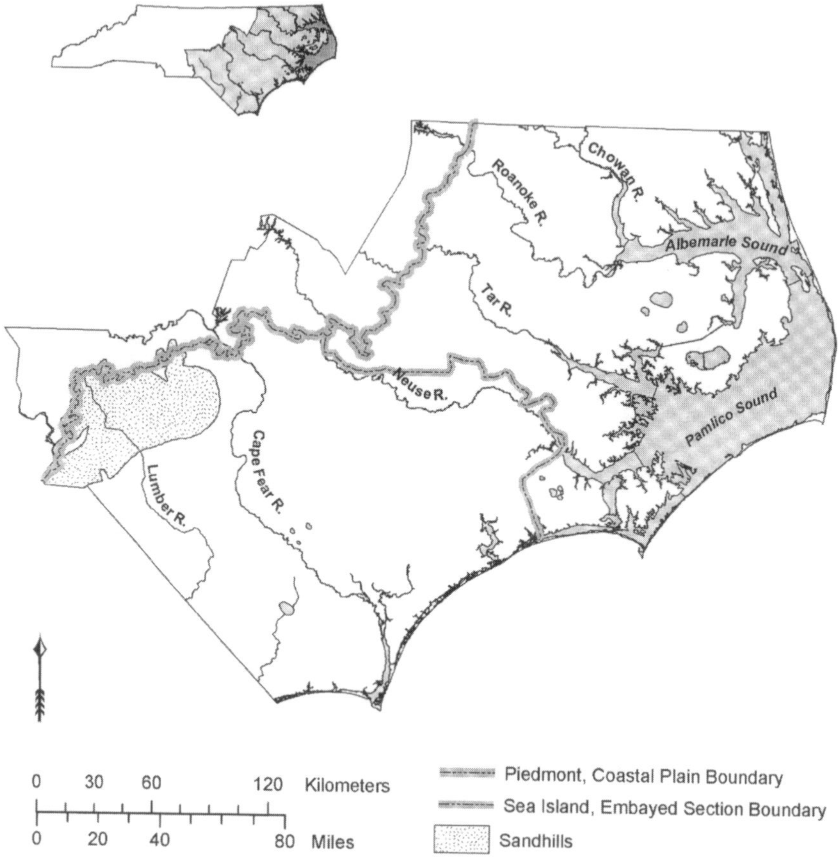

Figure P.1. Physiographic provinces of the study area.

spatial and temporal gaps, broad temporal and geographic patterns are reflected in the sample.

Over the past 50 years, several ceramic typologies have been independently designed for archaeological pottery collections from coastal North Carolina (Crawford 1966; Haag 1958; Loftfield 1976; Phelps 1983; South 1976). Some of these studies began with surface collections from sites in a specific area and generated taxonomic sequences that have come to be applied to a much broader geographic region (e.g., South 1976), while others worked from the excavated assemblages (Loftfield 1976; Phelps 1983). In each case, pottery types from adjacent regions were referenced, and similarity or isomorphism was acknowledged, but new pottery types were defined.

Consequently, when classifying sherds from a given region, the modern ceramic analyst must choose among several potentially applicable taxonomies. In some cases sequences have fallen out of use due to what appears to be purely historical circumstance, while others have persisted for decades despite meager substantiation of the estimates of the chronological placement of types. One of the goals of the present study, therefore, is to evaluate and synthesize various classification systems currently in use in the coastal region of North Carolina, in order to present a single unified scheme.

1

Sketch of the Region's Woodland History

The inception of pottery making that marks the beginning of the Woodland era lies far back in time, perhaps two millennia before the Christian era and more than three millennia before the first Europeans were noting linguistic differences and recording the whereabouts of the coastal Indian tribes. As we move back in time we quickly lose any surety that the cultural geography, as represented by regional similarities in language, remains faithful to those first ethnohistoric sketches. Nevertheless, it is assumed that the geography of precontact Indian cultures is reflected in the archaeological patterns of ceramic technological styles. Tracing the shifting boundaries of these ceramic techno-stylistic regions is one of the principal goals of this study.

For convenience, the Woodland era is divided into Early (2200–400 B.C.), Middle (400 B.C.–A.D. 800), and Late (A.D. 800–1600) periods. In theory, such boundaries are designed to coincide with fundamental shifts in technology and major differences in social and economic traditions. In practice, however, the data with which to measure shifting socioeconomic conditions are often uneven or totally lacking. In such cases, the temporal boundaries of subperiods are often based on differences in a limited suite of material culture traditions including pottery and are, more often than not, imposed as a convenient means of establishing a chronological framework. In many parts of eastern North Carolina, where even the most basic subsistence data are absent, economic model building must rely on inference.

Early Woodland Period (2200–400 B.C.)

The Early Woodland period in eastern North Carolina begins about 2200 B.C. and is distinguished from the preceding Late Archaic principally by the emergence of ceramic technology. Studies on the lower Savannah River and Coastal Plain of South Carolina have shown that the earliest pottery made in the Atlantic coastal region (fiber-tempered Stallings) has been found in contexts dated at least as early as 2500 B.C. (Sassaman 1993:102–110, Figure 11, Appendix). As the earliest Stallings pottery is contemporary with contexts bearing Late Archaic period Savannah River phase materials, many researchers prefer to assign the early portion of the Stallings phase to the Late Archaic period. Finding no advantage in assigning the North Carolina Stallings potters to the Archaic era, I have chosen to stick to the more traditional formula: as pottery emerges, so begins the Woodland era. Regardless of culture–era affiliation, ceramic technology first emerged on the Atlantic coast around 2200 B.C. and evolved into an essential technology over the next 500 years. In the Savannah River valley, perforated soapstone disks or slabs, presumably used in basket or bladder cooking, appeared about 3000 B.C. (Sassaman 1993:185). This was followed in about 300 years by the innovation of ceramic vessel technology, with which it coexisted for many generations. At present it appears that the practice of pottery making spread from the Savannah Valley into the North Carolina Coastal Plain during this same period, by both overland (inland) and maritime (coastal) transportation and trade networks.

Sassaman (1993) contends that the earliest fiber-tempered vessels in the Savannah region were not placed directly on cooking fires but were used as containers for boiling-stone cookery. This may also be true of early pottery from North Carolina, such as the Croaker Landing series (Byrd 1999; Egloff et al. 1988; Pullins et al. 1996). Although the Stallings and Croaker Landing pottery regions are found several hundred miles apart, they appear to reflect very similar technological styles. Vessels were typically thick-walled, slab-built, flat-bottomed containers that were inherently porous, rather soft as a result of low firing temperature, and probably cumbersome—in many ways, a poor substitute to soapstone bowls but eminently more efficient as one did not need to travel to the Piedmont to obtain the raw materials for making clay pots. In just a few centuries, this technological practice led the way to broad-scale experimentation in pottery making. On the southern and central coasts, quartz in a variety of sizes and densities became the standard ingredient in paste. The slab-built, flat-bottomed method of construction was superseded by coil building with the paddle-and-anvil system that produced thin-walled, conical-based pots that were fired at higher temperatures and, thus, represented extremely effective cooking vessels for use directly on the fire.

This second generation of Early Woodland vessels along the North Carolina coast were tempered with a variety of substances including primarily quartz sand (from fine to granule sized) and crushed rock (including quartz, sandstone, granite, and soapstone). Crushed metamorphic stone such as saprolitic granite was sometimes used to temper pottery found on sites in the Sandhills. Ingredients that reflect Piedmont sources suggest the perpetuation of the Late Archaic procurement networks by which soapstone slabs and bowls, along with rhyolite for projectile points and tools, were acquired (Culpepper et al. 1999; Sassaman 1993; Waselkov 1982).

Middle Woodland Period (400 B.C.–A.D. 800)

The greater archaeological visibility of Middle Woodland sites may be due to generally increased population size and dispersion, but it is also the result of more routine use, breakage, and discard of ceramic cooking vessels fired at higher temperatures, whose sherds preserve more readily than Early Woodland pottery. There were several significant changes in ceramic technology that occurred at this time. Fiber tempering was superseded by sand tempering on the South Carolina coast. Limestone tempering appears in the Hamp's Landing series on the southern coast of North Carolina and in the Wando series of northern South Carolina. For the Middle Woodland period in the northern coastal region, Phelps (1983) suggests that the size grade of sand temper used in the New River series (Deep Creek) shifts from coarse to medium, while the proportion of granule- and pebble-sized temper of the Mount Pleasant series increases (cf. results from the Bandon midden in Chapter 4).

Middle Woodland vessel shapes include larger jars with conical bases and straight walls, a transformation that emphasizes the intensified use of ceramic containers as cooking vessels. The carved-paddle stamping technique that emerged in the Refuge and Deptford phases in South Carolina and in the Hamp's Landing and New River series in North Carolina expanded to include wrapped-paddle cord marking and fabric and net impressing in North Carolina. Very few Middle Woodland sand-tempered specimens from the North Carolina Coastal Plain exhibit simple stamping. This stands in distinct contrast to the Early Woodland New River and Hamp's Landing series. Simple stamping occurs in both the Cape Fear and Hanover series in coastal South Carolina (Anderson et al. 1982) but not in North Carolina, where it is found to reappear only in the Late Woodland Townsend (Colington) and Cashie series (Phelps 1981a, 1983).

Late Woodland Period (A.D. 800–1600)

During the first centuries of the Late Woodland period, economic, organizational, and ideological structures in eastern Carolina are marked by increasing sedentism, tribalization, territoriality, and ceremonialism. Sedentary villages evidenced by site size, architectural and storage facilities, and the remains of cultivars such as squash, beans, and corn are particularly evident on the coast and in the tidewater region where abundant marine resources helped to sustain village life. Current evidence suggests significant differences in residential settlement strategies in the various areas of eastern Carolina. In the Sea Island and Sandhills sections of the Coastal Plain sites are small and broadly scattered, suggesting relatively high mobility and dispersed settlement (Culpepper et al. 1999). In the Embayed Section of the coast, larger village sites located along the sounds, estuaries, major rivers, and their tributaries suggest more sedentism and regionalization (Phelps 1983:39).

Three cultural regions have been proposed for coastal North Carolina that conform to ethnohistoric records of linguistic differences: Algonquian speakers resided in the northern and central Embayed Coastal region, Iroquoian speakers occupied the northern interior Coastal Plain, and Siouan speakers inhabited the southern Coastal Plain.

Archaeologically, these culture areas are recognized by regional differences in ceramics (Phelps 1983) and notable differences in burial customs and architectural forms (Loftfield 1990; Loftfield and Jones 1995). Phelps (1983:39) suggests that the southern extent of the Algonquian culture and the corresponding distribution of Colington ceramics were just south of the Neuse River (cf. Loftfield 1976). Loftfield and Jones (1995) have suggested that the distribution of Late Woodland Colington phase cultures may have extended as far south as Onslow County, North Carolina. These authors cite evidence including not only shell-tempered pottery but also mortuary and architectural features, for example, ossuary burials and long houses typical of Algonquian culture found to the north.

This regionalism, expressed in pottery technology, is perhaps best represented by the shell-tempered Townsend series Colington and White Oak types. Clearly bounded in geographic distribution, the makers of the shell-tempered Townsend series, found on the northern coast of North Carolina, constructed vessels with simple-stamped and fabric-impressed surfaces, often fired in a reduced atmosphere. Their southern neighbors made very similar shell-tempered ware with some interesting differences. The White Oak type, restricted to the central coast of North Carolina, does not appear to include a simple-stamped variant but does have a burnished type only rarely seen in Colington.

Archaeological data provide less evidence of Late Woodland adaptations on the southern coast and in the Sandhills. Whereas in the central and northern coastal regions evidence of small villages with several associated house structures has been found, both palisaded and open, nothing on this scale has been found on the southern coast or in the Sandhills. Although communication and social cohesion seem to have existed in these areas, extended-family dwellings appear to have been scattered across the landscape.

2

Explaining Ceramic Patterns

Any exposition of the behavioral and social causes lying behind the spatial and temporal patterning of pottery in a given region requires some explanation, and in this chapter I consider some of the issues involved.

Methodological Issues

Constructing Types and Varieties

The taxonomic classes of pottery used in this study are considered to be definitional referents, that is, products of observation that focus on the modal expression of a set of traits exhibited by specimens in an assemblage, rather than on the variability continuously expressed in the sample. The implication of using defined (static) sets of attributes to model continuous (dynamic) variation is what Dunnell (1995a) has referred to as the materialist paradox. This conceptual problem draws our attention to the critical importance of maintaining the distinction between empirical and theoretical units. Artifact classes do not evolve; classes are counting units that partition variation so that when arrayed chronologically, distinct classes are differentially represented over time (Dunnell 1995a; Jones et al. 1995; Teltser 1995). The usefulness of types for assessing or resolving questions about variation in space and time depends upon the sets of traits of which they are composed.

Traditionally, the process of defining pottery types has arisen from the desire to identify criteria (attribute sets) sufficient to segregate groups of potsherds thought to have culture-historical significance. Logically, the process has moved inductively from the observation of variation to the formation of classes. Reasoning has then worked from hypotheses (often including assumptions about the linkage between regularly patterned data and cultural behavior) to inferences about the empirical data; that is, if culture groups are differentiated in space and time, then so should pottery types be. If the observations of empirical phenomena conform to the implications, then the hypotheses appear to be supported.

Thus, if pottery types are found to cluster in space and time, they are interpreted as evidence of discriminate culture groups. The problem, as Jones et al. (1995:15) point out, is that "although the observations may be *sufficient* to support the hypothesis, they may not be a necessary consequent of *only that causal process* specified in the hypothesis" (emphasis added). In short, several explanations may account for the same observation. The problem of equifinality is similarly encountered in evolutionary narratives. A solution to this problem may be sought by employing multiple working hypotheses or differential scales of measure (Dunnell 1995b) or through actualistic studies (Binford 1989, 1992), both of which seek to evaluate the accuracy of alternative explanations.

The potential deficiency of relying exclusively on a typological approach for exploring ceramic boundaries is that important variation may be overlooked. The definition of a pottery type comprises a temporally variable cluster of attributes including temper, surface treatment, decoration, vessel form, and any attributes reflecting construction and firing methods. Each sort of attribute reflects a different step in the chain of operations performed in making pottery, and each may vary independently with respect to space and time. The imperative for all samples to be sorted into mutually exclusive classes composed of attribute clusters may draw attention away from variation existing within classes that may be important for identifying boundaries or relationships at different scales and for explaining or accounting for the mechanisms that may have caused the observed variation. A partial solution, therefore, is to report ceramic data both at the class and at the attribute level.

If a recurring attribute pattern is found to be chronologically or spatially circumscribed, there is little reason to doubt that a typological classification describing this pattern represents past technological traditions that have a cultural basis. The identification of the temporal and spatial dimensions of such traditions is, in fact, a primary objective of this study. The utility of characterizing assemblages or collections in terms of such types is obvious—it simplifies the denotation of attribute combinations so that their temporal and spatial variation may be more easily observed and it provides a means of exploring the way material culture was patterned by those who used it. This study, therefore, employs both attributes and types, the first designed to improve our understanding of the variation in specific technological practices independent of types, and the second designed to reduce the complexity of pottery-making practices into more easily observed units that are hypothesized to correspond to identifiable patterns of cultural behavior and social structure. Ultimately, the goal is to explain these behaviors and structures.

Dating and Sequencing

Ceramic chronology building typically begins with the sequencing of types based on relative dating techniques. Radiocarbon chronometrics are then used to refine age ranges in more absolute terms. Unfortunately, contextual factors related to the sandy Coastal Plain soil often limit opportunities for obtaining relative dating information or radiocarbon dates. Generally speaking, the soils of North Carolina's southern Coastal Plain are composed of unconsolidated sand, highly permeable and strongly acidic. In the few instances in which non-ossuary burials have been recognized by excavators—primarily in sand mounds—skeletal remains have often been so thoroughly decomposed that only a few fragmentary elements survive removal (Coe et al. 1982; Holmes 1916; Keel 1970; MacCauley 1966; MacCord 1966; Peabody 1910; South 1966; Wetmore 1978). Excessive leaching also promotes decomposition of carbonized plant remains and other organic materials. As a result, the soil staining associated with pits, hearths, post molds, burials, and other features is typically not observable by excavators working in the southern Coastal Plain and Sandhills provinces (e.g., Abbott 1993; Abbott et al. 1999; Cable et al. 1998; Gunn and Wilson 1993; O'Steen 1994). One exception occurs in soils underlying shell middens, where calcium salts neutralize pH levels.

In addition to excessive permeability and acidity, unconsolidated sand is unusually susceptible to bioturbation. It has recently been suggested that bioturbation is the principal geomorphic process responsible for artifact burial and site formation on upland or interfluvial landforms over much of the Coastal Plain (Leigh 1998a, 1998b; Michie 1990). Under such conditions, the boundaries between stratigraphic zones are typically diffuse. Artifacts ranging from the Early Archaic to the Late Woodland period are typically found within a homogeneous E-horizon (a leached transitional zone) undifferentiated by observable stratigraphy. The sequential deposition of artifacts does ensure some vertical sorting, but mixing is common. Features are generally defined on the basis of artifact clustering, not soil staining. Where carbonized plant remains are found together with diagnostic artifacts, their association is often open to question. This is especially true when charcoal for dating is recovered from the flotation of soil samples gathered around artifact clusters, as seen at the Riegelwood site (Abbott et al. 1999; Sanborn and Abbott 1999).

Because of poor preservation of charcoal for ^{14}C dating, this study relies primarily on two procedures for sequencing pottery types: the analysis of the relative stratigraphic position of sherds from excavated context and luminescence dating. Three small exploratory excavations conducted by W. G. Haag in 1955 provide the stratified site samples reanalyzed for this study. While this sample is relatively small, it provides valuable information about the regional sequence.

An equally important sequencing tool used in this study is thermoluminescence (TL) dating. The most important advantage of using TL for dating pottery is that it does not rely on associated organic material but dates the artifact itself (Aitken 1990:3; Feathers 1993:5; Godfrey-Smith et al. 1997:253). In a pilot study designed for this purpose, TL proved to be an effective method for dating sand- or grog-tempered pottery from the southern coastal area of North Carolina, where little opportunity exists for dating by the radiocarbon method (Herbert 1997). Given these encouraging results, an additional 20 TL dates for pottery from the upper Cape Fear River basin and 18 TL dates from the lower Cape Fear River basin were obtained for the current study. The methods used in TL dating are described in Chapter 3, and the results of this TL-dating project are presented in Chapters 6 and 7.

Mapping the Geography of Traditions

Determining geographic distributions and boundaries between different pottery-making practices at various times over approximately 3,600 years of the Woodland period is another major objective of this study. Previous studies have focused on the relationship of certain pottery types and ethnohistorically documented Native American groups occupying specific geographic areas of the coast (Loftfield 1976; Phelps 1983; South 1976). Ethnographic studies, however, provide little evidence that regional pottery-making traditions follow linguistic boundaries. Instead, pottery-making methods that can be recognized as regional styles respond to a very complex suite of environmental, demographic, social, economic, and political conditions that can affect decision making and technical choice. Certainly, the distributions of different pottery types identified in this study suggest numerous factors that may have contributed to their geographic arrangement, and some of these factors are reviewed below.

First, pots are tools and the variation observed in pottery may be explained in functional terms as suites of traits affecting vessel performance (e.g., Braun 1983, 1987; Bronitsky and Hamer 1986; Dunnell and Feathers 1991; Prezzano 1985; Schiffer and Skibo 1987; Steponaitis 1983). In this sense, pottery making as human behavior may be viewed as an adaptive response and, as such, an extension of the human phenotype (O'Brien and Holland 1995a; O'Brien et al. 1994). As an adaptive mechanism that is socially transmitted, pottery making exists within a selective environment composed of environmental and social contexts. This perspective has some interesting implications not only for the interpretation of the meaning of pottery variation but also for the way we conceive of the taxonomic units used to classify pottery.

For example, although surface treatment has been shown to affect the thermal conductivity of a vessel (Schiffer et al. 1994), the range of variation observed in net-impressed, cord-marked, and fabric-impressed vessels composing the majority of this study collection is not likely to result in significantly different thermal properties. Several ethnographic and archaeological studies, however, suggest that the specific structure of perishable materials stamped or impressed on vessel surfaces may reflect social groups (Drooker 1992; Petersen and Hamilton 1984; Maslowski 1984; Minar 2001). Cordage twist direction, for example, has been used as a tool to identify Middle Woodland culture phases on the Florida and Georgia coasts (Minar 2001). Therefore, although surface treatment may affect vessel performance it may also provide a tool for detecting social boundaries. The Late Woodland Iroquoian and Algonquian ceramics of southern New England and eastern New York are an example of technologically distinct wares also reflecting different cultural traditions (Chilton 1996, 1998). This may also be true of Late Woodland pottery from the northern coast of North Carolina thought to be associated with Iroquoian- and Algonquian-speaking groups.

The size, shape, proportion, and nature of tempering material can significantly affect vessel strength and thermal shock resistance (Bishop et al. 1982; Braun 1982, 1983; Bronitsky 1986; Bronitsky and Hamer 1986; Feathers 1989; Neff et al. 1989; Rye 1976, 1981; Steponaitis 1984) and vessel performance in cooking or storage. These same characteristics may also be considered as emblems of style, symbols of cultural affiliation, or vehicles for conveying cultural information. Choices about visual characteristics of artifacts may be intended to convey cultural meaning, personal identity, family or clan membership, or village, regional, or ethnic affiliation. Sackett (1973, 1990) refers to this as iconographic style and it is well documented ethnographically (Wiessner 1983, 1985). Indeed, material culture can be understood as a fundamental mode of human communication, no less important than language (Schiffer 1999). Intentional signaling, however, need not be involved for a pot to convey stylistic information. Pottery-making behaviors that are learned early in life in an apprenticeship and ingrained as habitual motor skills communicate group participation. A potter may reproduce a style simply because the apprenticeship process has instilled certain pottery-making techniques. Because social customs govern the apprenticeship process, similarities in pot-making styles (and hence pots) may parallel social groups. Such an inquiry into how pots were made moves beyond the argument of style and function and focuses on the relations between practice and society to identify technological traditions (Chilton 1998:133).

The sheer number of cultural factors that *could* account for stylistic variation in pottery, however, suggests a very complex relationship between archaeological evidence and their cultural causes. We have little direct information about the social contexts within which pots were designed, manufactured, distributed, and used on local and regional levels. Estimates of population density, postmarital residence rules, market systems, and political complexity must be inferred from archaeological data alone and for these social and cultural features, data are quite scarce for most periods. Even if these conditions were precisely known, ethnographic accounts provide little evidence of an invariable relationship among ceramic styles and tribal or ethnic groupings; rather often, pottery styles appear to co-occur with social groups of greater or lesser scale than that of the tribal or ethnic group (MacEachern 1998:113)

Nevertheless, the ceramic data examined in this study provide the temporal and geographic range necessary to test hypotheses concerning the existence and nature of social boundaries over much of North Carolina's Coastal Plain throughout the Woodland era. All technological styles are a product of social activities, and the broad aspects of social conditions potentially influencing pottery making in the region can be inferred with reasonable confidence. The distribution of site assemblages proposed for study represents both a north–south transect along the coast and an upper–lower Coastal Plain transect on the Cape Fear Basin.

Theoretical Issues

The goal of explaining the social behaviors that account for the temporal and geographic patterning of archaeological pottery is indisputably challenging; the social distance between the student and object of study and the nature of the evidence pose real constraints. To say simply that many theoretical issues are raised with any attempt to discover the social causes of cultural patterns does not do justice to the vastness of the anthropological literature written on the subject or to the variety that exists in conceptual and methodological approaches championed at various points in the history of this and other disciplines. It is imperative, then, to narrow the focus to a few key theoretical issues that are most relevant to the problems at hand. Aspects of evolutionary-selectionist theory, social agency, practice, and learning theory, often characterized as opposing ways of explaining the source of archaeologically observed variation, are employed here as a suite of approaches, each of which explores the nature of variation at a different scale.

I use the term *technology* in the following discussion in its etymological sense, derived from the Greek *techne* or "art" and *logos* or "word," thus defining technology as the study of practical arts encompassing both *knowledge and artistry* or practice (*sensu* Dobres and Robb 2000). From this perspective, *ceramic technology* does not refer exclusively to the functional characteristics of pottery and the host of ways that materials science studies measure the characteristics of ceramic vessel performance, but moreover to the whole package of knowledge and artistry arising in social context. The sherds that make up the study collections are seen as fragments of vessels, themselves the product of complex acts of performance artistry, and I refer to this package of knowledge and artistry in spatiotemporal context as "technological style." My view of the first component of this conjunction, technology, has been briefly defined. The second component, style, requires further consideration.

When ethnographers immersed in the living languages and cultures of existent societies have approached the problem of distinguishing ethnic groups and identifying territorial boundaries, the sheer complexity of the cultural systems seems often to have overwhelmed their best efforts to render dynamic processes into static entities (Leach 1954). The obviousness of these circumstances and other factors long ago led social anthropologists to move away from the idea that ethnic groups could be identified by a set of cultural traits (Barth 1969). Overwhelming evidence indicates that ethnic homogeneity may be maintained over a broad area despite a diversity of behavioral styles and forms of social organization and, similarly, ceramic technological styles often transcend ethnic boundaries (MacEachern 1998). So, it is important to understand at the outset of this discussion that the ceramic styles, periods, and areas under examination are not assumed a priori to represent bounded ethnic or social groups. At the same time it certainly is true that archaeologically observable temporal and spatial patterns in material culture are the expression of technological styles that are social and historical in nature.

In the middle of the twentieth century archaeologists underwent a philosophical transformation mirroring to some degree that of ethnography. In some ways the temptation to render dynamic cultural processes into static patterns is even more alluring for archaeologists than for ethnographers—the objects of study are, after all, objects, no longer associated with the dynamic cultural systems that created them. It is easy enough to conceptualize pottery of a distinctive style defined as representing a cultural tradition, period, and social group. Processualist theory reacted critically to the assumption that the goal of archaeology was to move conceptually from the creation of artifact classes to the idea of ethnically distinct groups behind those classes. Moreover, according to the "new" view of the middle twentieth century such conceptual connections explained little about the dynamic processes responsible for the observed archaeological patterns. Postprocessualist theorists in turn fashioned their approach on a foundation critical of the objective posture assumed by processualist archaeologists whose goal, for a short while at least, was the discovery of universal functional relationships between culture as an adaptive mechanism and the environment, to the exclusion of human intent. From our present vantage point we are fortunately able to avail ourselves of the strengths of both processual and postprocessual approaches.

Adopting an Evolutionary Perspective

The archaeological record is composed of empirical variants that are observed to persist at different frequencies through time. Sociocultural mechanisms exist for transmitting and preserving variation among and between generations. Prevailing conditions, both environmental and social, favor particular variants. Accordingly, it follows that "the differential persistence of cultural traits—behaviors, artifacts, or technologies—is significantly influenced by natural selection" (Jones et al. 1995:14). Although evolutionary explanations are historical narratives, they do more than sequentially order events; they require conscious model building (Jones et al. 1995; Leonard and Jones 1987). The purpose of evolutionary narrative in archaeological context is to explain variation that survives at such frequency and for sufficient time as to be archaeologically evident, and an evolutionary perspective is adopted to explain the patterns that emerge from the analyses presented in the chapters that follow.

An evolutionary approach is particularly well suited to archaeological studies for several reasons. Archaeological projects such as the present one consist of a phenetic taxonomy (a system in which phenotypic variation is classified without initial regard to phylogenetic relationships) and the exploration of spatial and temporal relationships among pottery types or traditions (phenotypic variants) that have the potential to illustrate homologous relationships (traditions related through cultural continuity). In an evolutionary account of the pattern of events, consideration is first given to how the substantive archaeological record expresses variation relevant to the causal processes believed to be significant in this case. The task then turns to showing the histories of the classes, or building an evolutionary phylogeny. Thus, the explication of the relatedness of types depends on the antecedent processes of classification and measurement, which therefore cannot include relatedness as part of the definition of classes (Jones et al. 1995).

The data used in this study represent a broad geographic region over which relatively uniform environmental conditions are expected to have prevailed over the approximately 3,750-year period in question. Broad-scale climatic changes may have affected the entire region, but faunal and botanical responses are not expected to have differed widely between each of the three coastal areas of North Carolina. An ample temporal span is represented by the data: cultural materials represent Early Woodland (2200–400 B.C.), Middle Woodland (400 B.C.–A.D. 800), and Late Woodland (A.D. 800–1600) periods. The comparative data sample comprises all of the artifacts exposed on the surface at the time the collections were made.

Operationalizing Function and Style

Dunnell (1978, 1995b) has proposed a fundamental dichotomy between stylistic and functional realms and this has figured prominently in the development of evolutionary theory in archaeology, and since these concepts are used here, consideration of Dunnell's arguments is useful. If stylistic and functional variation may be independently identified in the archaeological record, then these realms of variation may provide the basis for testing hypotheses at different scales and generating alternative explanations. Before determining how style and function might be operationalized with the proposed data, the strengths and weaknesses of this aspect of the theory are considered.

The notion that pottery traditions are simply the result of cultural choice among optional ways of doing things (Sackett 1977, 1982, 1985a, 1990:33) or just a "way of doing" (Hodder 1990:45) has been stridently opposed as having no explanatory value (Binford 1989). Pottery-making traditions, it has been argued, consist of information about the production and use of pots as tools (Braun 1983, 1987). From this perspective, if tool making is a mode of human adaptation, then the remains of tool-making activities are the physical evidence of the evolution of human adaptive behavior (Lipo et al. 1997; Neff 1992, 1993; Neiman 1995). The potential for variation in pottery traditions arises continuously as a result of differential opportunities for learning or implementing what is known (Neiman 1995), or as innovation— creating new techniques designed to improve performance (Rye 1976:118–119; Steponaitis 1984:112–114).

Much of the recent literature addressing the application of evolutionary theory in archaeological explanations suggests a direct relationship between artifact usage and the selection of cultural activities (Dunnell 1980, 1989, 1995a; Jones et al. 1995; Lipo et al. 1997; Neff 1992; Neiman 1995; O'Brien and Fox 1994; O'Brien and Holland 1990, 1992, 1995b; Teltser 1995). From this perspective, pottery-making traits that affect the operation of the vessel as a cooking or storage container (functional traits) tend to be perpetuated by virtue of their effectiveness in the specific context of the ecological and social niches in which they are employed. Ineffective techniques tend not to be perpetuated. The process by which traits not affecting vessel operation (stylistic or neutral traits) arise and are perpetuated can be thought of as sampling error (drift) in cultural transmission controlled by population size and the rate of introduction of new information (Dunnell 1978, 1989, 1995a; Neiman 1995).

Often, however, traits that at the prima facie level might be considered selectively neutral function as symbols that convey specific social meaning (Conkey 1978; Conkey and Hastorf 1990; DeBoer 1991; DeBoer and Moore 1982; Hodder 1982; Larick 1985; Sackett 1977, 1985a, 1985b; Sinopoli 1991; Wiessner 1983, 1984; Wobst 1977). If by virtue of this actively symbolic role such traits affect the adaptedness of the bearers, they must be considered selectively active. For example, if some feature of stylistic ornamentation signals inclusion in a group in which membership serves to reduce individual risk, then that trait, or more precisely the psychological and social impetus for signaling group identity through ornamentation, would be subject to selection. It is also true that variation in traits affecting vessel performance (e.g., shape, wall thickness, temper type) may not affect performance to such a degree that they are subject to selection. For example, within the class of conical-based vessels a range of variation in specific base shape is exhibited. While this represents variation within a performance-related class, it may not be sufficient variation to affect vessel performance as measured by cooking effectiveness. In this case, the variation observed in a performance-related trait would be neutral.

It must be concluded that any one trait may be selectively active and "functional" at one scale and selectively neutral or "stylistic" at another scale. Thus, while a pottery trait such as vessel form may indeed be explained as an expression of ethnically focused aesthetic choice or as the result of problem-solving behavior designed to affect a certain functional outcome, at the scale at which the trait is generated it may be interpreted as either selectively neutral or active. The degree and manner in which a trait is replicated at a transgenerational scale and observed archaeologically, it is argued, are affected by selective pressure that is detectable through modeling.

Accordingly, it follows that a taxonomic system composed of functional traits should not be expected to vary in the same manner as a system composed exclusively of stylistic traits. Functional traits should vary in a manner marked by relationships of similarity in form that affect performance. Search for an accurate explanation requires an account of the history of the system in which the artifacts were made, used, and deposited. Such an explanation seeks to examine the evolution of traditions of pottery making and use.

Before embarking on an examination of ceramic patterns armed only with the interpretive framework of selectionist theory as portrayed above, it is important to consider the limitations of that approach represented in the growing body of theory focused on an examination of the sociocultural processes that might have shaped ceramic technological styles. Typically, a selectionist account is not concerned with social agency, intentionality, modes of learning, practice, and ritual; viewed as modes of variation, these social factors are simply off the radar screen. The *source* of the variation, however, is of central importance in an explanatory narrative.

Integrating Learning and Practice

If the meaning of technological style is that it constitutes symbolic expression, then it stands to reason that the language or grammar of the symbolism and the context in which it is learned and practiced is critical to understanding how it influences the technology. For example, Wiessner (1984:191–192, 1989:56) proposes that the fundamental human cognitive process of social identification by comparison underlies the behavioral basis of style in material culture. This approach utilizes theory developed in the field of social psychology asserting that the negotiation of personal and social identity and the formation of self-image occur through a comparative process whereby individuals evaluate their own characteristics and abilities against those of others. Reciprocally, this process serves to form a collective image or ethnicity.

The influence of this psychological process might be expected to be very compelling in prehistoric settings in which group size was small and anonymity impossible. It is very likely that the women who made the vessels examined in this study made their pots in a community in which they and the products of their crafts were intimately known by most members of the community. In this heightened state of awareness there is little doubt that pottery making was learned and practiced in a highly charged environment of interpersonal comparison. Wiessner (1984:193) asserts that with few exceptions stylistic similarity is "stipulated culturally." This stipulation is described as personal choices "made according to existing cultural structures" and the restrictive or constraining effect of feelings of insecurity that arise from the perception that one's expression is different from others'. The fact that cultural stipulation or prescription constrains the process of personal choice implies that changes in personal choice will arise only with changes in existing cultural structures and perceived insecurities.

Stylistic variation and developmental change are the principal subjects of interest in most studies employing social agency theories. Focused as it is on change, this approach is most effective if the subject of study is artifacts made by members of a social group in which advantages accrue to those who differentiate themselves. But what about societies in which long-term stylistic and technological stability appears to have been obtained? By and large, the ceramic technological styles that are the subject of the present study were practiced with very little change (perceptible at the level obtained with the current data) for several hundred years, over areas encompassing major portions of several states. In such a case, should we expect the members of a social group with a uniform pottery-making style to have exhibited malformed or underdeveloped self-images?

Insights may also be sought in the theory of situated learning that focuses on the attainment of group membership and hence social identity as a function of participatory practice (Sassaman and Rudolphi 2001). The theory of situated learning, which resonates with practice theory in anthropology, proposes that learning is a process of participation in communities of practice—participation that is at first peripheral but that increases gradually in engagement and complexity (Lave and Wenger 1991:49–50). Similar to sociopsychological theories of the development of self-image through comparison, situated-learning theory asserts that the process of learning, consisting of group participation, evolves through one's lifetime as the roles of participation change. The difference between the two approaches appears to focus on the issue of individual motivation. In the "self-evaluative" approach the motivation for conformity is personal feelings of insecurity that arise when participants become aware that their practices depart from the norm (the expected behavior or outcome of practice). The personal insecurity felt by deviating participants is presumably enough to stimulate corrective measures without external coercive pressures. In the situated-learning approach, conformity is assumed as part of the learning process; one learns by participating and by participating conforms. In other words, learning is conforming through participation.

Sassaman and Rudolphi (2001) contend that there is no necessary connection between the community of practice and the content of that practice. As with the selfish gene, they reason that the function of a community is to reproduce itself, not specific practices. Sassaman and Rudolphi (2001:408) conclude that the histories of the technological styles of artifacts bear no necessary relationship to the histories of the social identities of the artisans, "rendering untenable the isomorphism that underlies archaeological time-space systematics."

In addition, Pfaffenberger (1992:498) reminds us that "those who seek to develop new technologies must concern themselves not only with techniques and artifacts; they must also engineer the social, economic, legal, scientific and political context of the technology." Often silent in practice and almost always silent in the archaeological record, ritual represents one of the most effective mechanisms for the coordination of labor under conditions of stateless or local autonomy.

The use of social artifacts is therefore a process of nonverbal communication. In this process, each new act of ritual framing is a statement in an ongoing dialogue of ritual statements and counterstatements that help to constitute social relations as a polity. Pfaffenberger calls this polity-building process a "technological drama."

Modeling Traditions

Among many potential explanations for ceramic variation it is useful to attempt to identify some factors influencing pottery technology as an adaptive response. Following this line of reasoning, this discussion examines some constraining factors arising from environmental, technological, and social sources.

Environmental Constraints

Potters must have access to suitable clay and temper sources. It is often assumed, by archaeologists at least, that the distribution of clay adequate for making pottery is essentially ubiquitous across the landscape. Although clay resources may be available throughout the Coastal Plain, their distribution is not continuous, and the pottery-making characteristics of specific clay resources certainly vary. Variation includes the characteristics of workability, drying, and firing performance. Although this study does not delve into the problem of identifying locations of usable clay deposits, recent research in the region strongly suggests that sources in some regions may have been much more restricted than initially assumed (Herbert et al. 2005; McReynolds and Herbert 2004).

Another important restriction of access to clay resources is intertribal competition for subsistence resource areas. If discontinuous subsistence resource distribution and attendant risk factors resulted in intertribal competition, resource restriction could also extend to the clay located in those areas.

The size of geographic regions of pottery-making information (areas with similar technological styles) may be related to regional population change. Larger ceramic areas may reflect a greater degree of social group integration or information exchange. Smaller ceramic areas may be related to an increased awareness of territorial boundaries. The fixity or definiteness of ceramic-area boundaries might be expected to become more evident as population increase raises demands on the local environment, thereby increasing the likelihood of competition between neighboring groups (Boyd and Richerson 1985; Cashdan 1992). The reduction in settlement mobility that accompanied the transition from foraging to farming in the Late Woodland period should also be reflected in a reduction in size of ceramic area and an increase in boundary definition (or resolution) of ceramic areas, but not necessarily for reasons of regional competition for scarce resources (Braun and Plog 1982). Long-term trends in regional social integration and the degree of technological information exchange may be related to the risks associated with an increased reliance on food production in the context of sedentism. Such trends are documented in the Illinois Valley (Braun 1983) and in the southwestern United States (Braun and Plog 1982) and are expected throughout the Southeast.

Braun and Plog (1982) articulate an evolutionary interpretation of patterns of social integration measured as the diversity of ceramic decoration on pots from Middle and Late Woodland sites in Illinois. Former theories interpreted homogeneity of artifact styles within smaller, well-defined regions, occurring primarily after A.D. 500, as evidence of increasing regional autonomy of social groups that evolved as a defensive response to increasing population density and competition for scarce resources. Braun and Plog explain the same pattern as evidence for an increase in the integration and formalization of regional social systems that were implemented as a means of avoiding the local risk associated with increasing dependency on food production in an unpredictable environment. Neiman's (1995:27) simulation model of the interassemblage distance, measured as the diversity of pottery decoration, indicates that the data tend to support the earlier population-competition hypothesis proposing intergroup transmission being at low levels, rising to a maximum during the Middle Woodland, and declining to new lows in the Late Woodland. The Hopewell climax corresponds with the highest level of movement within the region, and the Late Woodland is marked by social isolation among potters in different demes (Neiman 1995:28).

In portions of the current study area, ceramic data indicate that by Middle Woodland times, techno-stylistic areas assumed spatial extents that appear to coincide to some degree with environmental zones. South (1960) notes the presence of a ceramic area boundary along the coast that coincides with the boundary between the Sea Island (south of the Neuse) and Embayed (north of the Neuse) sections. Egloff (1985) has noted similar patterns in eastern Virginia. By Middle Woodland times culture areas corresponding to physiographic zones had become established between interior and estuarine Coastal Plain provinces when the Mockley series became ubiquitous in the Chesapeake region north of the James River. For the Late Woodland period, Egloff (1985) notes that the Cashie and Prince George series appear to be restricted to the interior Coastal Plain and Townsend to the estuarine Coastal Plain. Similar patterns have been recognized on the coast of North Carolina (Phelps 1983) for the Late Woodland period.

There is certainly ample evidence to distinguish at least three broad biogeographic zones in the study area (the interior or upper Coastal Plain, Sea Island, and Embayed sections) based on biomass richness, species diversity, and a host of specific environmental variables. There is also evidence that these factors affected the particular forms of human ecological adaptations and ultimately demographics. It would seem to follow that ceramic technological styles would also differ among these regions, but in fact the current data are inconclusive in this regard. The geographical positions of the triad of linguistically distinct historic Native American groups on the North Carolina coast—Siouan speakers south of the Neuse in both the Sea Island and interior sections, Algonquian speakers in the Embayed section, and Iroquoian speakers in the interior Coastal Plain north of the Neuse—appear to be the result of social or historical factors rather than ecological ones. The expectation has long been that Late Woodland period ceramic-area boundaries will be found to coincide with these ethnohistorically defined culture areas (Phelps 1983). Although the data sampled in this study are insufficient to test this model where it concerns the interior Coastal Plain on the northern coast, results thus far do support the hypothesis differentiating Late Woodland cultures of the Embayed section (the makers of Townsend series pottery) from those found in the Sea Island and interior sections of the southern coast. So, it seems that the argument for ceramic techno-stylistic boundaries coinciding with environmental boundaries is mixed, and not especially convincing.

Technological Parameters

A basic tenet assumed here is that pots functioned prehistorically as containers with specific purposes. Whereas textile bags and baskets served to store and transport items, pots were designed to function as cooking vessels, short-term storage containers (especially for liquid), and serving vessels. Cooking pots were clearly not a necessity for food processing during most of prehistory. Meat could be dried, smoked, broiled, or baked in the quarry's skin, and baskets were used for indirect (boiling-stone) cooking. Nuts, acorns, and roots could be parched in coals or steamed over stone hearths. It might be inferred from the dramatic increase in the frequency of cooking vessels that direct-heat cooking (with the pot on the fire) became much more important in coastal North Carolina sometime in the Early Woodland period (probably around 1500 B.C.) and especially in the Middle Woodland (400 B.C.–A.D. 800). On the contrary, Middle Woodland data are not characterized by a dramatic shift to greater reliance on plant foods requiring long periods of boiling, although the paleoethnobotanical record for the Middle Woodland in North Carolina is very limited. Judging from elsewhere in the United States, the rate of increase in the use of domesticates seems to be gradual, evolving at different rates according to environmental and social conditions, alongside traditional strategies for foraging wild plant foods (Fritz 1993; Yarnell 1993). The increased occurrence of coil-built, conical-based, straight-walled cooking pots that began in the Early and Middle Woodland with the Thom's Creek and Refuge traditions coincides with the period of very gradual intensification in the use of starchy seeds that eventually (post–A.D. 800) led to the cultivation of domesticates including corn (Yarnell 1993; Yarnell and Black 1985). Ethnohistoric accounts affirm the ubiquity of boiled meat-and-vegetable stews at the aboriginal hearth and it is reasonable to assume that this was the case over the entire coastal region throughout the late Late Woodland period (ca. A.D. 1100–1500). Although it may be assumed that the importance of clay cooking pots is temporally correlated to the intensification of plant-food production, this correlation alone is inadequate to explain the appearance of the various tempering and surface treatment traditions.

Varying rates of residential mobility may also have influenced the types of pots found in the archaeological record. The pottery technology of highly mobile band-level foraging groups might be expected to differ from that of village agriculturalists. Although there is little archaeological evidence at present to support the notion of intensive corn agriculture on the coast, a mixed economy of marine-resource utilization and plant-food production is well documented in European accounts of the coastal villages. Such shifts in residential mobility may have influenced the size, shape, and weight of pottery vessels (Schiffer and Skibo 1987; Skibo et al. 1989), as well as influencing the stochastic aspects of information transmission (Neiman 1995) and patterns of breakage and discard (Deal and Hagstrum 1995; DeBoer and Lathrap 1979; Longacre 1985).

Social Practices

Braun (1995:125) has defined social practices as "any cultural practices that specifically affect the flow of information and materials among people, the extent of peoples' cooperation or competition, the ways in which decision making takes place within groups, or the persistence of groups themselves." An almost endless variety of cultural practices might be identified as potentially influencing information flow and the development and persistence of particular pottery-making practices. For simplification, this model focuses on three classes of social practice specifically affecting pottery making: sex roles, kinship, and intergroup relations.

Although it is possible that men occasionally made pots, ethnogaphic data suggest that pottery was most often made at the household level by women (Skibo and Schiffer 1995). It is reasonable, then, to infer that the pottery that is the subject of this study was made by women to be used at the household level. This is not to suggest that the trade of pots did not take place or that pots were not sometimes made specifically for trade, but rather that the most common type of vessel represented in the assemblages examined in this study was the utilitarian cooking and storage vessel. Crafting pottery was very likely a lifelong task the learning of which began in childhood as imitation of the activities of the adult women in the community.

Dietler and Herbich (1994) make the very important point that variation in the social context of pottery production may be quite different from variation in the social context of consumption. Sassaman and Rudolphi (2001) focus on potential sources of variation in the social context of production, pointing out how variation in kinship systems and marriage rules might affect the system in which pottery making is learned.

Minimally, the production sequence included selection and preparation of the materials (including the clay body and tempering agents), forming the vessel, drying, and firing (Rye 1981). While the ceramic medium allows some variability, there are tolerance limits within each of these steps that, if violated, may result in vessel failure. By Middle Woodland times (ca. 200 B.C.), and perhaps much earlier, the process of building effective cooking pots was firmly established in the repertoire of skills routinely practiced by women inhabiting coastal communities in Carolina. From ethnographic and archaeological data we can infer that, in addition to child rearing, a woman's repertoire of skills probably included basket and textile making (without benefit of drop-spindle or loom), hide preparation, foraging and food preparation, cultivation of food plants, pottery making, and the preparation of all the tools necessary to these crafts—essentially all the skills necessary for subsistence. As the knowledge necessary for success in these crafts was paramount to the knowledge necessary to survive, significant deviation from a successful tradition would likely have incurred risks. The same mimetic learning process that assured a certain consistency in replication of techniques that produced effective cooking pots (reducing risk), therefore, also resulted in the faithful replication of traits we recognize as "stylistic" traditions.

Assuming that women were the ceramic artisans of prehistoric communities, kinship systems may have structured the parameters of the transmission of pottery-making traditions and trade or exchange of pottery vessels by gifting. If groups reckoned descent matrilineally and practiced matrilocal residence, as in fact ethnohistoric data suggest, we might expect a certain amount of conformity between regions of ceramic similarity and kin systems.

Additional permutations are presented in consideration of intergroup or intercommunity relations. It is not uncommon among ethnographic hunter-gatherers, for instance, for fictive kinship or special friendship status to be conferred on members of unrelated groups. Membership composition in such foraging bands can be quite fluid. Generally, strict incest taboos promote exogamy. Disagreements within communities often result in group fissioning. Intertribal or intergroup disputes or warfare may result in the delineation of territorial boundaries. Any of these and many other social practices may have influenced the manner in which information regarding pottery making was transmitted.

Developing Explanations

From the foregoing review of factors potentially influencing pottery traditions, it can be concluded that some method is needed to simplify the model. The data provide one means of simplification, as the classification of pottery series and types is based largely on variation in two classificatory dimensions, temper and surface treatment. The specific temporal and spatial patterns observed in these two dimensions may be interpreted with respect to environmental, technological, and social influences.

Temper

Most Woodland period pottery series from coastal North Carolina have for many decades been defined primarily by differing types and proportions of aplastic additive or temper. Using this taxonomic approach, pottery classes are distinguished by traits that may reflect significant differences in methods of construction, vessel performance, or simply cultural preference of materials. The proposition that pottery classes defined by sets of functional traits may also be used to identify ethnic groups or community boundaries requires careful consideration. Change in functional characteristics may reflect evolving technology not related to ethnic or cultural identity. The differential transmission of functional traits may be subject to selective pressures as well as stochastic factors. Features of the selective environment, such as conditions that impinge on vessel construction and performance, may affect the information passed from one potter to another. Consequently, functional change does not necessarily signal change in ethnic identity.

Each of the triad of influences—environmental, technological, or social—might be expected to result in different distributions of pottery series or temper types in space and time. In general, aspects of pottery making related to environmental resources, such as clay qualities, are known to vary geographically within the study area as a function of the distribution of different clay types. Features of pottery technology that affect vessel performance such as those related to the intensification of plant-food production and requisite cooking requirements might be expected to characterize certain periods over the entire study area. If the characteristics of ceramic technology are influenced primarily by social practices they might be expected to vary independently from clay or temper resource areas and technological changes that might affect cooking and storage procedures. Some hypotheses and expected patterns of artifact distribution may be proposed.

If variation in temper type reflects the need to improve the workability of the clay specific to certain areas, then temper classes should have a high degree of spatial discrimination. Series should occur in a single area during a particular period with few or no co-occurring series (or tempering traditions). Temper regions or series areas should conform to environmental features that provide only certain types of clay and temper. Such temper series should not co-vary with ancillary archaeological data that define culture periods or phases and, consequently, should not exhibit gradual increase and decrease in popularity over time but should show a rapid increase and sustained presence in the series area until the advent of historic depopulation.

If variation in tempering methods reflects the performance requirements of finished vessels, then it should be associated with temporal trends in other technological systems. Temporal patterns should be long term, but potentially punctuated, and should be correlated with relevant aspects of technology in specific ways. For example, late-period vessels required to do heavy service as cooking vessels for settled-village agriculturalists should have temper characteristics that serve to mitigate the negative effects of thermal stress, while exhibiting characteristics of thermal conductivity as great as, or greater than, those of differently tempered vessels typical of preceding culture periods. The inception and increase in frequency of a series in a given area should coincide with other significant shifts in technology such as the intensification of plant-food production and corn agriculture. Such traditions should encompass long periods of time (several hundred years) but not necessarily exhibit gradual increase and decrease. The lower limits of the historical trajectory could be steeply increasing and the upper limits steeply decreasing in cases in which one technological process is quickly replaced by another. This could be expected whenever there is a significant differential in effectiveness or efficiency between two technologies that serve the same purpose. If primarily technologically determined, pottery series should not be spatially discriminate. Technological processes are expected to transcend geographic or cultural boundaries and to be expressed panregionally over long periods of time.

If variation in temper type is primarily stylistic it should not exhibit a strong correlation with geophysical or environment discontinuities. Neither should it be strongly correlated with long-term temporal trends in other technological traditions. If stylistic, temper types should exhibit historical trajectories of shorter duration than those exhibited by technological traits. Some difference in duration of trends in stylistic traits could also be expected on stochastic grounds, however. During the Early Woodland period when population was sparse, a few longer-term trends might be expected while in the Late Woodland period when population was relatively dense and territorial ranges circumscribed, several shorter-term trends would be expected. Similarly, spatial discrimination of stylistic trends should increase with time and the intensification of regionalization.

Surface Treatment

If surface treatment is hypothesized as a neutral variant, that is, having no effect on storage or cooking performance, then certain considerations should be made. First, few actualistic studies have been conducted to determine how different surface treatments are produced and how their production relates to the structural mechanics of the building process, for example, in shaping the vessel or annealing coils. Second, while techno-functional studies have shown measurable, but slight, differences in the performance of vessels with different surface treatments (Schiffer 1990), no actualistic studies have investigated the potential differences in performance among the types of surface treatments represented in the sample used in this study, namely, carved-paddle stamped, simple stamped, net impressed, cord marked, or fabric impressed. If surface treatment is actually a neutral variant then its frequency should vary independently from environmental and technological traits, except that it can only occur on coil-built vessels. In general, the frequency of types of surface treatment often exhibits greater variability over time and between geographic areas than either environmental or technological traits.

Summary

In summary, each of the goals of this research entails certain practical conditions and theoretical possibilities. Aspects of evolutionary-selectionist theory, social agency, practice, and learning theory, often characterized as opposing ways of explaining the source of archaeologically observed variation, are employed here as a suite of approaches, each of which explores the meaning of variation at a slightly different scale. Consideration is given to the use of ceramic series, types, and varieties as units of measure that parse the continuous variation that exists in the archaeological record. Variation in any attribute state, whether temper, surface treatment, or vessel form, may be independent of the other and may reflect a unique response to changing social or environmental conditions. Functional and stylistic variations, often used by archaeologists as opposing categories, are viewed as manifestations of learning, practice, and individual agency expressed in the pottery-making craft as women reaffirm group membership through the replication of technological styles. The concepts of ethnicity, ethnic groups, and ethnic boundaries are of central importance in modeling how cultural information is shared within and between groups. These concepts are equally important in understanding how archaeologically observed patterns of apparent homogeneity, continuity, and stability in ceramic technological style emerge from systems that are essentially diverse, dynamic, and continuously evolving.

As the conceptual bridge from broken bits of pottery on the sorting tray to a regional perspective of the sequence of ceramic stylistic horizons across the coast is complex, it is essential to begin with a description of the methods used to traverse this connection. In the following chapter I review the methods used for classifying and sorting pottery, analyzing temper and surface treatment, sequencing types with relative and absolute dating techniques, and assessing the geographic distribution of types across the region.

3
Techniques of Analysis

The goals of this study are to refine the definitions of pottery types and synthesize regional taxonomies, augment the chronological data that allow us to understand the temporal relationships of the types, and determine the geographic distribution of the types. The methods used in each phase of the study are described below.

Classification System and Sorting Criteria

Issues concerning the classificatory method that is used to compare existing collections of Coastal Plain pottery require clarification. In the present study it was desirable to keep the classification system comparable to existing typological schemes. In some cases several different type descriptions applied to a single class of pottery and, unless there was some demonstrable difference in characteristics between regions, only one type name could apply. In part, this study was designed to synthesize independently constructed taxonomic classes and monitor variation within and between classes. Therefore it was important that pottery not simply be classified to one or the other existing type but that the attribute states composing classes be observed across the data spectrum without regard to types. Therefore, an attribute analysis was employed that recorded the details of temper, surface treatment, decoration, vessel form, and manufacturing technique. In the analysis of attributes, data were first analyzed on several scales, independently or lumped into composite classes. Once attribute-level variation was understood, existent types were evaluated, modified, or, when necessary, disregarded for the purposes of this study.

Fortunately, there are some very clearly articulated statements on taxonomic issues presented by contemporary ceramicists working in this and other regions of the Southeast (Anderson et al. 1982; Espenshade 1996; Steponaitis 1983). I made use of these statements to develop the system used in this study and to draw distinctions between their approaches and my own when necessary.

The system of classifying pottery by series, types, and varieties is hierarchical, employing three levels of inclusiveness. A series may comprise several types, each of which may include several varieties. Type descriptions used by earlier researchers were in some cases too broad to explore potential temporal and spatial variation on the desired scale. The use of the type-variety system allows the recognition of finer categories (varieties) without having to discard the structure of previously identified types. It also has the advantage of making the local typology more consistent with the system recently introduced on the South Carolina coast (e.g., Anderson et al. 1982, 1996). In fact, although a type-variety system is used, there are very few cases in which varieties are actually needed. This occasional need, however, warranted use of the system.

Series are generally defined on the basis of characteristics of paste, and types are typically defined on the basis of surface-finish characteristics. For some series, it is adequate to know only the sort of temper to classify the sherd. For other series, the temper in combination with surface treatment is necessary. Types are generally defined on the basis of fairly broad differences in surface treatment and occasionally varieties are used to sort out more specific surface treatment. Once defined, series and types are typically given proper names. In this study, as in others from this region (see Anderson et al. 1996), varieties are denoted by descriptive terms rather than formal names. In cases in which attributes do not fit existing type descriptions, they are listed as unspecified.

The relationships among the attributes that define the series and types are illustrated with a dendritic key (Figure 3.1). The typology is a tree-type classification (Whallon 1972) in which there is a hierarchy of importance of attributes that determines the order in which attributes are considered in determining class inclusion. The criteria for classification may also vary depending on which branch of the tree one is following. The primary attribute is temper type. Once this determination is made, a broad set of surface treatment attributes is considered. This is all that is necessary to determine most types. For example, if a sherd is shell tempered and simple stamped it is classifiable as Townsend series, Colington Simple Stamped type. A more specific set of surface treatment attributes is necessary for distinguishing certain types such as sand-tempered fabric-impressed and cord-marked types.

Every pottery type in this system was drawn from the existing literature. When it was determined that more than one previously published type description defined a single class of pottery, one of the type descriptions was chosen to best represent the class. In such cases, the historical precedence, completeness of description, current popularity, and relation to the concept of regional culture phases were considered when selecting which type description to use. A few of the types that appear here, while commonly used by archaeologists in the region, have yet to be adequately defined. It is hoped that more thorough descriptions for these types will be crafted in the near future.

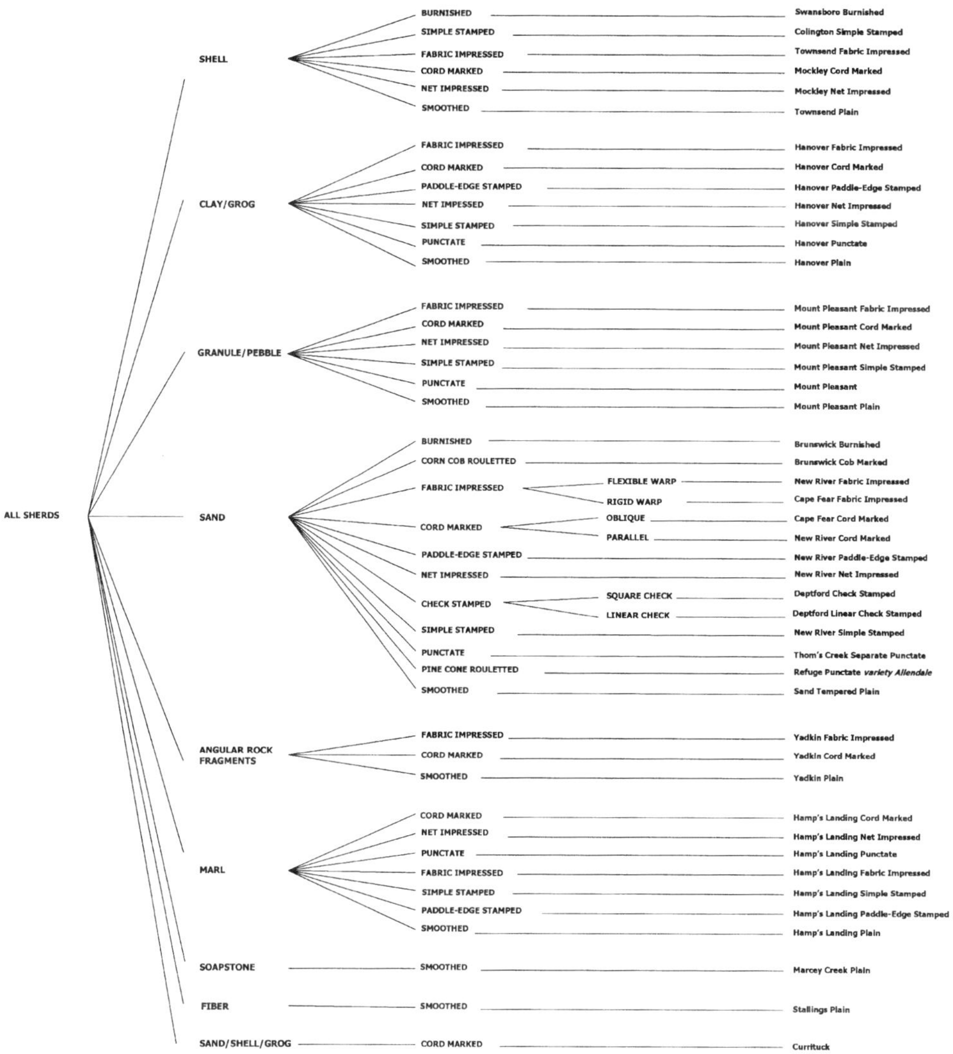

Figure 3.1. Dendritic key for classifying coastal North Carolina pottery types.

Temper Analysis

Temper classes were determined on the basis of the results of observation of freshly broken sections. For the excavated sample of North Carolina coastal sherds, temper particle size, shape, and proportion were described using low-powered microscopy. A binocular microscope with fiber-optic light was used to assess the characteristics of temper particles. Particle dimensions were measured at ×10 magnification with an ocular micrometer. Size classes follow Wentworth standards (medium, <.5 mm; coarse, .5–1 mm; very coarse, 1–2 mm; granule, 2–4 mm; pebble, >4 mm). Temper particles in the fine (.25–.5 mm) and smaller size range are considered less likely to have been purposefully added and small enough to be commonly found in the clay matrix. It is recognized that this lower limit is substantially higher than the .05 mm size suggested by Rice (1987:412) as the appropriate boundary. Two broad categories are used: (1) fine, medium, and coarse size grades (.125–1 mm) are referred to as sand and (2) very coarse and granule size grades (>1 mm) are referred to as grit. Sand-and-grit–tempered, or sand/grit-tempered, ware, therefore, includes sand in the fine through coarse fraction as well as grains in the very coarse and larger fraction. The proportion or density of grain size fractions in the matrix was estimated (e.g., 3–5 percent very fine–medium or 1–3 percent medium–granule), but the precision of these data is not appropriate for defining classes based on exact proportions of each Wentworth size grade. In most cases, the sand was quartz in either a monocrystalline or polycrystalline (less frequent, but common) form, but microline, feldspar, epidote, and plagioclase minerals were also commonly observed at proportions less than 3 percent. Sand grains were found most often to be of subrounded or subangular shape, but angular grains were also occasionally noted.

Most ceramic studies in this region have not utilized microscopic measurements of temper sizes. Consequently, sherds typically classified as tempered with "fine sand" probably have included grain sizes that feel fine to the touch, perhaps up to 1 mm in diameter. Since most former studies have not employed attribute analyses using Wentworth size grades, the results of those studies are not necessarily comparable to the conclusions of this one.

Point counting was not used to determine temper proportions, but the largest five particles in the field of view (typically the broken section of a sherd) were taken as characterizing the temper. Temper proportions for excavated samples were estimated following Rice (1987:349, Table 12.2). Temper proportions were not estimated for surface-collected samples. Temper particle angularity was subjectively sorted into four classes, rounded, subrounded, subangular, and angular, for sherds tempered with sand or crushed rock. Grains with any rounding at all were considered to have been derived from a naturally occurring sedimentary context. Angular grains (with no rounding whatsoever) were interpreted as crushed rock prepared especially for use as temper. It should be noted that this distinction is not without its problems. Angular grains of quartz ranging in size from fine sand to pebbles can be created by the natural weathering of quartzite. Handfuls of sharply angular small bits of quartz may be found throughout the eastern Piedmont where quartz veins in residual clay are freshly exposed by erosion.

Whereas the classificatory approach taken here identifies series in large part on the basis of size, shape, and type of temper, not all archaeologists have agreed about the effectiveness of this approach. For example, Haag (1958:69) cautioned that "[i]f pottery types were erected for the Banks area and variation in temper were considered sufficient justification for a new type, the number of types within this limited area would be great. It is probable that they would also be useless for comparative studies." Although Haag's conclusion is perhaps excessive, his point is well taken: sand (<1 mm) and grit (1–2 mm) temper are most problematical traits upon which to define pottery types.

Sand-tempering traditions that began in the Early Woodland appear to persist into the Middle and Late Woodland periods. A similar pattern is observed on the central coast of South Carolina, where the Deptford, Oemler, McClellanville, Santee, and Savannah series represent sand-tempered wares ranging in time from the Early Woodland to the Mississippian period (Poplin et al. 1993). Under such circumstances, series may be distinguished on the basis of other variables such as the size or proportion of sand, wall thickness, or other aspects of vessel form and surface treatment. But most surface treatment types appear to be very long lived. Given the current level of knowledge about the use of sand as temper, classification based upon variations in sand size and shape should perhaps be viewed more as an exploratory process, partitioning the range of traits into classes hypothesized to reflect temporal units that are designed to be tested.

Crushed Rock. Crushed rock, occasionally from Piedmont sources, was found in several of the Coastal Plain Sandhills samples. Rock fragments were angular, subangular, or irregularly shaped medium to very coarse grains of quartz or granitic igneous material. The composition of the igneous rock was some combination of plagioclase and one or more other minerals including quartz, K-feldspar, amphibole, epidote, opaques, and biotite. Crushed-rock temper fragments were often macroscopically visible on the surfaces of hand samples but did not exceed 10-percent density in the thin-section analysis.

Marl or Limestone. The term *marl* is used as shorthand for a group of calcareous materials potentially including fossiliferous sand, fossiliferous clay, marl, calcarenite, molluscan mold, and bryzoan-echinoid skeletal limestones found in the Tertiary deposits of the Coastal Plain, including the Waccamaw, Yorktown, Belgrade, River Bend, Castle Hayne, and Beaufort Formations (North Carolina Geological Survey 1988). Since the calcareous material used as temper has not yet been specifically linked to any of these sources, the single term *marl* is used here as a convenience to denote them all.

Grog. For quite some time ceramicists working with assemblages from the Mid-Atlantic coast have been struggling with the problem of distinguishing naturally occurring clay clasts, mineralized lumps, and crushed potsherds in grog-tempered pottery such as the Wilmington and Hanover series. Further confusing the issue, Thomas Loftfield (1976:154) described his clay-tempered Carteret series in the following way: "The temper consists of intentional inclusions of aplastic clay. These were either old sherds or fire-hardened pieces of clay added to the wet, plastic clay of which the vessel was formed. The pieces of aplastic tended in the construction process to begin to soften and lose definition in relation to the plastic portion of the paste."

This is an unfortunate characterization of grog as it conflates crushed sherds and "fire-hardened clay," placing both in the class of "aplastic clay." A dried lump of clay may be understood as aplastic, but definitely not as a ceramic, and it is unclear whether "fire-hardened clay" refers to ceramics or something else. The statement that the source of analytical difficulty in distinguishing clay lumps has to do with their loss of "definition" when they are added to wet clay paste suggests that Loftfield was not referring to a ceramic but rather to desiccated clay, which is not grog.

Alternatively, Espenshade (1996:44) has argued for a tripartite definition as follows: "[1] Sherd-tempered for bodies with discernible crushed sherds; [2] grog-tempered for bodies with distinct clay lump inclusions; [3] clay-tempered for bodies of small or extremely weathered sherds in which indeterminate temper (sherd or lump) is present." Although this solution is more efficient and more in keeping with the facts as we currently understand them, it is also problematic. The term *grog* has long been understood as crushed sherds, ground brick, tile, or other ceramic (Rice 1987:74, 409; Rye 1981:33; Shepard 1956:25). To apply this term to clay lumps of uncertain origin is potentially confusing.

In the current analysis, the grog class was split into two categories on the basis of attributes observable in a hand sample using low-powered microscopy. The distinction was made between clay temper (rounded inclusions or lumps distinguished from the surrounding matrix primarily by contrasting color and texture) and grog temper (angular inclusions distinguishable as remnant sherds). While this distinction was attempted in the analysis, it soon became clear that the difference between clay and grog could not confidently be ascertained and that only the most obvious examples of crushed sherds were being identified. Analysis of thin sections with petrographic microscopy stands a better chance of distinguishing grog by identifying diagnostic characteristics of suspected grog particles such as angularity, presence of a shrink rim, internal microstructure, composition distinct from the host matrix, difference in proportion and sorting of grain size, distribution and proportion of inclusions within host matrix, color, and presence of remnant surfaces (Cuomo di Caprio and Vaughan 1993:25, Table 1; Whitbread 1986, 1989). In addition to the fact that most of these distinguishing characteristics can be routinely recognized only through petrographic analysis, the small size and low proportion of grog particles may prevent recognition with macroscopic or low-powered microscopic techniques. In one petrographic study of Lowland Maya pottery, grog particles were typically less than 1 mm and less than frequent (Jones 1986:20). The results of the petrographic analysis of samples from the upper Cape Fear presented in this study describe many sherds containing grog particles in fine to granule size grades, in proportions from 3 to 15 percent, occasionally found alongside clay lumps also ranging from fine to granule size. These results suggest that the distinction between crushed sherds and clay lumps is difficult with petrographic techniques and probably very unreliable in a hand sample.

Nevertheless, the distinction between grog (crushed sherds) and clay (clay clasts of uncertain origin) temper was attempted in this analysis both macroscopically and with low-powered microscopy and, when possible, the results are considered.

The foregoing discussion raises the question, why attempt to distinguish clay lumps from crushed sherds anyway? There are several reasons for attempting to distinguish grog from clay temper. The techniques used to prepare the two tempering agents stand to be quite different and may therefore be linked to different communities of practice. One might expect the process for preparing grog (crushed sherds) to be well understood in archaeological context and fully documented ethnographically. In fact, although materials science–based studies have discussed the theoretical advantages of grog-tempered pottery in terms of performance characteristics (Rice 1987:229–230; Rye 1976:117; Steponaitis 1984:111), there are few studies from the Eastern Woodlands with explicit descriptions of grog.

For a very small number of sherds in this study, the presence of crushed pottery or clay lumps was positively identified through the petrographic analysis of thin sections to identify the mineralogy, particle size, shape, and proportion of temper from each thermoluminescence (TL) dated sample. The petrographic methods used in this study have been previously published (Herbert et al. 2002), and readers are encouraged to refer to these, as well as Ann Cordell's (1983, 1984, 1993) work for a description of procedural details.

Petrographic analysis allowed temper identifications to be clarified and in some cases the assignment of pottery classes depended on the petrographic identification of inclusions. This was particularly true with the identification of grog, where type identifications based on low-powered microscopy were occasionally revised based on the results of Cordell's petrographic study. Classes based on petrographic data, however, do not necessarily reflect classes based on macroscopic analysis and so are only replicable with petrography. While this may be viewed as a limiting factor from the perspective of the mass analyst (obviously, sectioning all sherds in a collection is impossible), classes based on petrographic information are assumed to be more accurate characterizations.

Surface Treatment Analysis

Surface treatment is often considered to be a decorative embellishment or a secondary process of building pots by the paddle-and-anvil technique (Rye 1981:69–70). In this technique, the exterior of the vessel is struck with a paddle, backed on the interior by an anvil, while the clay is in a plastic state. This process anneals the coils, smooths the surfaces, thins and shapes the vessel walls, removes air bubbles from the clay body, and aligns temper particles. A perfectly flat paddle face tends to stick to the surface of the wet clay, and in drawing it away the shape of the vessel may be deformed. If the paddle face is carved or wrapped with thong, net, cord, or fabric and then wetted, it will not stick to the surface. So textured, paddles leave distinctive impressions on the surface that, no doubt, had the added attraction of embellishing the appearance of the pot.

Surface treatment categories were evaluated in this study by making casts of archaeological samples and comparing these to experimentally produced test tiles impressed with replicated cordage and textiles (Herbert 1999a). The impressions observed on the surface of prehistoric pottery were made by netting, cordage, or fabric that was wrapped around the paddle or, with simple, checked, or complicated stamping, by the carved surface of the paddle face itself. In addition to providing information about the structure of the perishable materials, the impressions also hold clues to the techniques of the paddling that appear to have varied in space and time. The pottery sample is divided into four broad classes of surface treatment: net impressing, cord marking, check stamping, and fabric impressing. The netting used to impress vessel surfaces was made by knotting (as opposed to looping, for example) and this class was further subdivided by the width of the mesh (<5 mm, closed mesh; >5 mm open mesh).

Cord-marked wares almost always showed evidence of overstamping. Two distinctive varieties of overstamping were recognized in the analysis of materials from the Papanow and Pond Trail sites (Herbert 1997). One variety, referred to as "parallel," exhibited overstamped cord impressions that were roughly parallel or slightly oblique. A second variety, "perpendicular," showed cord impressions that were distinctively perpendicular or nearly so. Early interpretation of the perpendicular variety was purposefully vague about its structure, characterizing it as "over-stamped with perpendicular cords, or impressed with open, twined textile" (Herbert and Mathis 1996:170). The interpretation of the perpendicular variety as twined or plaited, netlike, open-weave textile was prompted by close analysis of casts. This interpretation has since been found to be wrong. This "interwoven textile," it was proposed, could only be created if the cords were first interwoven and then applied to the surface. Other researchers in the region who have paid close attention to casts of overstamped, cord-marked wares have come to similar conclusions (Steen 2000:135, Figure 110). A series of replication experiments subsequently demonstrated that perpendicular cord marking could indeed be made by overstamping with a cord-wrapped paddle, effectively eliminating the necessity of the alternative interpretation of perpendicular impressions as interwoven netting (Herbert 1999a).

An interesting conclusion of the study was that a very different set of paddle-stamping behaviors is needed to produce parallel and perpendicular varieties of overstamped cord-marked ware. Although both parallel and perpendicular types appear to be made by overstamping with a cord-wrapped paddle, the techniques used to produce each are different enough to warrant the exploration of how these surface treatments might vary independently in space and time.

Although there is some evidence from the Eastern Woodlands that cordage twist direction is diagnostic of geographically or temporally distinct cultural traditions (Johnson 1996; Johnson and Speedy 1992; Minar 2001; Petersen 1996, 1999; Petersen and Hamilton 1984) no temporal patterning was observed in the twist direction of cordage in the sample of sherds studied for the current study.

Fabric-impressed wares were subdivided into five categories. Three of these categories consist of wares impressed with weft-faced fabric made of plied cordage weft elements interwoven over rigid (noncordage) warp elements. The three categories are distinguished by the diameter of the weft cordage (fine, <1 mm; medium, 1–2 mm; coarse, >2 mm). A fourth category, also based on weft-faced, interwoven fabric, is distinguished by flexible (cordage) warp elements of approximately the same diameter as the weft, yielding a more elastic textile than those of the first three classes. The fifth category of fabric-impressed wares is characterized by very broad (approximately 5 mm) warp elements and, typically, fine weft elements (1 mm or less in diameter). The weft elements in all five categories are assumed to have been plied cordage.

In addition to the net-impressed, cord-marked, and fabric-impressed specimens, one sherd in the sample was check stamped.

Sequencing with Relative and Absolute Dating

Temporal sequencing of types was achieved with two techniques: (1) the analysis of assemblages from excavated contexts and (2) absolute dating. The first pottery assemblages analyzed were those excavated from sites with stratified geomorphological deposits. With these assemblages, vertical sorting of pottery classes within the soil column was analyzed to establish the broad trend of attribute sequencing. Determination of the absolute ages of 43 sherds with thermoluminescence (TL) dating was then undertaken, and this method is discussed below.

Excavated Samples

Samples from excavated contexts analyzed for vertical sorting include assemblages from three sites in the northern area: (1) the Bandon site (31CO1), with an assemblage of 847 sherds from 15 3-inch levels (Haag 1958); (2) the Cape Creek site (31DR1), with 238 sherds from five 3-inch levels (Haag 1958); and (3) the Whalen site (31BF26), with 46 sherds from five 3-inch levels. Each of these sites was excavated by William G. Haag and reported in *The Archaeology of Coastal North Caro-*

lina (1958). These three sites represent three areas of the northern coast where clusters of sites were surface collected by Haag. The surface-collected assemblages form the basis of the geographic analysis and the excavated assemblages provide an important means of discerning temporal trends apparent in pottery attributes.

Thermoluminescence Dated Samples

The potential of the TL dating method has not yet been realized by archaeologists in the southeastern United States for a variety of reasons including availability, cost, and perceived reliability (Feathers 2000). The accuracy of dating pottery by TL has been established for 30 years, however, and improvements in technique through that time have increased precision (Adamiec and Aitken 1986; Aitken et al. 1964; Barnett 1999, 2000; Dunnell and Feathers 1994; Dykeman 2000; Dykeman et al. 2002; Feathers 2001; Feathers and Rhode 1998; Fleming and Stoneham 1973; Godfrey-Smith et al. 1997; Ichikawa et al. 1978; Mejdahl and Bøtter-Jensen 1994; Prescott et al. 1993; Prescott and Hutton 1988; Sampson et al. 1972; Whittle and Arnaud 1975; Zimmerman and Huxtable 1969, 1971). Costs per sample are currently less than those for AMS (accelerator mass spectrometry) dating and with the increasing use of automated equipment may soon approach those of conventional radiocarbon dating.

The most important advantage of using TL for dating pottery is that it does not rely on associated organic material but dates the artifact itself (Aitken 1990:3; Feathers 1993:5, 1997a; Godfrey-Smith et al. 1997:253). TL dating is based on radiation-induced stored energy that has accumulated since the time when the material was last heated to at least 450–500°C. For pottery, this event corresponds in most cases to the time of manufacture or use, precisely the event of archaeological interest. Energy accumulates continuously in the molecular matrix of ceramic material beginning from the time the pottery vessel is fired. The energy is released as luminescence or light when the material is heated under controlled conditions in the laboratory. The luminescence is measured, and the intensity of this light is proportional to age.

Principles of TL are described in much greater detail by Aitken (1990), and applications to a variety of archaeological contexts have been demonstrated (Dunnell and Feathers 1994; Dykeman et al. 2002; Feathers 1997a, 1997b, 1997c; Huntley et al. 1993). The TL procedures used for the pottery in this study may be summarized as follows.

Pottery samples for TL dating were drawn from three excavated site assemblages, the Papanow (31NH690) and Riegelwood (31CD114) sites in the lower Cape Fear River valley, and the several sites from Fort Bragg in the upper Cape Fear valley (Herbert et al. 2002). The sampling strategy for pottery for TL dating was based on the variation observed in temper and surface treatment attributes.

Samples were selected to represent a range of temper and surface treatment characteristics commonly observed among sherds from sites across the study area. Sherds to be dated were selected from excavated contexts where the spatial relationships of associated artifacts were controlled and where soil samples were collected specifically for assessing the background radiation dose rate.

With samples from both regions of the Cape Fear valley, attributes of weight, thickness, color, porosity, temper, and surface treatment were measured and recorded for each sherd, and permanent casts and digital images were made of the exterior surfaces. Munsell color values were determined using clean, freshly broken cross sections at the exterior, interior, and middle of each cross section. Casts were made with commercial modeling compound ("Sculpey"). Following attribute analyses, a small portion of each sherd to be dated was removed to provide a thin-section sample for petrographic analysis.

The methods used by the University of Washington Luminescence Laboratory to estimate the age of pottery in this study have been described in a previous publication (see Herbert et al. 2002) and the interested reader is directed to this source for procedural detail.

Radiocarbon-Dated Samples

Every radiocarbon date associated with pottery from Coastal Plain sites in North Carolina up to the year 2003 is presented in this volume. Each of these dates was carefully reviewed for accuracy and recalibrated with the Calib 4.3 program using the INTCAL98 calibration curves (Stuiver and Reimer 1993). Nonmarine radiocarbon samples were calibrated with the decadal atmospheric/inferred atmospheric curve. Marine-shell samples were calibrated with the marine data set to compensate for differences in availability of radiocarbon in reservoirs. Organisms from marine (and lacustrine) environments have been exposed to different levels of ^{14}C than their terrestrial counterparts. The marine calibration incorporates a time-dependent global ocean reservoir correction of about 410 years. Local reservoir effects were corrected by applying the ΔR value derived from coral dates in the Bahamas (–5 ± 20), which is the closest analog for coastal Carolina samples (P. Reimer, personal communication 2002; Stuiver and Braziunas 1993). For samples of human bone collagen, the carbon was assumed to be derived from a mixture of 50-percent marine and 50-percent terrestrial carbon. These proportions are estimates based on recent stable isotope data indicating that marine resources were a very significant part of the diet of coastal populations up to about A.D. 1500, even after the advent of the introduction of corn agriculture around A.D. 1000 (Hutchinson 2002).

All radiocarbon data that appear in this volume have been corrected for $\delta^{13}C$ isotope fractionation. This was accomplished with the assistance of the staff of

Beta Analytic, who provided information from their records about the status of $\delta^{13}C$ correction (R. Hatfield, personal communication 2002). Information about corrections made for $\delta^{13}C$ isotope fractionation is typically not reported along with ^{14}C age estimates in the published literature. In cases in which Beta Analytic's records indicated that a sample had not been corrected, the correction was applied. In cases in which there were no records indicating whether a particular sample had or had not been corrected, a determination to correct the sample was based on the date the sample was run. Samples processed prior to 1990, for which laboratory records were ambiguous on this point, were corrected.

The ^{14}C age estimates that appear in this volume are calculated with Calib 4.3, Method A (simple intercepts with linear interpolation of data points on selected calibration curve) with the standard lab-error multiplier k. Results are presented with calibrated intercepts and minimum and maximum calibrated 2σ (.95) ranges. Multiple calibrated intercepts for error ranges are not reported.

Geographic Information Analysis

The exploration of potential prehistoric ceramic-area boundaries relies on mapping the occurrence of attributes and taxonomic classes along what might be envisioned as two transects. The first encompasses the entire length of the outer coast (tidewater) and the second an east–west transect comprising the upper and lower Cape Fear River basin. Surface collections were selected for this study for several reasons. The number of surface-collected assemblages is far greater than the number of excavated samples from this region and their spatial distribution provides a denser coverage of the coastal region. Among thousands of sites and hundreds of thousands of sherds available for study, two collections (the Haag collection and the Loftfield collection) were chosen on the basis of their size (number of sites and sherds) and site area of coverage (Figure 3.2). The Haag collection, made in 1956, is composed of 14,204 sherds from about 222 sites in 10 counties. This collection provides a sample of sites and assemblages from several major river basins in the tidewater region of the coast of North Carolina. The Loftfield collection, made in 1979, consists of 2,987 sherds from 127 sites in three counties, providing a representative sample of sites and assemblages from the portion of the upper Cape Fear River basin within the 648-km^2 (250 square miles) area of the Fort Bragg military reservation (Table 3.1).

The Haag collection is housed at the University of North Carolina, Research Laboratories of Archaeology (RLA). Collections made by federal contractors on the Fort Bragg military reservation (including the Thomas C. Loftfield collection) are housed at the Fort Bragg Cultural Resources Curation Facility. These two collections are large enough to provide ample opportunity to observe the major types of variation and small enough to be manageable for this project. Using just two collections minimized variability in collecting methods among individual site

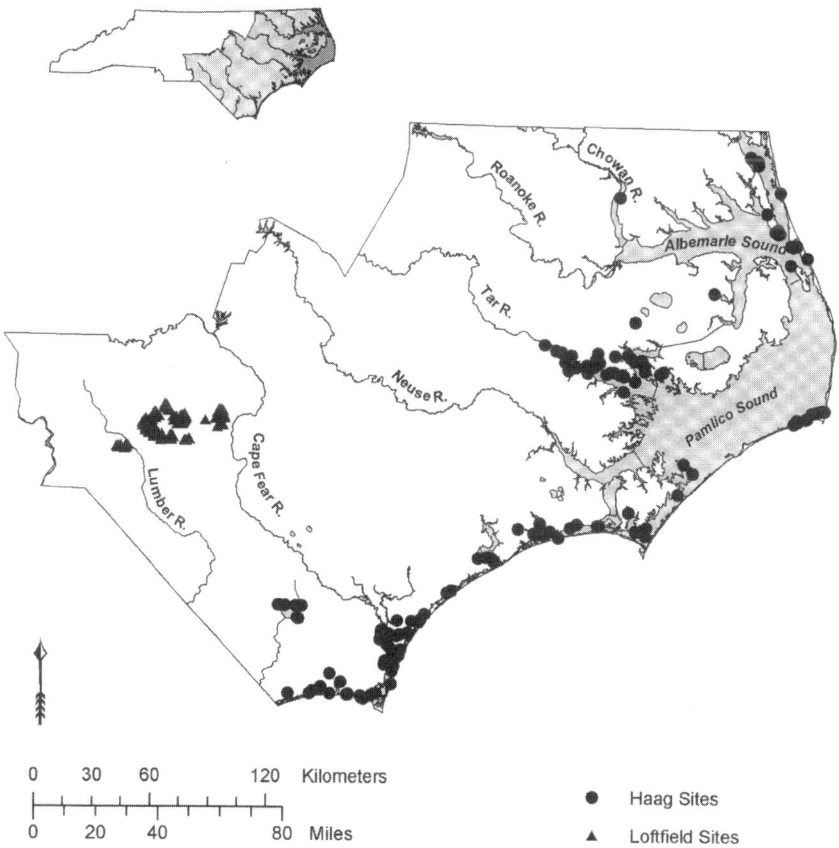

Figure 3.2. Location of surface-collected site assemblages used in this study.

samples, but there were some differences between the two collection methods. The sample is unquestionably uneven; sites are clustered geographically, due to sampling logistics, with some rather large spaces between. A few Haag site samples are quite large (more than 1,000 sherds) while most of the site samples in the Loftfield collection have fewer than 10 sherds. Nevertheless, the pattern of site samples is considered adequate to reflect regions of technological style and any boundaries that may exist within the region represented by the site samples.

Geographic distributions of the pottery classes were mapped using GIS (geographic information systems) software (ArcMap 7). As relative frequencies or proportions (percentages) of trait occurrence at each site may be masked by problems of multicomponency in surface collections, several alternative measures are used to look for patterns. Among these are raw frequencies and frequencies within subsets of types that are roughly contemporary. Analyzing maps of counts (the raw frequency of traits, or sherds of various types), it is apparent that most surface treatment types, if viewed independently from series, occur rather uniformly

Table 3.1. Surface Collection Sample

County	Sites (count)	Sherds (count)
Beaufort	30	4,707
Brunswick	23	1,848
Carteret	16	1,401
Columbus	7	589
Cumberland	24	627
Currituck	7	887
Dare	19	2,138
Hoke	181	2,177
Hyde	6	567
New Hanover	22	1,444
Onslow	9	456
Pender	1	167
Scotland	22	183
Total	367	17,191

across the study area. In part, this may be due to the analytical method. The relative frequency of a type or trait, calculated as a percentage of the total pottery from a site, is a more sensitive indicator than raw counts for illustrating both the location and the relative importance of traits. An inherent problem with this approach when applied to surface collections, however, is that it may simply monitor settlement history at each site. In other words, when the data are multicomponent assemblages derived from site-occupation periods of unknown duration, the potential for mixing may mask variation if the trait of interest is known to occur in more than one period. To minimize this problem, samples were classified according to approximate age (Early, Middle, or Late Woodland period), then relative frequencies were calculated for site assemblages from each period. This does not eliminate the problem but mitigates it somewhat by calculating trait frequency relative to one period in which, it is assumed, the duration of site occupation would be similar. This assumption rests on our knowledge of the economic differences among the periods and the effects that these differences might have had on residential mobility.

4
Haag's Excavation of Bandon, Cape Creek, and Whalen

This chapter is concerned with three key sites, Bandon, Cape Creek, and Whalen, that are found on North Carolina's northern Coastal Plain and are uniquely important in providing evidence for sequencing pottery types from stratified geomorphological context. The information presented in this chapter derives from assemblages excavated in 1956 by William G. Haag as he worked his way down the coast of North Carolina with the aim of learning what he could of the lost colony of Croatan and the Native American sites from that period. In practice, it appears that his sense of scientific exploration and the lure of Atlantic prehistory led him far beyond his original study area as he extended his work through coastal North and South Carolina and into Georgia, surface collecting the largest sites, occasionally excavating test units, and amassing a wonderful comparative collection of pottery. There has been a great deal of archaeology conducted on sites in this region since Haag's time, of course, and information from these investigations provides the backdrop for interpreting the Haag collection. David S. Phelps recently conducted extensive excavations at the Cape Creek site and graciously provided information about his findings, which are included in this chapter, but the data presented here are from Haag's 1956 excavations.

While it is certainly true that three test units do not a regional pottery sequence make, the Bandon, Cape Creek, and Whalen assemblages provide a remarkably unified picture of the basic temporal trends in temper and surface treatment types for the region. Refining and dating the sequence will be left to future research, but the basic structure of the history of cultures, insofar as we may discern from pottery, comes to light in a careful inspection of the collections from these three sites.

Bandon

The Bandon site is a rich prehistoric shell midden on what was formerly the John and Inglis Fletcher plantation on the Chowan River. The site was well known to avocational and professional archaeologists working in the mid-fifties (Haag 1958:47), although Bill Haag was the only one of his contemporaries fortunate enough to excavate there. In *The Archaeology of Coastal North Carolina,* Haag (1958:47) began his discussion of the Bandon site in the following way: "This fine midden is one of the largest in northeastern North Carolina. It is most probable that an extensive excavation would prove rewarding." In addition to the shell midden, he noted the presence of two sand mounds known to the local residents as Indian mounds. Unfortunately, professional excavations have never been conducted at the Bandon site since Haag's initial exploration in 1956, and in the intervening time much of the site has been destroyed by residential development.

The Bandon site is located about 15 miles north of Denton on a high bluff overlooking the Chowan River, just above the Albemarle Sound (Figure 4.1). The Chowan is fresh at this location and Haag reported that none of the shell composing the midden was oyster. At the time of his visit, the shell midden was about 1,000 feet long and 200 feet wide. Haag judged the maximum thickness (depth) of the shell midden to be slightly less than 10 feet. In the location where his excavation unit was placed, the midden was just over 6 feet deep. It is reported that the shell from this deep midden was mined for agricultural lime in the years before (and possibly after) excavation and it is likely that the upper portion of the midden was significantly disturbed in many areas. Haag indicates that he consciously selected the placement of his excavation in an area he thought to be least disturbed by farming. The 5-×-5-foot unit, excavated in arbitrary 3-inch levels, represents an unparalleled opportunity to explore the prehistoric ceramic sequence from the lower Chowan Basin and upper Albemarle Sound.

Haag's analysis reported 847 sherds from 15 excavation levels (all were 3-inch levels except Level 1, which was 9 inches, bringing the total depth of the pottery-bearing zones to 48 inches). In addition, 92 sherds were reportedly recovered from a pit intruding into the subsoil beneath the midden (Haag 1958:101, Table 5). The upper 9 inches of fill was almost certainly plow zone and contained numerous historic artifacts including pig bones, bricks, plaster, glass, crockery, and kaolin pipe fragments. Haag (1958:102) made two observations of note: that shell-tempered ware was absent and that an abundance of net-impressed wares was found in the lower levels. The latter observation he said demonstrated "the cultural position of the site to be quite different from the Cape Creek site and other Outer Banks sites." The first of these observations was uncharacteristically imprecise; shell-tempered Townsend series pottery is represented in low frequency in the upper levels. It is certainly true, however, that the majority of the midden fill reflects a very long occupational history spanning the Middle and Early Woodland periods, quite distinct from Outer Banks middens, which very often lack these early components.

Differences between Haag's (1958:101, Table 5) results and those presented in

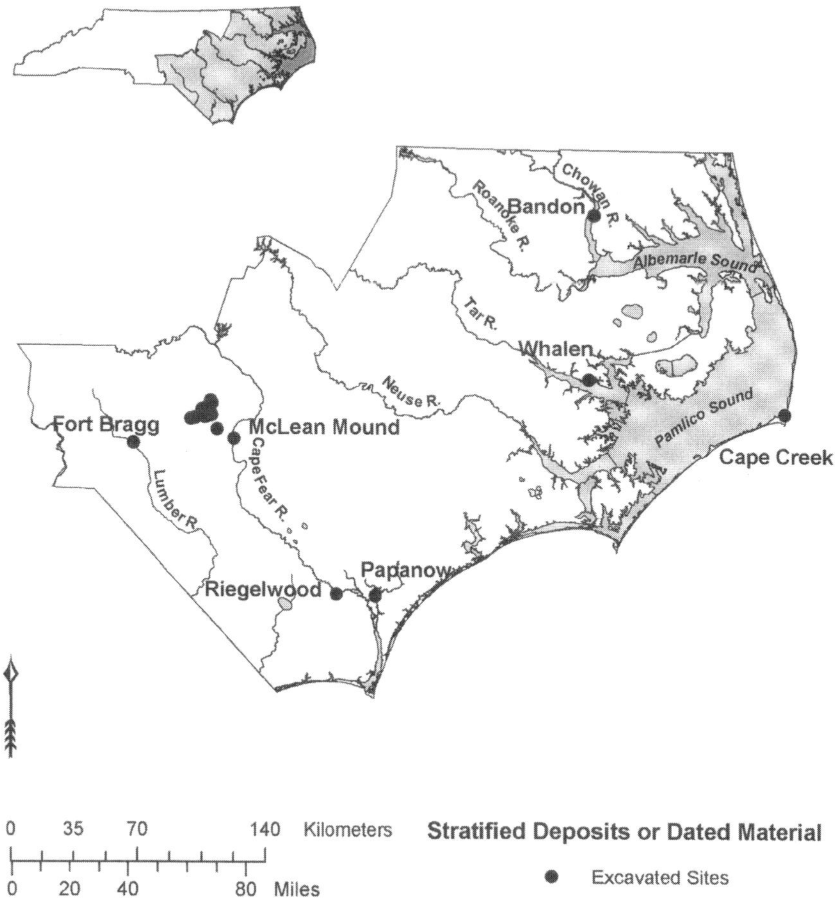

Figure 4.1. Location of excavated sites with stratified or dated assemblages.

this analysis regarding the total number of prehistoric sherds and attributes observed are due in part to the use of different class definitions and analytical techniques. Pottery from the Bandon site analyzed for this study includes 910 sherds from 15 levels and those from the submidden pit. Sherds are distributed among eight temper classes and eight surface treatment classes. The majority (90 percent) of the sherds are tempered with quartz sand and most include some very coarse or granule-sized grains. Smaller numbers of sherds with clay or shell temper were observed. Most sherds (73 percent) are fabric impressed, with fewer having net-impressed, cord-marked, stamped/smoothed, or simple-stamped surfaces.

The relative frequency of various temper types among excavation levels indicates the presence of multiple temporal components, or pottery series (Table 4.1, Figure 4.2). Although frequency percentage graphs appear similar to seriation

Table 4.1. Temper Type by Level from the Bandon Site

	Temper								
Level	None	Medium Sand	Coarse Sand	Very Coarse Sand	Granule	Clay	Shell	Granule/ Shell	Total
1			1	2					3
2				17			1		18
3	1		3	2			2		8
4			1	25			4		30
5				52			24		76
6				71			13		84
7			2	76			4		82
8		1	7	55	6		3		72
9		3	6	74	1	1	1		86
10			6	68	2				76
11		2	1	8	59	8			78
12		1	5	1	51	10			68
13		5		1	38				44
14		8	12	12	18			8	58
15	4	6		2	22		3		37
Pit		11	2		71	4	2		90
Total	5	37	46	466	268	23	57	8	910

charts, the box sizes in each row correspond to the frequency of types in each excavation level, standardized as a percent of the total sherds from that level. Sample size obviously affects the appearance of this chart (and those that follow) as it is percentages of the total for each level that are shown, regardless of the number of sherds in each level. With such a limited portion of the midden represented, the remains of single pots could strongly influence the appearance of the graph. It should also be noted that the vertical patterning of types may reflect some post-depositional movement of sherds within the soil column, as well as any temporal trends in technological style that might be apparent.

The pattern exhibited by sherds tempered with granules as opposed to those

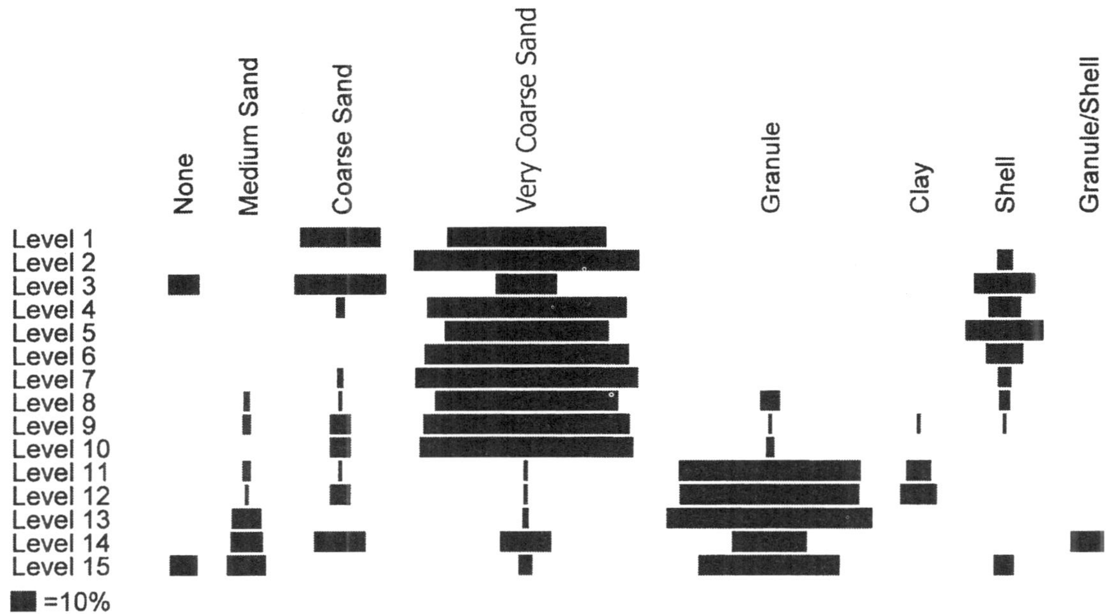

Figure 4.2. Frequency percentage chart of temper by level from the Bandon site.

tempered with coarse sand suggests the influence of small sample size. The majority of sherds above Level 11 are tempered with coarse sand and below Level 10, with granules. Rather than suggesting a population replacement or a technological transition in tempering at about the time Level 10 was laid down, this pattern more likely reflects the influence of a few vessels. In contrast, the pattern illustrated by shell-tempered sherds suggests shifts in site occupational patterns. Shell-tempered sherds occur primarily in the upper nine levels, but there are also a small number of sherds in Levels 14 and 15 and the submidden pit that are tempered with shell or mixtures of shell and coarse sand or shell and granules occasionally also including clay lumps. In addition, three of the four clay-tempered sherds found in the submidden pit appear to include some marl. Although lumped with the clay-tempered sherds in Level 15 (Figure 4.2), the sherds including marl are classified as Hamp's Landing in the discussion of series and types that follows. The sherds in the submidden pit include mostly granule-tempered ware, but also found in this context are sherds with odd mixtures of clay, shell, and marl, suggesting an eclectic tempering tradition early in the occupational sequence. This early component suggests some relation to the Currituck Beaker ware described by Painter (1977), although no evidence of beaker vessel forms was discovered.

Several components are also indicated by proportions of surface treatment types in each level (Table 4.2 and Figure 4.3). Fabric impressing contributes the greatest proportion in every level except Level 1 (where sample sizes are too small to be representative), but proportions are slightly reduced in the lower levels. Net-impressed ware is not represented above Level 6 and is most frequent in Level 13, placing it early in the sequence. Cord marking is represented in low frequency in almost every level below Level 3. One cord-marked sherd was found in the plow zone, Level 1, but no cord-marked sherds were found in Levels 2 and 3. The only evidence that might provide a clue as to the temporal placement of cord marking is its absence in Levels 2 and 3, where all sherds were fabric impressed, suggesting that cord marking is not late in the series at the Bandon site. Simple stamping is almost completely absent; three simple-stamped sherds were noted in Level 5.

There is also some indication of temporal variation in the structure of fabric impressed on vessel surfaces (Table 4.3). Two sorts of fabrics were recognized: those with rigid warp elements and those with flexible warp elements. Samples impressed with rigid warp textile were further subdivided according to weft diameter into coarse (>2 mm), medium (1–2 mm), and fine (<1 mm). In almost all cases the fabric was weft faced, such that weft elements were packed tightly together, leaving the warp elements completely covered except where weft cords were worn through. A small subset of rigid warp fabric, however, exhibited wefts that were interwoven with spaces between them, usually about the width of the diameter of the weft cord itself.

Table 4.2. Surface Treatment Type by Level from the Bandon Site

Level	Surface Treatment								Total
	None	Smoothed	Smoothed/ Stamped	Simple Stamped	Net Impressed	Cord Marked	Fabric Impressed	Eroded	
1		1	1			1			3
2							18		18
3							8		8
4			2			1	27		30
5				3		4	69		76
6		1			1	2	80		84
7		1			2	1	78		82
8		6			10	4	52		72
9		4	2		9	5	60	6	86
10	5		4		3	2	61	1	76
11			1		11	3	56	7	78
12		1	3		9	2	40	13	68
13					16	2	26		44
14					15		34	9	58
15			3		8	2	22	2	37
Pit	9				31	27	23		90
Total	14	14	16	3	115	56	654	38	910

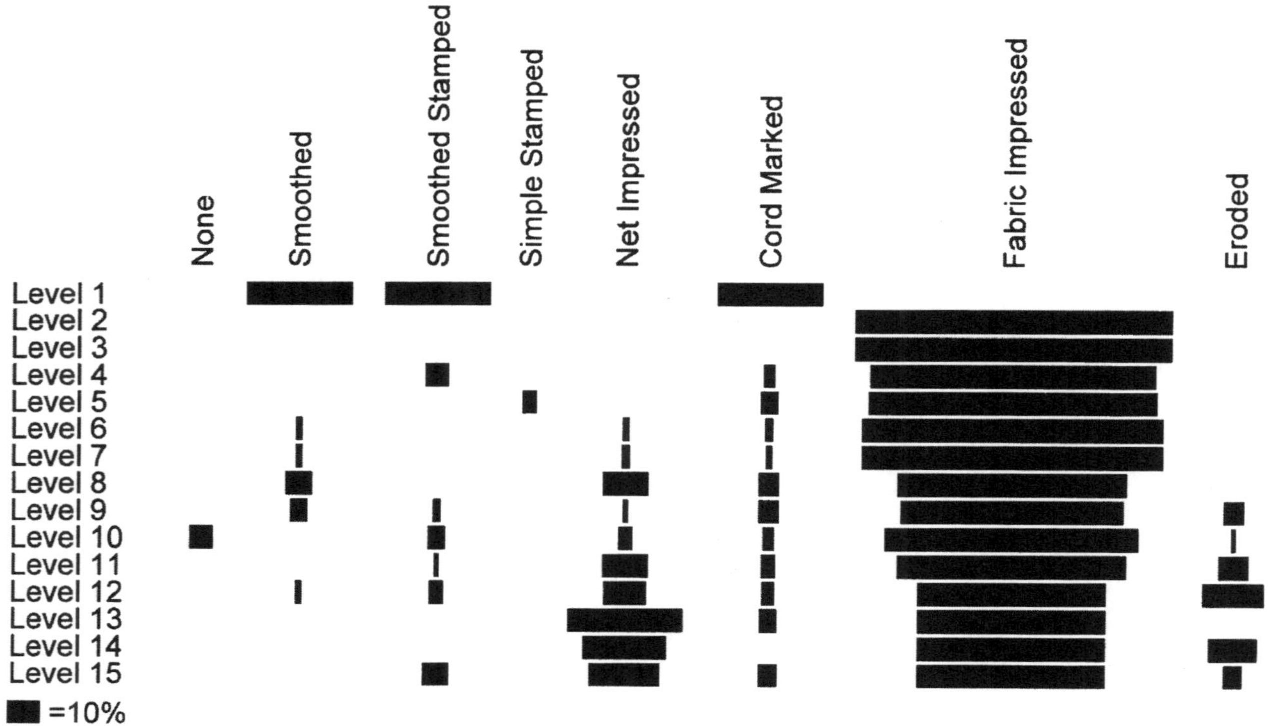

Figure 4.3. Frequency percentage chart of surface treatment by level from the Bandon site.

Table 4.3. Fabric Type by Level from the Bandon Site

	Fabric Structure						
Level	Indeterminate	Coarse Weft	Medium Weft	Fine Weft	Spaced Weft	Flexible Warp	Total
1							
2			18				18
3			8				8
4			21	6			27
5		3	50	11		5	69
6	16	4	41	14		5	80
7	29	2	29	15		3	78
8		2	29	6		15	52
9		4	25	9		22	60
10		7	42	9		3	61
11	1	3	29	9		14	56
12		4	28			8	40
13		1	20			5	26
14			21	2	11		34
15			5	2	15		22
Pit		1	18	1		3	23
Total	46	31	384	84	26	83	654

In small sherds or special cases, this "spaced weft" variety is difficult to distinguish from surfaces stamped with the paddle edge. In general, however, the rigid warp, medium weft interwoven (or plaited) textile was most common in every level. There is some suggestion that rigid warp, fine weft fabric occurs later in the sequence than flexible warp fabric, but this pattern is not especially strong. Spaced weft fabric was identified only in the lower two levels (14 and 15), suggesting it may be an earlier variant.

The structure of the cordage used in marking pottery was also investigated as a potential temporal indicator (Table 4.4). Cord-marked wares were divided into two categories, those with cord impressions that were essentially parallel and those exhibiting cord impressions that were overstamped at nearly perpendicular angles.

Table 4.4. Cordage Type by Level from the Bandon Site

	Cordage Structure					
Level	Parallel	Parallel (S-twist)	Parallel (Z-twist)	Perpendicular (S-twist)	Perpendicular (Z-twist)	Total
1					1	1
2						
3						
4					1	1
5				2	2	4
6		1		1		2
7				1		1
8	1		2		1	4
9				5		5
10			2			2
11			1	1	1	3
12		1			1	2
13			2			2
14						
15		2				2
Pit		11	14	2		27
Total	1	15	21	12	7	56

There is some evidence that the parallel cord-marked variety is earlier than the perpendicular variant in the series, but the data are merely suggestive. Cord-marked sherds occasionally exhibited such clear impressions that the twist direction of the cordage could be determined. The Bandon data reveal no preference for one or the other of these cord-marking techniques at any point in time.

Given this arrangement of traits and based on the series and type definitions (Chapter 3), it can be concluded that seven ceramic series are represented in the assemblage from the midden at Bandon: Hamp's Landing (represented by the three clay- and marl-tempered sherds from the pit), New River, Hanover, Mockley, Mount Pleasant, Cape Fear, and Townsend (including Colington Simple

Stamped) (Table 4.5 and Figure 4.4). Although the application of taxonomic series defined for the southern or central coastal areas, such as Hamp's Landing, New River, and Cape Fear, may appear inappropriate for the Chowan Basin, it should be remembered that individual sherds were assigned to series and type classes on the basis of attributes and the taxonomic system described in Chapter 3. Applying this analytical procedure to pottery from the Bandon midden provides some very interesting results. The series illustrated in Table 4.5 and Figure 4.4 are arranged in approximate chronological order (oldest to youngest reading left to right), based on current interpretations. Given the definitions provided in Chapter 3, however, it appears that certain series and types are out of order. New River Net Impressed (its northern series equivalent being Deep Creek) is most frequent in the lower third of the midden (Levels 11–15) as expected, and New River Fabric Impressed is more common in the middle third (Levels 6–10). This arrangement agrees well with what we expect, given previous investigations in the region (e.g., Phelps 1983). Other series do not seem to be arranged quite as we might expect.

The Mount Pleasant series (granule and larger quartz temper) should follow Deep Creek and therefore occur in greater frequency in the middle levels of the midden. In fact, sherds with granule inclusions occur almost entirely in the lowest five levels, apparently contemporary with New River Net Impressed sherds. A sand/grit-tempered, fabric-impressed ware, here defined as the Cape Fear series, is most frequent in the upper two-thirds of the midden, co-occurring with shell-tempered Townsend series sherds.

The pottery from the Bandon midden raises a number of intriguing questions. Obviously, the classification of the major component of the pottery from the middle or late portions of the sequence as Cape Fear series is provocative in terms of the prehistory of the northern coastal region as we now know it. As current type descriptions stand, the sand/grit-tempered ware here classified as Cape Fear could not be classified to either the Cashie or Mount Pleasant series. Detailed attribute analyses of large assemblages of Mount Pleasant series pottery have yet to be published, but given the detailed description of the Cashie series offered by Phelps and Heath (1998), it is very unlikely that this material is Cashie. No folded or decorated rims were noted in the assemblage and vessel interiors seemed to be normally treated, not extensively smoothed or floated. There are two remaining taxonomic options: (1) that this sand/grit-tempered, cord-marked, and fabric-impressed material represents a variant of the Middle Woodland Mount Pleasant series without the characteristic granule or pebble temper or (2) that it represents a Late Woodland sand-tempering tradition that has yet to be defined and reported for assemblages from sites in the northern coastal area. Lacking chronometric data from the strata in question at the Bandon midden, or thermoluminescence (TL) dating of the pottery itself, it is impossible to determine whether this material represents a Middle Woodland or Late Woodland component. Its position in

Table 4.5. Pottery Series and Type by Level from the Bandon Midden

	Hamp's Landing	New River			Hanover				Mockley
Level	Net	Net	Cord	Fabric	Net	Cord	Fabric	Plain	Net
1									
2									
3									
4		1							
5				5					
6		1	1	5					
7		2		3					
8		5	2	15					
9		9		22				1	
10		3	2	3					
11		7	1		3		3		
12		3		1	6	1			
13		6							
14		11		9					
15		8	2						
Pit	3	1	10		1				2
Total	3	57	18	63	10	1	3	1	2

[a]The Townsend series is made up of the White Oak Fabric Impressed and Colington Simple Stamped types.

the stratigraphic column certainly suggests that it coexisted with Townsend series shell-tempered ware. Overall, what these data indicate is that the taxonomic and chronological differences among sand-tempered, sand/grit-tempered, and sand/granule-tempered wares are not very well understood in the northern coastal region. Much more work is needed to fully characterize the differences between New River, Mount Pleasant, and any Late Woodland sand-tempered series that may exist in this region.

Mount Pleasant				Cape Fear		Townsend[a]		Sand Tempered	
Net	Cord	Fabric	Plain	Cord	Fabric	Fabric	Stamped	Plain	Total
				2				1	3
					17	1			18
					6	2			8
				1	24	4			30
				4	43	21	3		76
				1	62	13		1	84
				1	71	4		1	82
5	1			1	34	5		4	72
		1		5	44	1		3	86
		2			56			4	70
1	1	56	1	1	2				76
1	1	47	2		1				63
10	2	20							38
		15			11				46
		22				3		2	37
23	15	24		2					81
40	20	187	3	18	371	54	3	16	870

Cape Creek

The Cape Creek site (31DR1), thought to be the historically documented Algonquian village of Croatan, is located on the Outer Banks near Cape Hatteras, northeast of Buxton, near the mouth of Cape Creek on the Pamlico Sound (Figure 4.1). W. G. Haag visited this site during the summer of 1956 as part of his survey of coastal North Carolina and reported it "the best midden found on the Outer

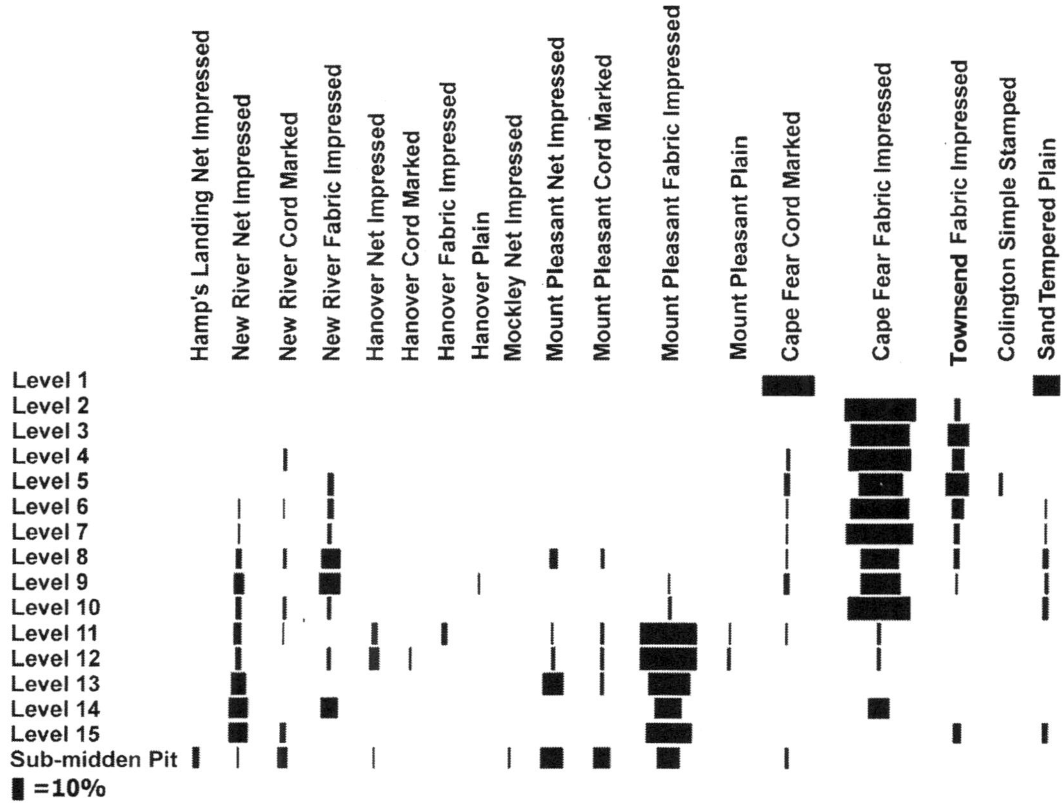

Figure 4.4. Frequency percentage chart of ceramic types by level from the Bandon site.

Banks" (Haag 1958:28). He was preceded by H. R. Harrington and Joffre L. Coe, both of whom made collections from the site.

Haag found the site to be an extensive midden consisting of shell and bone, drifted over with 1 to 5 feet of sand (Haag 1958:26). He estimated the midden occupied an area 500 feet square, with a depth, in the locations tested, rarely exceeding 2 feet. He speculated, however, that its size had been greatly diminished by shoreline erosion, attested by the local residents to be a consistent seasonal phenomenon and not the result of exceptional storms. Haag noted that no construction, plowing, or previous archaeological investigation had disturbed the site, but he speculated that borrowing shell for road material had reduced the upper portion of the midden in some locations, especially where two roads transected the midden. Accordingly, Haag situated his 5-x-10-foot excavation "in the most propitious spot, that is, the least disturbed." Excavating in arbitrary 3-inch levels, Haag found a rich humus zone beneath the shell midden, suggesting to him the existence of a forest cover prior to prehistoric settlement. In the upper 9 inches of the midden Haag found a number of historic artifacts including pipe bowl and stem fragments (of both Native clay pipes and English kaolin pipes obtained in trade), a metal button (Level 1), iron spikes, a cut brass fragment, a gun flint, and a historic potsherd. Only the pipe fragments and gun flint are reported in his published volume (Haag 1958). A great deal of research was conducted at the site in recent years by David S. Phelps and currently by Charles L. Heath. Artifacts suggest that the period of the site's European occupation was between 1690 and 1730; early in the historic era to be sure, but many decades later than the Roanoke colony that Haag and Phelps hoped to find and for which Heath continues to search.

Haag's (1958:97, Table 3) tabulation of pottery from the excavation included 238 sherds. The analysis conducted for this study includes 442 sherds, the discrepancy possibly being due to the large number of eroded sherds that Haag may have ignored.

The pottery assemblage from Cape Creek is distinctly different from that from the Bandon site. Among the Cape Creek sherds, 80 percent are shell tempered, only 9 percent are tempered with sand of any size grade, and only 8 percent include granule-sized quartz. Fifty-one percent of sherd surfaces are fabric impressed and 34 percent are simple stamped. Only three sherds are net impressed and two are cord marked. Although the shallowness of the midden where the excavation was placed prompted Haag (1958:97) to underestimate its utility, temporal patterning is discernable among pottery attributes observed by level (Table 4.6). Historic artifacts were found in Levels 1–3, but none were found in Levels 4 or 5. The fact that historic materials are found to a depth of 30 cm below the surface suggests some degree of vertical mixing had taken place within the midden at the test location. Shell-tempered sherds, while present in every level, were most numerous

Table 4.6. Temper Type by Level from the Cape Creek Site

	Temper								
Level	None	Medium Sand	Coarse Sand	Very Coarse Sand	Granule	Sand/ Granule	Clay	Shell	Total
1		2	1					36	39
2				1	2			59	62
3	1	3	1					88	93
4		31				35	9	131	206
5			2					40	42
Total	1	36	4	1	2	35	9	354	442

in Level 4. Also found in Level 4 were a significant number of sand/granule- (or sand/grit) and fine sand–tempered sherds. The near absence of these temper types among sherds found in Levels 1–3 suggests that these tempering traditions may not have persisted into historic times but were present in the precontact period. Although relative frequencies of temper types in each level do not exhibit increasing or decreasing trends, the differences between the upper three levels and the lower two are apparent (Figure 4.5).

Surface treatment frequencies also show some temporal patterning (Table 4.7). The number of simple-stamped sherds is greatest in Levels 2–4. The number of fabric-impressed sherds is greatest in Levels 4 and 5. Smoothed (plain) sherds are most common in Level 3, smoothed-over stamped (or smoothed stamped) sherds are most common in Level 2, and smoothed-over fabric-impressed (or smoothed fabric) sherds occur in Levels 1, 2, and 4. Relative frequencies of surface treatments in each level illustrate the trends more clearly (Figure 4.6). Fabric impressing has the highest proportion in Level 5 and decreases throughout the levels above. The greatest proportion of simple-stamped sherds occurs in Level 2, and proportions decrease in successively deeper levels.

When considered from the perspective of attributes composing the taxonomic classes defined for this study, the ceramic series within the midden at Cape Creek is much more complex than might be expected (Figure 4.7). As the chart indicates, there are several Early and Middle Woodland sherds mixed with the Townsend series material. New River Net Impressed and Mount Pleasant Net Impressed reflect an early component. That a few New River Net Impressed sherds were found in the first level probably reflects a certain amount of vertical mixing due to

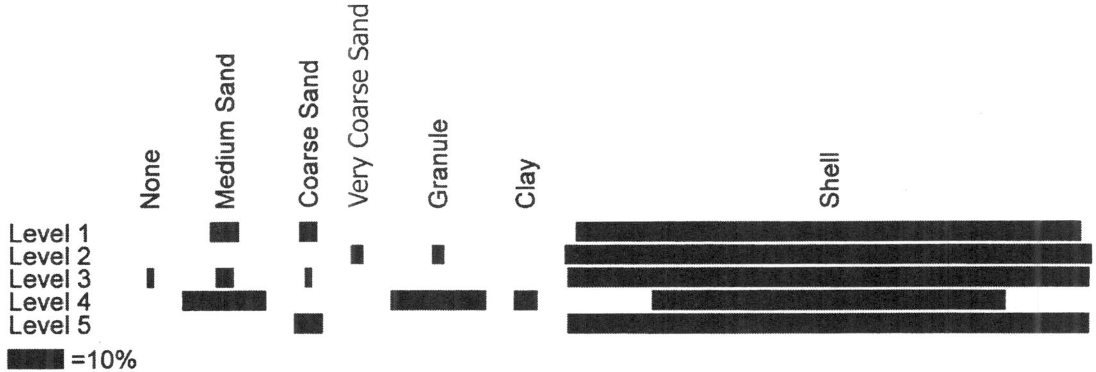

Figure 4.5. Frequency percentage chart of temper by level from the Cape Creek site.

Table 4.7. Surface Treatment Type by Level from the Cape Creek Site

	Surface Treatment								
Level	None	Smoothed	Smoothed/ Stamped	Simple Stamped	Net Impressed	Cord Marked	Fabric Impressed	Eroded	Total
1		1	2	7	1		5	23	39
2			9	37		1	4	11	62
3		20	5	38	1		4	25	93
4		7	14	48	1	1	60	75	206
5	2			3			15	22	42
Total	2	28	30	133	3	2	88	156	442

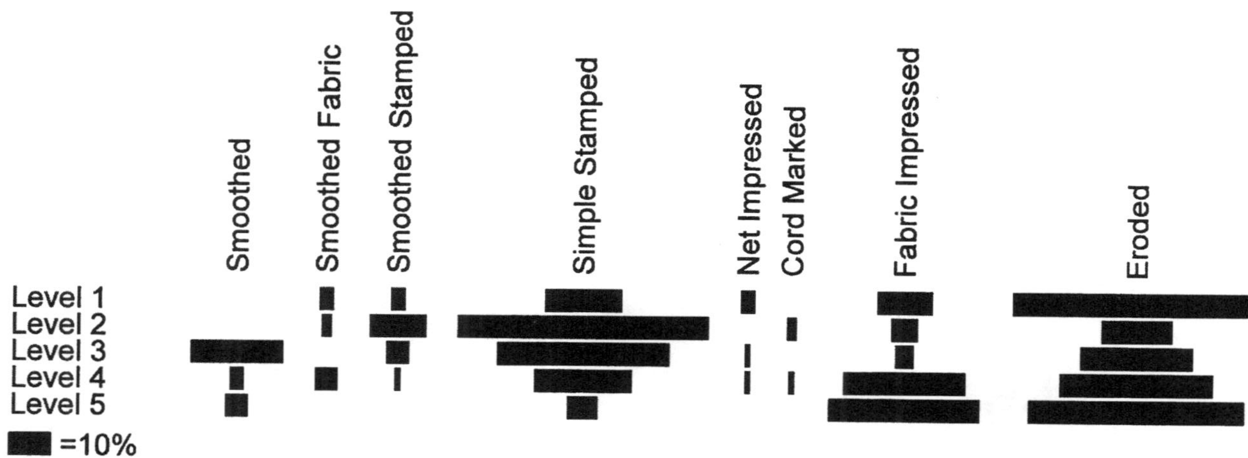

Figure 4.6. Frequency percentage chart of surface treatment by level from the Cape Creek site.

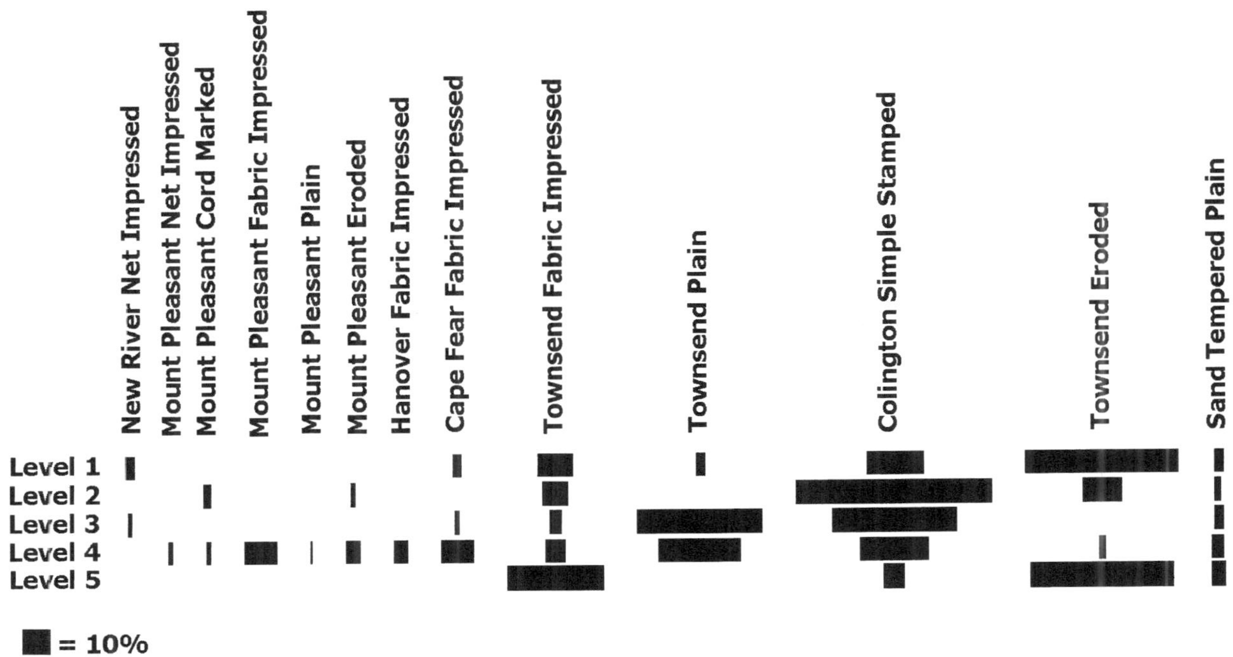

Figure 4.7. Frequency percentage chart of ceramic types by level from the Cape Creek site.

postdepositional disturbance. Mount Pleasant Plain, Mount Pleasant Fabric Impressed, Hanover Fabric Impressed, and Cape Fear Fabric Impressed types are all represented in Level 4 in very small amounts. The distribution of the Townsend series sherds illustrates the temporal relationships of types in this series. Townsend Fabric Impressed and Plain are more frequent in the lower levels, with Colington Simple Stamped predominating in the upper levels. Throughout the column are found a small number of plain sand-tempered sherds.

Whalen

The Whalen site (31BF26) is located on the west bank of St. Clair Creek at its conjunction with the Pamlico River (Figure 4.1). At this spot, a bluff extends for about 800 feet and upon it is situated the Whalen site, which Haag (1958:48) referred to as "an excellent midden." Although the midden shape was irregular at the time of Haag's visit, he estimated based on surface indications that the site extended at least 600 feet back from the bluff edge in some places. As might be imagined, the site had long been known to local residents and previous "investigations" were reported, but none that Haag could "specifically determine."

Haag (1958:98) reported that storms in 1954 had cut away about 25 feet of the site and serious damage was also reported in 1955. A 5-×-5-foot test unit was placed in an area of the site Haag thought never to have been plowed and excavation proceeded in 3-inch arbitrary levels. The top 3 inches yielded soil mixed with shell and the next 6 inches "was nearly solid shell." Below 9 inches "the shell was nearly absent although potsherds were more numerous. The soil gradually decreased in humus content and was quite clean at a depth of two feet."

Unfortunately, the size of the sample of pottery recovered at the Whalen site was quite small. Haag (1958:99, Table 4) tabulated 42 sherds recovered from his excavation. The reanalysis of that sample for this study includes 51 sherds. The distribution of temper attributes among the six excavation levels, therefore, provides only a suggestion of relative temporal sequence. Most sherds (50 percent) were found in Level 5 and most of these (76 percent) were tempered with clay (Table 4.8). There is some suggestion that clay/granule-tempered sherds occupy a position later in the sequence than sherds tempered with clay alone, and the fact that the only shell-tempered sherds (n = 2) were found in Level 1 suggests that they make up the latest position in the sequence (Figure 4.8).

Evidence for sequencing surface treatment attributes must also be considered tenuous because of the small sample size. Most (59 percent) of the sherds were fabric impressed and these occurred in every level except Level 6 (Table 4.9). A small number (n = 10) of sherds with smoothed-over stamped surfaces were found in Levels 2 and 3, and five net-impressed sherds were found in Levels 4–6 (Figure 4.9). Comparing the relative frequency of surface treatment types in each level

Table 4.8. Temper Type by Level from the Whalen Site

	Temper						
Level	Medium Sand	Coarse Sand	Granule	Clay	Clay/ Granule	Shell	Total
1		2		1		2	5
2				2	3		5
3		1			6		7
4		1		5	2		8
5	1	2	1	19	2		25
6		1					1
Total	1	7	1	27	13	2	51

suggests that net-impressed sherds are among the earliest, and surface smoothing appears to occur late in the sequence.

The vertical distribution of ceramic types among the levels at Whalen indicates that New River Net Impressed materials are among the oldest (Figure 4.10). Interestingly, the Hanover Fabric Impressed and Mount Pleasant Fabric Impressed sherds appear in reverse order, with the Hanover series appearing earlier than Mount Pleasant. This arrangement may be due, in part, to the fact that most of the sherds classified as Mount Pleasant were so classified on the basis of their including granule-sized quartz inclusions, while many also contained some clay temper. The sherds containing both granules and clay temper may represent an early component of the Hanover series or a late component of the Mount Pleasant series. Cape Fear Fabric Impressed sherds are only very slightly represented in Level 4, and a few eroded sand-tempered sherds were found in the uppermost level. Townsend Fabric Impressed occurred only in the uppermost level, suggesting that it is the youngest of the series represented.

Summary

The pottery from the Bandon midden is more diverse than that from Cape Creek and Whalen and, perhaps because of the depth of the deposit, more clearly stratified. In the deepest levels, about 37 percent of sherds tempered with medium sand were net impressed, 29 percent cord marked (parallel), and 20 percent fabric impressed (flexible warp). Two varieties of net impressing were observed: knotted open weave and knotted closed weave, sometimes referred to as "knot-roughened." The data do not suggest any particular sequence for these varieties.

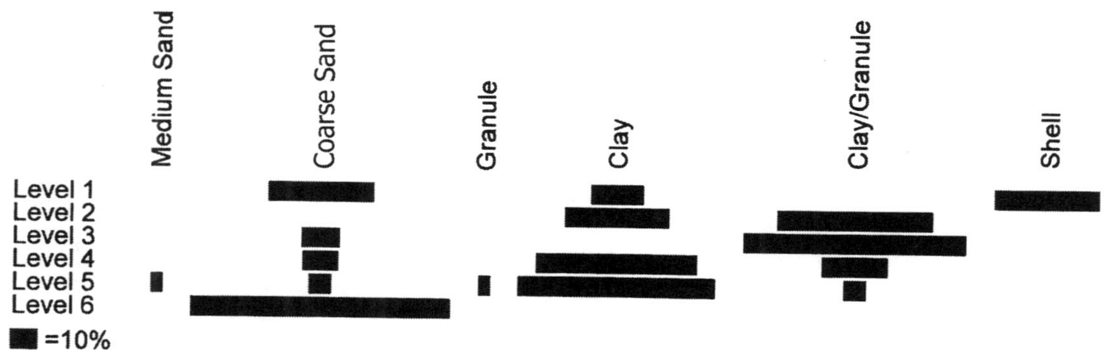

Figure 4.8. Frequency percentage chart of temper by level from the Whalen site.

Table 4.9. Surface Treatment Type by Level from the Whalen Site

	Surface Treatment						
Level	Smoothed	Smoothed/ Stamped	Net Impressed	Cord Marked	Fabric Impressed	Eroded	Total
1	1				2	2	5
2		4			1		5
3		6			1		7
4	2		1		5		8
5			3	1	21		25
6			1				1
Total	3	10	5	1	30	2	51

Although net-impressed surface treatment and sand tempering may also be found in the Mount Pleasant series (Phelps 1983:33), such pottery is here classified as New River series. Apparently, both sand tempering and net impressing are traditions that spanned many generations, finding expression in the wares of both Early and Middle Woodland potters. Phelps (1983:33) suggests that the frequency of net impressing increases through time, with a greater proportion of net impressing found in the Mount Pleasant series than in the Deep Creek phase. Data from the midden at Bandon, however, simply indicate higher percentages of net-impressed wares in the lower levels. The distinction between New River and Mount Pleasant series sherds in the Bandon assemblage was made by identifying quartz sand grain sizes and proportions in fresh breaks under low-power (×10) magnification. Sherds with a high proportion (>20 percent) of medium or fine sand, lacking granule-sized grains, were classified as New River. Those tempered principally with either fine sand or very fine sand, with granule-sized sand grains occurring in low proportion (<10 percent), were classified as Mount Pleasant. In most cases, the distinction between these wares was relatively clear; in hand samples the surfaces of sherds classified as New River feel rough to the touch, while those classified as Mount Pleasant feel smoother, with obvious, occasional larger grains. The attribution of either ware to a unique culture phase associated with the series, however, would be inappropriate based on these data.

It is worth noting that the distinction between these two wares, the size and proportion of sand in the ceramic matrix, is a functional feature that may relate to technological changes in ceramic use. Phelps (1983:33) suggests that the Deep Creek (New River) and Mount Pleasant ceramic series represent phases of a continuous technological tradition. However, whereas Phelps (1983:33) suggests that

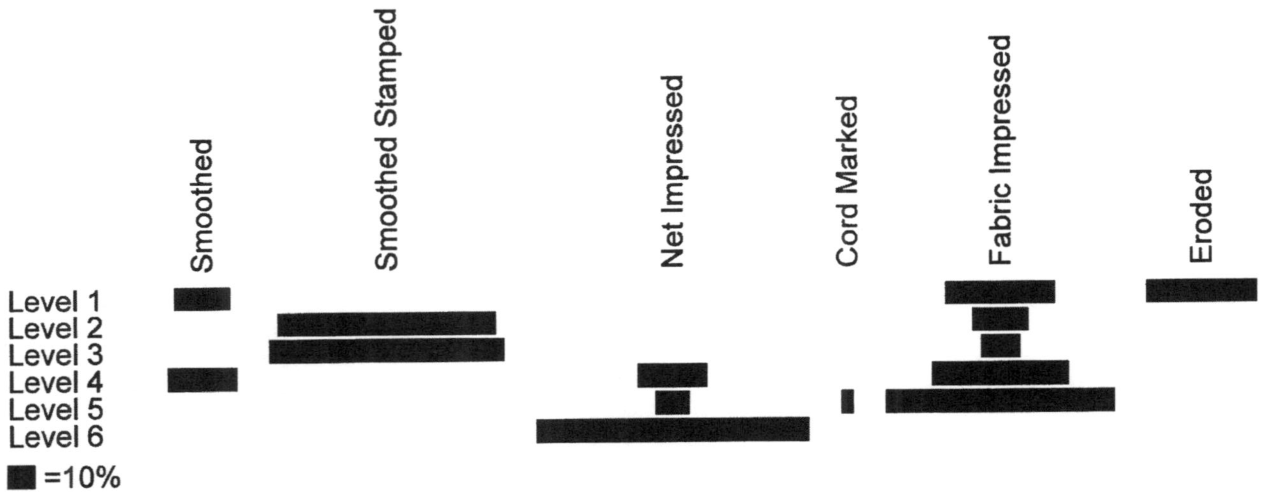

Figure 4.9. Frequency percentage chart of surface treatment by level from the Whalen site.

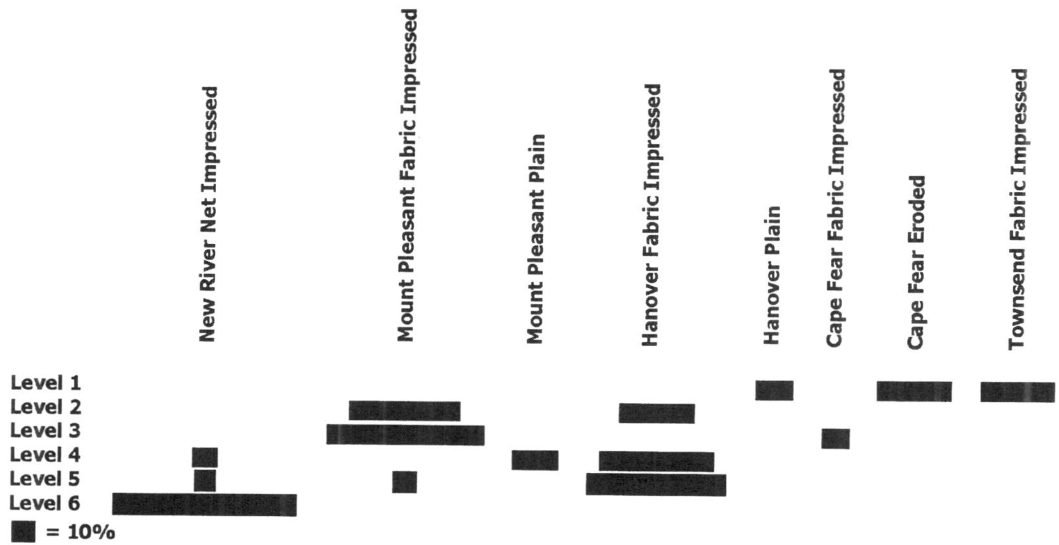

Figure 4.10. Frequency percentage chart of ceramic types from the Whalen site midden.

the proportion of granule- or pebble-sized grains increases in proportion through time from the Deep Creek to Mount Pleasant series, data from the Bandon midden show a shift from a higher frequency of the use of granule grain sizes in the lowest levels to an increased incidence of grains in the coarse and very coarse sand size range in the middle levels. The presence of clay-tempered sherds in Levels 11 and 12 might be taken as markers of the Middle Woodland tempering tradition associated with the Hanover series except for the fact that they are principally net impressed. The fact that they could only be identified as tempered with clay lumps, not clearly recognized as crushed pottery, or grog, leaves open to question whether or not the inclusion of clay pellets was incidental to the technological process.

The presence of identical surface treatment types among the New River and Mount Pleasant series pottery sample from the Bandon midden illustrates a continuation of traditional practices through the Early and Middle Woodland periods. The Mount Pleasant and New River series at Bandon included both open- and closed-weave net-impressed types. Both series also included parallel and perpendicular cord-marked types. The Mount Pleasant series sherds included four types of fabric-impressed ware. There are two broad categories of fabric-impressed ware: those with flexible (cordage) warp and those with rigid (noncordage) warp. The New River series wares included only medium weft–faced, rigid warp and medium weft–faced, flexible warp types.

Townsend series pottery occurred in the upper nine levels, mostly above Level 7 (Table 4.5, Figure 4.4). Most (58 percent) of the Townsend ware was impressed with medium weft–faced, rigid warp fabric and 25 percent was impressed with fine weft–faced, rigid warp fabric. A few Colington Simple Stamped Townsend series sherds were found in Level 5. Inspection of the casts of the surfaces of simple-stamped sherds suggests that the structure of the implement used to create the surface texture was not a carved wooden paddle but several reeds, or similar plant stems, arranged parallel to one another and used as a paddle. Two separate lines of evidence support this interpretation. First, the cast of one of the simple-stamped sherds reveals the remnants of fine cordage interwoven in weft-faced fashion over a few millimeters of the central portion of the cast. Such interwoven cordage would serve well to bind several reeds into the shape of a flat-surfaced paddle. A second form of evidence for this interpretation is provided by several Mount Pleasant Fabric Impressed sherds that exhibit worn or widely spaced weft elements that reveal the noncordage structure of the supporting warp. These examples leave little doubt that the warp foundation of much of the fabric used to impress pottery in both the Middle Woodland Mount Pleasant and Late Woodland Townsend series traditions was not cordage but a rigid plant stem similar to a reed.

In conclusion, the pottery from the Bandon, Cape Creek, and Whalen sites analyzed for this study appears to conform in large part to the existing sequence developed by Phelps, with a few notable deviations that suggest possible grounds for adjustment. Evidence from Haag's excavated materials from these three sites indicates that net-impressed or cord-marked, fine sand–tempered and fine sand/granule-tempered wares are early in the sequence. These are primarily New River and early Mount Pleasant series. There is some indication from the Bandon site that the distinction of these two series, currently made solely on the presence or absence of granule temper, can be refined as more becomes known about the variability in each of these series. Granule-tempered, net-impressed wares were among the earliest at the Bandon site, possibly prior to the Mount Pleasant phase or part of the New River series. Granule-tempered ware was more common early in the sequence, with coarse sand-tempered ware gaining dominance through the middle period of the sequence. There is also evidence that shell was occasionally added as temper in a small number of sherds that appeared to be very early in the sequence. Early wares exhibiting mixtures of tempering materials including shell, sand and granule, grog, and even possibly bone are suggested from several sites in the northern coastal region, including Long Point on the White Oak River (Shumate and Evans-Shumate 2000), the Currituck site (Painter 1977), and White Oak Point (Waselkov 1982) on Virginia's Northern Neck. The Hamp's Landing series was also represented in the lower levels of the Bandon midden by a few sherds containing leached limestone voids.

Fabric-impressed wares were most common in every part of the sequence, but the relative proportion of fabric-impressed wares was especially high in the middle portion of the sequence. Among fabric-impressed wares, there is some suggestion that textile stamps with flexible warps were used more often early in the sequence, with rigid warp textiles more commonly used later in the sequence. It is possible that the textile weaving technology may have changed in this way and that the impressions on clay vessels reflect this technological trend.

Perhaps the most intriguing aspect of the assemblage from the Bandon midden is that shell-tempered Townsend series wares are a minority, the majority ware being sand tempered. There is little doubt that this sand-tempered material is contemporary with the Townsend ware of the circum-Chesapeake and Virginia coastal region, suggesting the possibility of a Late Woodland sand-tempered ware as yet not defined in the northern coastal region. A careful inspection of the rims of sand-tempered vessels from every level of the Bandon midden assemblage indicates that rim treatments were plain in this series—no folded rims or special decorative elements occur, unlike Cashie series vessels and most Late Woodland and proto–Historic period series throughout eastern North Carolina. The classification of the sand-tempered materials from the Bandon midden as Cape Fear series is, ultimately, neither very accurate nor satisfying and illustrates the need for an additional series in the regional sequence currently being used.

The Cape Fear series in the southern coastal region appears to be related to the

Refuge-Deptford tradition of the Early and Middle Woodland periods, and TL dates obtained for Cape Fear sherds from the Riegelwood site and Fort Bragg sites suggest an age range from about 400 B.C. to A.D. 400. At present, there appears to be somewhat of a hiatus in the sequence of dates for pottery from the northern coast from this period. As additional data come to light, it is possible that the classification of sand-tempered wares from the Middle and Late Woodland period in the northern region will be reconsidered. Meanwhile, additional information from sites on the southern coast can be brought to bear on this problem and, as we shall see in the next chapter, many of the broad patterns in the sequence of temper and surface treatment choices represented at sites on the northern coast are duplicated on the southern coast.

5
Recent Excavations at Papanow, Pond Trail, and Riegelwood

Papanow (31NH690), Pond Trail (31NH465), and Riegelwood (31CB114) are sites that provide critical data for developing a Woodland ceramic sequence for the lower Cape Fear River valley. Papanow and Pond Trail are short-term habitation sites, in no way remarkable in terms of site structure, representative of the thousands of such sites that are scattered up and down the Cape Fear Valley. Riegelwood is somewhat more complex, with features and burials suggesting longer term habitation. The value of these sites for the current study, however, lies not in site structure or function but in the fact that thermoluminescence-dated pottery and ^{14}C-dated contexts were recovered at each of them, thus providing a unique opportunity to explore the sequence of stylistic traditions expressed in the Woodland period pottery of North Carolina's southern coast.

Papanow and Pond Trail

The vertical distribution of ceramics in the soil column at the Papanow site provided some clues about sequential patterning, but in order to strengthen chronological estimates of the variation observed in the Papanow and Pond Trail assemblages, thermoluminescence (TL) dating was used (Herbert 1997). The pottery samples submitted for TL dating were part of a pilot study of the efficacy and utility of TL dating on North Carolina's Coastal Plain. The method was found to be both effective and useful, and the study results are the focus of the following discussion.

The Papanow and Pond Trail sites, located adjacent to one another in the floodplain of the Northeast Cape Fear River, in New Hanover County (Figure 4.1), were discovered during an archaeological survey of the proposed Wilmington bypass (Klein et al. 1994). The Papanow site is situated on a slight rise or hammock surrounded by dense pocosin vegetation and longleaf pine forest. The Pond Trail site is about 1 km east of the Papanow site, lying on the shoulder of the terrace overlooking the floodplain escarpment.

Clusters of positive shovel tests (those yielding artifacts) concentrated on the terrace edge overlooking the floodplain or on raised hammocks within the floodplain identified the location of these sites. Six 1-x-1-m units were excavated in order to acquire pottery and soil samples suitable for analysis and TL dating. Five of these (four adjacent units in one 2-x-2-m block and one additional 1-x-1-m unit) were excavated at the Papanow site, and a single 1-x-1-m unit was excavated at the Pond Trail site. Vertical provenience was maintained in 10-cm arbitrary levels. The location of larger sherds, potentially classifiable to series, was mapped in situ and soil samples were collected for measuring radiation.

Although the Papanow and Pond Trail sites are about a kilometer apart, TL-dated pottery from the two sites was found to be contemporaneous. Therefore, their assemblages are combined in this study to increase the sample size. Five temper classes were defined for the 290 sherds recovered from excavations at the Papanow and Pond Trail sites. The largest group (68 percent) was composed of specimens tempered with medium and coarse quartz sand with occasional granule-sized particles. This assortment of grain sizes is referred to as sand/grit for shorthand and it is characteristic of both the Cape Fear and New River series. Judging from the surface treatments, at least four vessels are represented in this temper class. Grog-tempered sherds from at least two Hanover vessels make up the next most populous series (27 percent). Seven sherds from at least four vessels were found to be tempered with medium sand, and seven sherds from a single simple-stamped vessel were tempered with marl (Table 5.1).

The vertical distribution of sherds of various temper classes appears to be patterned (Table 5.2). The majority of the grog-tempered sherds were found in Level 2 (10–20 cm below the surface [cmbs]). The majority of the sand/grit-tempered sherds were found in Level 3 (20–30 cmbs), and the marl-tempered sherds were found only in Levels 3 and 4 (20–40 cmbs). Medium sand–tempered sherds were recovered in Levels 2–4 (10–40 cmbs). Judging from these data, the sequence of temper types appears, from youngest to oldest, to be grog, sand/grit, and marl, with medium sand occurring somewhere in the middle of the sequence. Although the sample size is quite small and the potential for mixing is considerable, these patterns do suggest a sequence that warrants testing.

Stratigraphic patterning is also evident among the surface treatment types from the two sites (Table 5.3). Excluding sherds with eroded or indistinct surface impressions, 277 specimens were classified according to surface treatment. The majority of the sherds impressed with fabric with medium weft diameter interwoven over rigid warp elements were found in Level 2. These appear to be the youngest of the sequence. Most sherds marked with a cordage-wrapped paddle and stamped in a perpendicular pattern were found in Level 3, in the middle of the sequence. Also in Level 3 were found the majority of the sherds whose surfaces were impressed with fabric constructed with flexible warp elements. Sherds with simple-stamped,

Table 5.1. Temper and Surface Treatment Attributes in the Papanow and Pond Trail Assemblages

Surface Treatment	Temper					Total
	None	Medium Sand	Sand/ Grit	Grog	Marl	
Simple stamped, broad					6	6
Net impressed, knotted		3				3
Cord marked, parallel			1			1
Cord marked, parallel (Z-twist)			4			4
Cord marked, perpendicular			1	3		4
Cord marked, perpendicular (S-twist)		2				2
Cord marked, perpendicular (Z-twist)			156	47	1	204
Fabric impressed, medium weft				27		27
Fabric impressed, fine weft		1				1
Fabric impressed, flexible warp		1	23			24
Punctate, stick bundle	1					1
Eroded			6	1		7
Eroded, stamped			6			6
Total	1	7	197	78	7	290

Table 5.2. Temper Type by Level from the Papanow and Pond Trail Sites

Level	Temper					Total
	None	Medium Sand	Sand/ Grit	Grog	Marl	
1			7	1		8
2		3	29	35		67
3	1	3	141	29	6	180
4		1	20	13	1	35
Total	1	7	197	78	7	290

Table 5.3. Surface Treatment Type by Level from the Papanow and Pond Trail Sites

	Surface Treatment								
Level	Simple Stamped	Net Impressed	Cord Marked, Parallel	Cord Marked, Perpendicular	Fabric Impressed, Medium	Fabric Impressed, Fine	Fabric Impressed, Flexible	Punctate	Total
1				7			1		8
2				35	21		9		65
3	5	2	2	142	5	1	11	1	169
4	1	1	1	28	1		3		35
Total	6	3	3	212	27	1	24	1	277

net-impressed, and parallel cord-marked surfaces were restricted to Levels 3 and 4 and these appear to be the earliest in the sequence.

Five TL-dated pottery samples from the sites range in mean age from 1221 B.C. to A.D. 1319 (Table 5.4). In general, the dates agree with the sequence suggested by the vertical arrangement of sherds. The parallel variety of cord marking and flexible warp fabric impressing are the earliest surface treatment styles, occurring in the Early Woodland and earliest portion of the Middle Woodland periods. This is followed in the Middle Woodland period by the perpendicular variety of cord marking and fabric made by interweaving weft cordage of medium width (1–2 mm) over rigid warp elements.

The oldest luminescence date (1221 ± 436 B.C.) was obtained for a New River Cord Marked specimen (Figure 5.1). An Early Woodland date (434 ± 250 B.C.) was also obtained for a sand/grit-tempered, fabric-impressed (flexible warp) New River series sample (Figure 5.2).

A date of A.D. 173 ± 228 was obtained for a sand/grog-tempered Hanover Cord Marked vessel (P2) from Papanow (Figure 5.3). The tempering material used in preparing this vessel was sand and crushed pottery, with grog fragments as large as 4 mm seen in broken cross sections and lumps protruding from the interior of the vessel wall. Petrography established the presence of medium to very coarse grog in 1-percent proportion, most with the same paste as the matrix.

The surface of the vessel was carefully overstamped at angles of nearly 90 degrees with a paddle wrapped with Z-twist cordage of 1-mm diameter, spaced about 2 mm apart. Several fragments of this vessel were also conjoined to reconstruct a partial base (Figure 5.4), which was stamped differently from the middle and upper portions of the vessel, with repeated overstamping with the edge of the cord-wrapped paddle. Obliquely overstamped cord impressions on the upper portion of the basal section are similar to those on sherds from the upper vessel walls.

Another Hanover vessel (P1), represented by 27 pieces from Levels 1–4 was TL dated A.D. 680 ± 145 (Figure 5.5). The largest grog particles in this fabric-impressed vessel were 3–4 mm and often created pronounced lumps on the interior. In thin section, grog particles in 1- to 3-percent proportion were in the coarse to granule size. The fabric impressed on the surface was constructed of weft cordage, 1–2 mm in diameter, interwoven or twined around rigid warp elements of 2 mm diameter. Some overstamping was apparent.

The youngest TL date (A.D. 1319 ± 192) for pottery from the Papanow site was obtained for a fragment of a sand/grog-tempered Hanover Cord Marked vessel (P3, Figure 5.6). The quartz sand temper, in 10-percent proportion, ranged from fine to very coarse size. Cord impressions were identical to those from the Hanover vessel dated A.D. 173 ± 228. Two-ply, Z-twist cordage of 1-mm diameter, spaced about 2 mm apart, was overstamped at an angle of about 45 degrees.

The five TL-dated vessels represent five pottery classes making up most of the

Table 5.4. Temper and Surface Treatment Attributes of TL-Dated Pottery from the Papanow and Pond Trail Sites

		Proportion of Temper Constituents (%)[b]						Surface Treatment Characteristics				
Sample[a]	Temper Type	Quartz vf–f	Quartz m–vc	Other vf–vc	Quartz/ Other Total	Grog	Surface Treatment	Secondary	Tertiary	Twist	Ceramic Series	TL Date
P1	Sand/grog	5	<1	2	8	1–3	Fabric impressed	Rigid warp	Medium weft		Hanover	A.D. 680 ± 145
P2	Sand/grog	5	1–3	2	8–10	1	Cord marked	Over-stamped	Perpendicular	Z	Hanover	A.D. 173 ± 228
P3	Sand/grit-grog	3	7	2	12	1	Cord marked	Over-stamped	Perpendicular	Z	Hanover	A.D. 1319 ± 192
P4	Sand/grit	5	6–8	1	12–15		Fabric impressed	Flexible warp	Medium weft		New River	434 ± 250 B.C.
P5	Sand/grit	3–5	7–13	2–4	9–17		Cord marked	Over-stamped	Parallel	Z	New River	1221 ± 436 B.C.

[a]University of Washington Luminescence Laboratory sample numbers: P1, UW-222; P2, UW-223; P3, UW-224; P4, UW-226; P5, UW-225.

[b]Key to size-grade abbreviations: vf = very fine; f = fine; m = medium; vc = very coarse. Other minerals include polycrystalline quartz, microline, rock fragments, feldspar, and microperthite.

Figure 5.1. New River Cord Marked sherds from Levels 3 and 4 at the Papanow site. A similar sherd from this context, probably from the same vessel, was TL dated 1221 ± 436 B.C.

sherds found at the sites. In addition, several vessels were represented by a few undated sherds. Two vessels reflecting Early Woodland occupations are represented by six marl-tempered sherds (Figure 5.7). The presence of marl temper is inferred from the blocky voids or pores that result from the dissolution of calcareous material, visible on the surface and in cross section.

The identification of limestone or marl temper on the basis of voids in the clay matrix is not a foolproof system. The presence of former limestone temper in the simple-stamped sherds (Figure 5.7) was easily identified by the size and shape of voids, but the voids in the cord-marked ware were much smaller. It is possible that voids created by the oxidation of noncalcareous organic material may be mistaken for marl voids. The identification of marl tempering in the cord-marked specimens is, therefore, less certain. In addition to the marl-tempered sherds, one simple-stamped sherd was noted to have no temper at all. The apparent absence of temper is common to some other Early Woodland series such as Thom's Creek.

Also represented in the Papanow assemblage was a small vessel tempered with medium sand and impressed with knotted net (Figure 5.8, A and B). The thin-walled (about 6 mm), slightly inverted rim section suggested a small bowl or jar with a rounded, smoothed lip. The net was knotted and had relatively narrow mesh openings (about 4 mm). This probably represents an Early Woodland vessel.

Also found in the Papanow excavation were remnants of a Cape Fear Fabric Impressed vessel. It was tempered with medium sand and stamped on the exterior with fabric constructed of fine weft (1 mm or less) interwoven over rigid warp elements of a wider dimension (3–4 mm) (Figure 5.8, C). Overstamping on this

Figure 5.2. New River Fabric Impressed sherds from Levels 1–4 at the Papanow site. A similar sherd from this context, probably from the same vessel, was TL dated 434 ± 250 B.C.

sherd prevented the recognition of any larger section of fabric and, consequently, overstamping with the edge of a cord-wrapped paddle cannot be ruled out.

These assays provide an Early Woodland age (1221 ± 436 B.C.) for New River Cord Marked and a somewhat later date for New River Fabric Impressed (434 ± 250 B.C.) and suggest that the New River series includes an earlier thick-walled, coarse sand–tempered, cord-marked type and a later type that is less thick, tempered with medium sand, and impressed with fabric. Obviously, the confirma-

Figure 5.3. Hanover Cord Marked sherds from Levels 1–4 at the Papanow site. This vessel (P2) was TL dated A.D. 173 ± 228.

Figure 5.4. Hanover Cord Marked conjoined fragments from basal section of vessel P2 (A.D. 173 ± 228).

tion of this trend awaits further dating opportunities. It is noteworthy, however, that this work at Papanow and Pond Trail is the first to establish the presence of an Early Woodland sand-tempered series in the southern coastal area. Such documentation is not surprising given what is known from the neighboring regions, but it is notable in that no such series was provided in the sequence first hypothesized by South (1960).

Figure 5.5. Hanover Fabric Impressed sherds. Samples A and B, from Pond Trail (vessel P1), were dated A.D. 680 ± 145. Samples C–F, from sites in Brunswick County, are impressed with fabric consisting of 1- to 2-mm weft cordage interwoven or twined around rigid warps.

Figure 5.6. Hanover Cord Marked rims (vessel P3), TL dated A.D. 1319 ± 192.

Dating from the Papanow and Pond Trail sites also confirms the position of the Hanover grog-tempered series in the Middle Woodland period as anticipated by South (1960) and suggests that Hanover Cord Marked may, generally speaking, predate Hanover Fabric Impressed. Again, the data are much too sparse to consider this hypothesis finally substantiated, but these dates do tend to agree with trends in surface treatment practices observed elsewhere on the coast.

A Late Woodland date (A.D. 1319 ± 192) obtained for the sand/grog-tempered, cord-marked (perpendicular) vessel, classified as Hanover, is at variance with the current understanding of the temporal placement of the Hanover series in the Middle Woodland period. The first and most obvious place to look for an explanation for this outlying date is with the dating process. The TL date obtained for

Figure 5.7. Hamp's Landing Cord Marked (A and B) and Hamp's Landing Simple Stamped (C–E) sherds.

this sherd was, in fact, problematic for several reasons and is best considered as a minimum age, although we can be confident of a post–A.D. 800 age for this vessel. This assay, therefore, indicates that the grog-tempering tradition extended into the Late Woodland period. As will be seen in subsequent chapters, the inclusion of grog in minor amounts in an otherwise sand-tempered paste seems to have been commonplace in the Late Woodland period on the southern coast. It should be acknowledged that identifying grog in such a low proportion and small size is difficult macroscopically. In fact, grog was not identified in Papanow vessel P3 until the petrographic results were obtained.

Figure 5.8. New River Net Impressed (A and B) and Cape Fear Fabric Impressed (fine weft) (C) sherds from the Papanow site.

In conclusion, it might be useful to note that the Papanow and Pond Trail sites were not in the least unusual or outstanding among the thousands of such sites that may be found on slightly elevated ground in the broad lower Cape Fear floodplain. The suggestion of vertical patterning of cultural material was not observed as stratigraphy in the excavations but was discernible only in the laboratory as the data were analyzed. Corroboration of the pattern observed in the data was possible with TL dating, which has the distinct advantage of providing an age estimate for the object, not the context in which it is found. Similar independent age assessments for pottery using radiocarbon would not have been possible, as the amount of vertical mixing and absence of features would have made the association of carbonized plant remains and pottery little more than guesswork.

With the use of petrography and TL dating, a sequence of tempering and surface treatment styles was confidently identified in the Papanow and Pond Trail sample. Combined, these data provide the basis for a pottery sequence for the lower Cape Fear basin. In the next section I describe how data from the Riegelwood site, also found in the lower Cape Fear valley, corroborate and strengthen this initial sequence.

Riegelwood

The Riegelwood site (31CB114) encompasses some 24,000 m^2 on a broad terrace lying about 3 m above sea level on the bank of the embayed lower reach of the Cape Fear River in Columbus County (Figure 4.1). Pottery found at this location represents the ceramic industries of the lower Cape Fear valley through much of the Woodland era.

The site was discovered and initially tested by Coastal Carolina Research to evaluate the potential effects of the proposed installation of a wastewater facility at International Paper's Riegelwood Operations (Lautzenheiser et al. 1997; Lautzenheiser et al. 1995). Following testing, the site was determined eligible for nomination to the National Register of Historic Places. It was during the data-recovery phase of investigations conducted by New South Associates (Abbott et al. 1999) that the features and associated pottery described in this section were found.

Data-recovery procedures at Riegelwood consisted of the mechanical removal of the topsoil to expose prehistoric features and the excavation of the locations where artifacts were observed. In most cases features were identified by the presence of artifacts, the organic residues of prehistoric activities having long since been leached from the sandy soil. Among the many features so exposed, five yielded 18 pottery samples selected for TL dating. Each pottery sample was associated with a soil sample collected from 20 to 50 cm below the pre-excavation surface within the context thought to be within the feature. Each context is described below.

Feature 1 was originally described as the remains of a single Hamp's Landing series vessel, sherds of which were dispersed in a 56-cm semicircular pattern along with bone fragments (Lautzenheiser et al. 1997). Excavation of this feature by New South exposed a variety of pottery types including Cape Fear Fabric Impressed, Hanover Cord Marked, New River Fabric Impressed, New River Cord Marked, Hamp's Landing Simple Stamped, Hamp's Landing Cord Marked, and Hamp's Landing Fabric Impressed (Abbott et al. 1999:131). The human bone was found over a 1.5-m-diameter area, extending about 35 cm beneath the surface. Charred plant remains derived from the fine-fraction flotation sediment produced a ^{14}C date of 2470 ± 40 B.P. (787–405 cal B.C. [p = .05]) (Table 5.5). Based on current radiocarbon evidence for the Early Woodland period in this region, it is likely that this radiocarbon date is associated with the New River and Hamp's Landing pottery. As part of this study, a Hamp's Landing Cord Marked sherd (Sample R10,

Table 5.5. Radiocarbon Dates from Features at the Riegelwood Site

Sample	Context	Target Pottery	Minimum (Mean) Maximum[a]
B-115425	Feature 1	New River, Hamp's Landing, Hanover, and Cape Fear series	–785 (–750, –695, –540) –410
B-115428	Feature 7	Thom's Creek Cord Marked?	–2198 (–2012, –2000, –1978) –1773
B-115427	Feature 6	Hamp's Landing Simple Stamped	–2273 (–2129, –2082, –2043) –1943
B-115429	Feature 10	Hamp's Landing Simple Stamped and Cord Marked	–2200 (–2129, –2082, –2043) –1957
B-115426	Feature 3	New River series	–3018 (–2898) –2764

[a]Minimum, mean, and maximum dates are 2σ intercepts calibrated with the Calib 4.3 program using the atmospheric decadal data set (Stuiver and Reimer 1993). Date ranges with ages B.C. are shown as negative numbers.

Vessel 1) from Feature 1 was TL dated 221 ± 249 B.C. (709 B.C.–A.D. 267 [p = .05], UW-654; see Table 5.6).

Features 4 and 5 consisted of the partial remains of two prehistoric ceramic vessels (Abbott et al. 1999:56, Figure 6.4). Feature 4 was identified as the remains of a Hanover Cord Marked vessel spread over the 2-×-2-m excavation unit. One sherd (Sample R7, Vessel 2) from this vessel was TL dated A.D. 675 ± 172 (A.D. 338–1012 [p = .05], UW-651; see Table 5.6). Also within this unit were the partial remains of a Hanover Fabric Impressed vessel identified as Feature 5 (Abbott et al. 1999:56, Figure 6.4).

Feature 7 consisted of the fragments of a conjoinable vessel section classified by New South as Thom's Creek Cord Marked. As Thom's Creek Cord Marked has yet to be described and formally defined in the literature, it is considered a provisional type and a question mark follows this type name in Table 5.5. The sherds were dispersed over a 1-×-1-m area in Unit N228 E164 (Abbott et al. 1999:58, Figure 6.7). Also found in this location were fragments of Hanover Cord Marked, Cape Fear Fabric Impressed, and sand-tempered, net-impressed ware. Although the sand-tempered, net-impressed ware was classified by New South as Cape Fear series, by the system employed in this study it should be classified as New River series. Found in association with this pottery were three cremations (Features 1, 3, and 6) and a hearth (Feature 10). Carbonized plant remains recovered from the flotation of sediments where the pottery was most dense were radiocarbon dated to 3630 ± 70 B.P. (2198–1773 cal B.C. [p = .05]).

Six TL dates were obtained for pottery from Feature 7 (Tables 5.6 and 5.7). Petrographic data suggest that among the six TL-dated samples from the area near Feature 7 there are a minimum of four vessels, with five possible. The youngest sample (R12) was from a Hanover Cord Marked vessel (Vessel 3) dated A.D. 931 ± 154. Although Samples R6 and R11 (Vessels 4 and 5) are both classified as Cape Fear Cord Marked and have very similar ages (A.D. 5 ± 206 and A.D. 4 ± 184, respectively), their constituents differ enough to warrant their assignment to different vessels (Table 5.7). Samples R8 and R9 are almost certainly from the same vessel (Vessel 6). This is the vessel that was identified by Abbott et al. (1999:58, Figure 6.7) as Thom's Creek Cord Marked. The difference in the dates for Samples R8 (199 ± 185 B.C.) and R9 (1000 ± 819 B.C.) may be due to the fact that R9 exhibited significant anomalous fading. Although the age estimate for R9 was corrected, the date for R8 is probably the better estimate of the age of Vessel 6. Despite the fact that the paste constituents of Sample R14 are very similar to those of Vessel 6 (R8 and R9), Sample R14 is interpreted as Vessel 7 because the width and spacing of cords impressed on this vessel were different from those observed on Vessel 6. Vessel 7 (R14) is provisionally classified as Thom's Creek Cord Marked, following New South.

Feature 10 consisted of the fragments of a conjoinable Hamp's Landing Simple Stamped vessel and a fire hearth (Abbott et al. 1999:61, Figure 6.9). Hamp's Landing sherds were dispersed over a 1-x-1-m area and were associated with a fire-cracked-rock hearth. Also found in association with, or near, the hearth and remains of the Hamp's Landing vessel were fragments of Hanover Cord Marked, Refuge Punctate *variety Allendale,* New River Fabric Impressed, and New River Cord Marked vessels. A charcoal sample obtained from a flotation sample taken from the area near the Hamp's Landing vessel and rock hearth yielded a radiocarbon date of 3700 ± 40 B.P. (2200–1957 cal B.C. [p = .05]) (Table 5.5). Six TL dates were obtained for pottery associated with Feature 10 (Table 5.8).

Among the seven sherds that were submitted for TL dating from the area in and around Feature 10, six vessels are represented. A New River Fabric Impressed sherd (Vessel 8, Sample R2) was found to be undatable by the TL method. Sample R3 was a Hanover Cord Marked jar (Vessel 9, A.D. 701 ± 311) represented by a rim sherd. Vessel 10 was represented by a rim sherd (Sample R1) of a Refuge Punctate *variety Allendale* jar. Unfortunately, this sample exhibited high scatter in growth curves so that its date (A.D. 634 ± 393) is unreliable. Vessel 11 was represented by two Hanover Cord Marked rim sherds (Samples R4 and R5). The difference in the dates for Samples R4 and R5 (A.D. 184 ± 241 and A.D. 462 ± 148, respectively) is possibly due to the fact that Sample R4 exhibited anomalous fading, rendering its age estimate less reliable. There is some suggestion from the petrographic data, however, that Samples R4 and R5 may have been from distinct vessels, although their appearance macroscopically suggested they were from the same vessel. A very

Table 5.6. Temper and Surface Treatment, TL Dates, and Ceramic Series for the Riegelwood Samples

Sample	Temper Type	Proportion of Temper Constituents (%)[a]				
		Quartz vf–f	Quartz m–vc	Other vf–vc	Quartz/ Other Total	Grog
R1 (UW-645)[b]	Limestone	3	1–3	5–7 (3%–5% voids)	9–13	
R2 (UW-646)	Medium sand	3	6–9	3–5	12–17	
R3 (UW-647)	Sand/grog	3–5	2–4	1–2	6–11	3
R4 (UW-648)[c]	Sand/grog	3–5	6–7	2	11–14	3
R5 (UW-649)	Sand/grog	3–5	4–7	3–6	10–18	3
R6 (UW-650)	Sand/grit	3	9–13	5–8	17–24	
R7 (UW-651)	Sand/grog	3–5	4–5	3–7	10–17	3
R8 (UW- 652)	Fine/medium sand	10	6	6–8	22– 24	
R9 (UW-653)[c]	Fine/medium sand	10	6–8	6–10	22–28	
R10 (UW-654)	Limestone	10	4–5	4–6 (3% voids)	18–21	
R11 (UW-655)	Fine/medium sand	10	8	6–8	24–26	
R12 (UW-656)	Sand/grog	3	4	2	9	3–5
R13 (UW-657)[c]	Limestone	5	3–6	8 (5% voids)	16–18	
R14 (UW-658)	Fine/medium sand	5–10	6–9	6–8	17–27	
R15 (UW-659)[b]	Sand/grog	5–10	3–4	6	14–20	3
R16 (UW-660)	Sand/grit	3	7–9	2	12–14	
R17 (UW-661)	Fine/medium sand	5	8	6–9	19–22	
R18 (UW-662)	Sand/grit	5	9–14	5	19–24	

[a]Key to size-grade abbreviations: vf = very fine; f = fine; m = medium; vc = very coarse. Other minerals include polycrystalline quartz, microline, rock fragments, feldspar, and microperthite.

[b]Samples R1 and R15 exhibited intolerably high scatter in the growth curves and, thus, high error. Consequently, their age estimates are unreliable.

Surface Treatment	Surface Treatment Characteristics			Ceramic Series	TL Date
	Secondary	Tertiary	Twist		
Punctate	Bundled drag-and-jab	Left-to-right		Refuge	A.D. 634 ± 393
Fabric impressed	Flexible warp	Medium weft		New River	No TL signal
Cord marked	Overstamped	Parallel	Z	Hanover I	A.D. 701 ± 311
Cord marked	Overstamped	Perpendicular	Z	Hanover I	A.D. 184 ± 241
Cord marked	Overstamped	Perpendicular	Z	Hanover I	A.D. 462 ± 148
Cord marked	Overstamped	Perpendicular		Cape Fear	A.D. 5 ± 206
Cord marked	Overstamped	Perpendicular	Z	Hanover I	A.D. 675 ± 172
Cord marked	Overstam ped	Perpendi cular	Z	Cape Fear	199 ± 185 B.C.
Cord marked	Overstamped	Perpendicular	Z	Cape Fear	1000 ± 819 B.C.
Cord marked	Overstamped	Parallel	Z	Hamp's Landing	221 ± 249 B.C.
Cord marked	Overstamped	Perpendicular	Z	Cape Fear	A.D. 4 ± 184
Fabric impressed	Rigid warp	Fine weft		Hanover I	A.D. 931 ± 154
Simple stamped	Wide, flat	Round-edged		Hamp's Landing	3056 ± 2598 B.C.
Cord marked	Overstamped	Perpendicular		Cape Fear	1247 ± 329 B.C.
Fabric impressed	Rigid warp	Medium weft		Hanover I	A.D. 528 ± 301
Cord marked	Overstamped	Parallel		New River	1385 ± 569 B.C.
Cord marked	Overstamped	Perpendicular		Cape Fear	168 ± 186 B.C.
Cord marked	Overstamped	Perpendicular	Z	New River	1765 ± 714 B.C.

[c]Samples R4, R9, and R13 showed significant anomalous fading. Although corrected for fading, high scatter reduced precision dramatically.

Table 5.7. Petrographic Data for TL-Dated Vessels from Feature 7

Sample	Vessel No.	Proportion of Temper Constituents (%)[a] Fine Sand	Medium Sand	Coarse Sand	Grog	Sponge Spicules	Phytoliths	Muscovite Mica	Ceramic Series	TL Date
R12	3	3	3	1	3–5			1	Hanover I	A.D. 931 ± 154
R6	4	3	3–5	5		<1	<1	3	Cape Fear	A.D. 5 ± 206
R11	5	10	5	3		5	3	3	Cape Fear	A.D. 4 ± 184
R8	6	10	5	1		3–5	1	3 (w/biotite)	Cape Fear	199 ± 185 B.C.
R9	6	10	5	1–3		3–5	1	3 (w/biotite)	Cape Fear	1000 ± 819 B.C.[b]
R14	7	5–10	5	1–3		3–5	1	1–3 (w/biotite)	Thom's Creek (?)	1247 ± 329 B.C.

[a]These values are for quartz sand only.

[b]The age estimate of R9 is unreliable due to anomalous fading.

Table 5.8. Petrographic Data for TL-Dated Vessels from Feature 10

Sample	Vessel No.	Proportion of Temper Constituents (%)[a]							Ceramic Series	TL Date
		Fine Sand	Medium Sand	Coarse Sand	Grog	Sponge Spicules	Phytoliths	Muscovite Mica		
R2	8	5	1–3	<1	1	5	>1	1–3	New River	No TL signal
R3	9	3	3	3	1			5 (w/biotite)	Hanover	A.D. 701 ± 311
R1	10	5	<1		1–3		>1	1–3 (w/biotite)	Refuge	A.D. 634 ± 393[b]
R5	11	3–5	3–5	3–5		3	>1	1–3 (w/biotite)	Hanover	A.D. 462 ± 148
R4	11	5	3	3–5	<1			1–3 (w/biotite)	Hanover	A.D. 184 ± 241[c]
R16	12	3	3–5	3				1	New River	1385 ± 569 B.C.
R13	13	5	3–5	<1				1–3	Hamp's Landing	3056 ± 2598 B.C.[c]

[a]These values for quartz sand only.

[b]The age estimate of R1 is unreliable due to high scatter in the growth curves.

[c]The age estimates of R4 and R13 are unreliable due to anomalous fading.

small proportion (<1 percent) of green pleochroic mineral and chert was found in R4, while none was found in R5. Small amounts (1 percent or less) of plagioclase and feldspar were found in Sample R5, but not in R4. Sample R16 represented a New River Cord Marked vessel (Vessel 12) dated 1385 ± 569 B.C. Sample R13 represented a Hamp's Landing Simple Stamped jar (Vessel 13). Unfortunately, the TL date for this sample (3056 ± 2598 B.C.) is unreliable due to anomalous fading.

Two samples (R17 and R18) not associated with features were TL dated. Sample R17 was a Cape Fear Cord Marked (perpendicular overstamped) vessel dated 168 ± 186 B.C. Sample R18 was a New River Cord Marked (parallel to oblique overstamped) vessel dated 1765 ± 714 B.C.

The range of the mean values of the 12 TL dates (excluding unreliable dates) for pottery from Riegelwood spans 2,696 years from 1765 B.C. to A.D. 931. This range of age estimates may be parsed into four segments based on petrographic data that reveal four classes of temper: sand/grit, fine/medium sand, crushed limestone, and sand/grog. The three sherds (R6, R16, and R18) classified as sand/grit tempered incorporate quartz sand grains in several sizes including very fine (vf, .0625–.125 mm) through very coarse (vc, 1–2 mm). The threshold for inclusion in this class is the presence of at least 1 percent very coarse sand (and no grog). A box plot of the distribution of the mean TL dates indicates an extensive age range for this group from 1765 B.C. to A.D. 5 (Figure 5.9). Ratios of sand- (very fine–fine) to grit-sized (medium–very coarse) grains do appear to be temporally patterned, such that the proportion of the grit (very coarse and larger grains) included as temper in the ceramic matrix tends to be lower (<1 percent) in younger samples (in the Cape Fear series, typically post–400 B.C.). Among sand/grit-tempered sherds, the oldest have the highest proportion of sand, grit, or rock temper and the youngest sherds the lowest.

Of three sherds tempered with crushed limestone (R1, R10, and R13), only one (R10) produced a TL date that was reliable, 221 ± 249 B.C. (Table 5.6). Sample R1, a Refuge Punctate *variety Allendale* sherd with 3- to 5-percent limestone voids, exhibited an intolerably high scatter and therefore the age estimate from this sample is not considered reliable. Sample R13, a Hamp's Landing Simple Stamped sherd with 5-percent limestone voids, showed significant decay, or anomalous fading, after one week. Although the age estimate of this sherd was corrected for fading, the data were highly scattered, thereby reducing the precision so dramatically that the estimate is not considered reliable.

Six sherds were tempered with varying proportions of fine, medium, and coarse sand, but less than 1 percent very coarse sand (Samples R2, R8, R9, R11, R14, and R17). These were classified as fine/medium sand tempered (Table 5.6). Sample R2 produced no measurable natural luminescence signal and did not respond with a measurable signal when exposed to a standard dose of radiation. The sensitivity of this sample was extremely low, preventing any reasonable dating. Sample R9 was

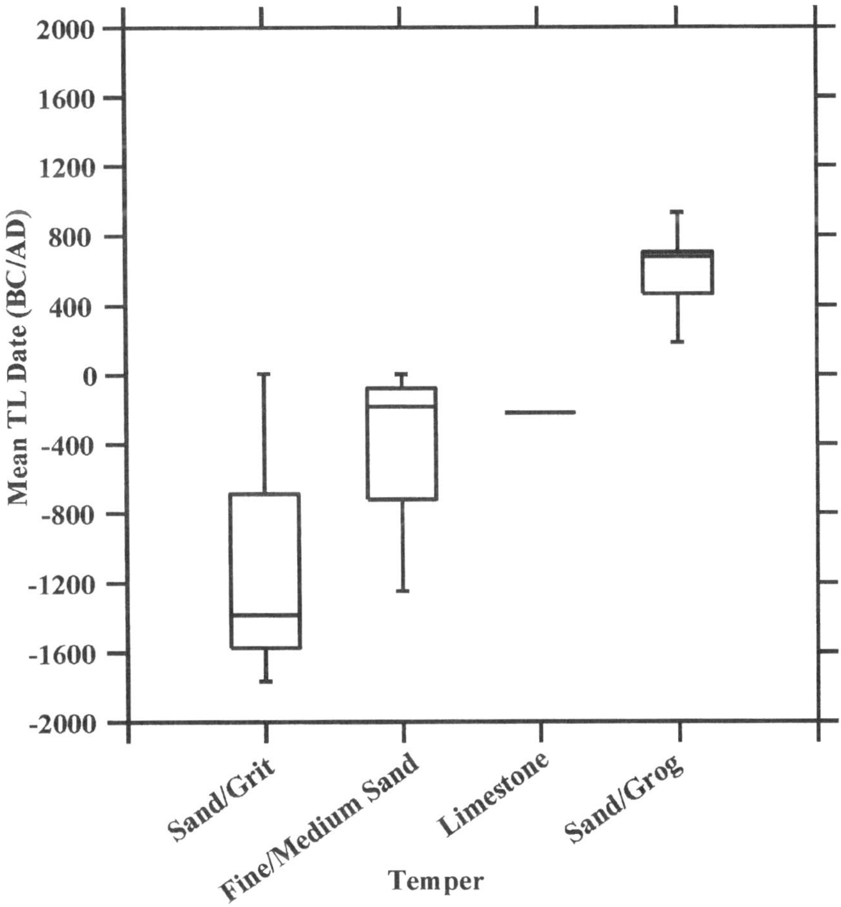

Figure 5.9. Mean TL dates for temper types in the Riegelwood sample.

classified as Cape Fear Cord Marked. This sample showed significant anomalous fading after one week and although corrected for fading, the highly scattered data reduced the precision so dramatically that the estimate is not considered reliable. Although the range of mean TL dates for this temper group is again quite broad, 1,251 years (1247 B.C. to A.D. 4), the median age of this group is A.D. 184.

Six sherds tempered with sand and grog were submitted for TL dating (R3, R4, R5, R7, R12, and R15). Of these, five produced reliable age estimates ranging in mean age from A.D. 184 to A.D. 931, with the median age being A.D. 675 (Table 5.6, Figure 5.9). Sample R4 showed significant anomalous fading after one week of storage. A correction for this was applied and, because the data were less highly scattered, the precision was better than that of other samples that faded (Sample R4 exhibited 13-percent error, while Samples R9 and R13 had 27.3- and 51.2-percent error, respectively). Therefore the age estimate for Sample R4 (A.D. 184 ± 241) was considered acceptable, while R9 and R13 are not included in the summary statistics. Sample R15 also is not included, as it exhibited intolerably high scatter.

The principal component of the temper in the sand/grog-tempered sherds is sand. Grog in fine to granular size ranges was found in the matrix in proportions between 3 and 5 percent. Sherds with 3-percent grog were the mode and all were also classified as Hanover series in the original analysis based on macroscopic, not petrographic, data (Abbott et al. 1999). No sherds were found to have a higher proportion of grog than sand.

Three surface treatment classes are represented among the TL-dated samples from Riegelwood: cord-marked overstamped parallel (variety 1), cord-marked overstamped perpendicular (variety 2), and fabric impressed (Figure 5.10). Three sherds are from vessels overstamped with a cord-wrapped paddle, producing a parallel pattern of cord impressions. This group of cord-marked sherds ranges in mean age from 1385 B.C. to A.D. 701, with a median value of 221 B.C. (Table 5.6). All samples, whether having parallel or perpendicular overstamped cord impressions, exhibit Z-twist cordage.

The youngest sample in this group (R3) is a sand/grog-tempered rim sherd. Found associated with this rim were many perpendicular cord-marked sherds that were thought to be associated with this rim. Parallel (vertical) cord marking is sometimes found on vessels whose body walls are stamped with perpendicular cord marking. As the vessel was not reconstructed, it could not be determined with certainty that this parallel cord-marked rim conjoined perpendicular-stamped body sherds, and therefore Sample R3 is included in the parallel-stamped group. If such a determination had been made and R3 not included in this group, the range of dates for the parallel-stamped cord-marked samples would have been 1385 to 221 B.C., with a median value of 803 B.C.

Seven perpendicular cord-marked sherds range in age from 1247 B.C. to A.D. 675, with a median age of A.D. 4 (Figure 5.10). Only one fabric-impressed sherd, with a mean TL date of A.D. 931, is included in this sample. The textile impressed on the surface of this sherd was weft-faced, interwoven fabric with a weft cordage diameter of less than 1 mm and a rigid warp diameter of about 2 mm.

In summary, determining the temporal relationships of temper and surface treatment types at Riegelwood provided a means of exploring the trends in these technological traditions over the Woodland era in the southern coastal region of North Carolina. Four ceramic series were identified among the 18-sherd sample from the Riegelwood site selected for TL dating: the New River, Hamp's Landing, Cape Fear, and Hanover I series (Figure 5.11). Sand appears to have been included as a tempering agent in every period from 1200 B.C. up to the Late Woodland (A.D. 900) and occurred mostly in combination with grog after A.D. 400. In contrast to results in a 20-sherd sample from the Sandhills (Herbert et al. 2002),

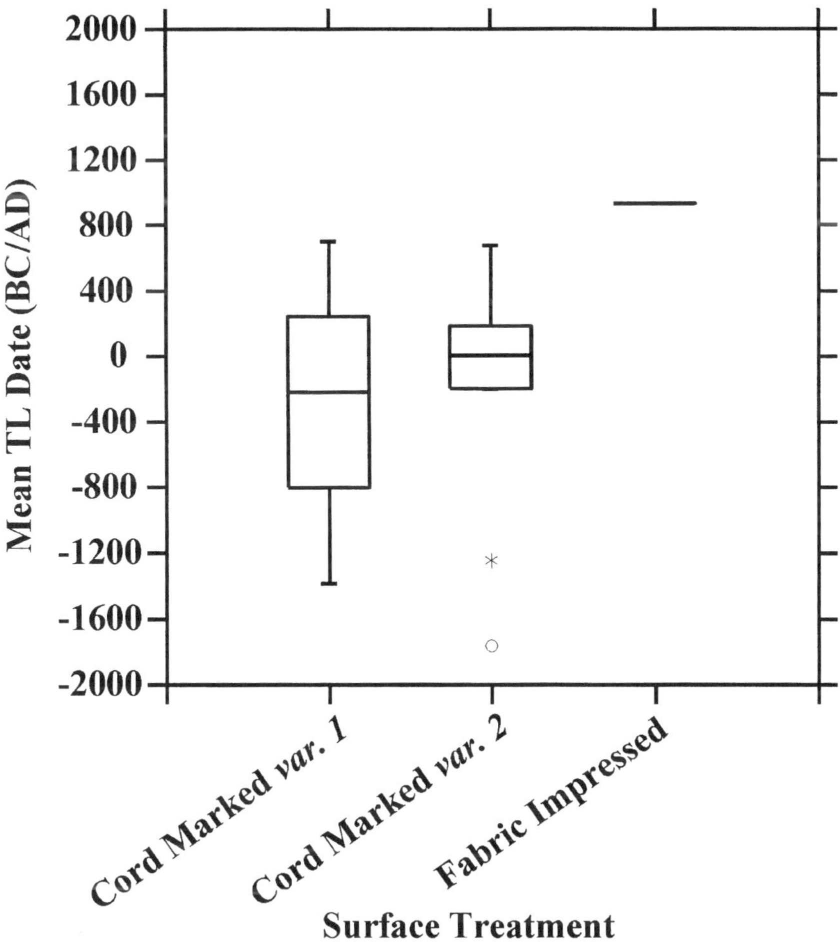

Figure 5.10. Mean TL dates for surface treatment types in the Riegelwood sample (star and circle symbolize outliers).

there is some evidence of changing preferences for sand grain sizes expressed in this sample. Two of the three sherds including 1 percent or more of quartz sand grains (and no grog) in the very coarse and granule sizes are classified as New River series. The range of mean TL dates for these sherds (1765–3185 B.C.) indicates an Early Woodland placement, but very coarse grains commonly appear in very low proportion throughout most of the Woodland era, including in sherds with grog temper. While grain size alone has not proven an especially powerful indicator of temporal trends in technological traditions in the region, sand size may be a valuable indicator in combination with other attributes such as the proportion of sand and the surface treatment type. It should also be noted that one of the sherds

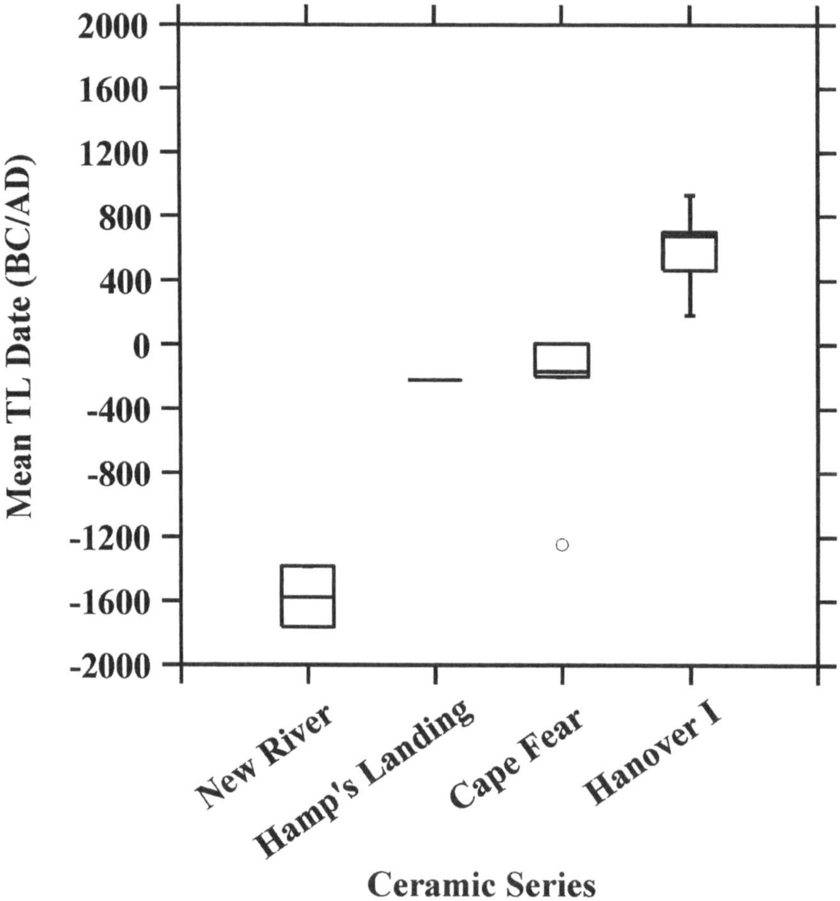

Figure 5.11. Temporal relationships of ceramic series from the Riegelwood site based on 13 TL-dated sherds.

(R18) classified as New River Cord Marked seemed to be overstamped in a perpendicular fashion (a technique that is suspected to be more frequent in the Middle Woodland than is parallel overstamping). This distinction is, in fact, one of the attributes used to distinguish Middle Woodland Cape Fear from Early Woodland New River series sherds. In the Riegelwood assemblage, however, overstamping seemed to prevail in every period. In part, difficulty in classifying surface treatment types among the Riegelwood sherds was due to the degree of erosion, which was considerable, and the fact that most stamping seemed to be rather haphazard and shallow, perhaps because it was executed on a partially dry vessel.

Of three limestone-tempered samples from the Riegelwood site submitted for

TL dating, only one, Hamp's Landing Cord Marked, produced a reliable date (R10, 221 ± 249 B.C.). This date is significantly younger than three radiocarbon dates currently thought to be associated with Hamp's Landing sherds from other sites in the southern coastal region. The calibrated intercepts of these three ^{14}C dates range from 2025 B.C. to 1890 B.C., suggesting a much earlier placement of the Hamp's Landing series in the ceramic sequence than is indicated by the Riegelwood TL date (Figure 5.11). It is very important, however, to consider the context of the radiocarbon dates when evaluating this information. Two of the three ^{14}C dates were obtained for charred wood derived from flotation samples taken from Features 6 and 10 at the Riegelwood site. Feature 6 was a human cremation found in a shallow pit containing charcoal and bone. Fifteen fragments of pottery were recovered in the excavation units in which this feature was found. Six sherds were classified as Hamp's Landing, two as New River, and four as Thom's Creek series. Abbott et al. (1999) associate the date of the cremation with the Hamp's Landing sherds, but the disassociation of the other pottery types does not seem justifiable on the basis of spatial context alone.

Similarly, Feature 10 is described as "a concentration of grog tempered (Hanover) ware" under which was found a partial Hamp's Landing vessel and a hearth remnant (Abbott et al. 1999:61, Figure 6.9). No pottery was found in the hearth feature itself, but sherds recovered from the excavation unit in which the hearth was located included 35 Hanover (including smoothed, cord-marked, and fabric-impressed types), 2 Cape Fear Cord Marked, 4 New River series, and 57 Hamp's Landing Simple Stamped—no fewer than six vessels represented (Abbott et al. 1999:133, Tables 8–12). Stratigraphic assessments were difficult, but the excavators interpreted the Hanover ware as intrusive and associated the date derived from carbon in the hearth area with the Hamp's Landing vessel.

Although these radiocarbon dates may indeed be associated with Hamp's Landing pottery, the complexity of the contexts of associations leaves in doubt the discrepancy between the early Middle Woodland TL date for Hamp's Landing and the very early Early Woodland radiocarbon dates for that series that have thus far been secured.

The classificatory distinction between New River and Cape Fear sherds from the Riegelwood site was particularly challenging. The distinguishing attributes of sand/grit temper density and cord impression orientation, found to be effective elsewhere, were not particularly satisfying in establishing mutually exclusive classes in the Riegelwood assemblage. This was because no significant differences in temper density were noted, and cord orientation tended to be oblique (neither precisely parallel nor perpendicular) in most samples. Three TL dates for New River pottery obtained from sherds from the Riegelwood site range in mean age from 1765 B.C. to 1247 B.C. (Table 5.6, Figure 5.11). Several other TL-dated New

River sherds from Fort Bragg sites and the Papanow site extend that range to about 400 B.C. (374 ± 259 B.C.) and there is even one date as young as A.D. 405 ± 272, although this is considered to be an outlier.

There are also two radiocarbon dates from the Riegelwood site associated with Features 1 and 3, where New River pottery was found. As mentioned, Feature 1 was a human cremation from which charred wood recovered from flotation was dated 2470 ± 40 B.P. (785–410 cal B.C. [p = .05]). As with other features from the Riegelwood site, Feature 1 was contextually complex. Fifty-seven sherds were found in the excavation unit in which the cremation was observed. These represent no fewer than 12 vessels, including Hamp's Landing, New River, Cape Fear, and Hanover series. Stratigraphic analysis provides little means of sorting out the problem of association—15 sherds were found on the surface after plow zone removal, 3 sherds were found in Level 1, and the remaining 39, including all four series, were found in Level 3 (Abbott et al. 1999:132, Tables 8–11).

On the basis of contextual information observed in the field, analysts originally associated the ^{14}C date with the Hanover pottery. The calibrated intercept for the Feature 1 charcoal date (695 B.C.), however, is 868 years older than the oldest mean TL date for Hanover series sherds (A.D. 173). Therefore it seems more likely that the date may be associated with the New River or Hamp's Landing ceramic components.

The Cape Fear series holds the distinction, temporary though it may be, of being the only pottery series in North Carolina (or probably the Southeast in general) whose chronological placement in the Woodland era relies solely on thermoluminescence dates. The range of six TL-date means for Cape Fear series pottery from the Riegelwood site is 1247 B.C. to A.D. 4 (Table 5.6, Figure 5.11). With the addition of four TL dates from sites on Fort Bragg (Herbert et al. 2002), this range may be extended to A.D. 997. The oldest and youngest dates in this group appear to be outliers from a core cluster that ranges in mean age from 278 B.C. to A.D. 118, placing the series confidently in the first half of the Middle Woodland period (400 B.C.–A.D. 900) prior to the period in which grog-tempering technology was fully expressed.

As mentioned above, the distinction between New River and Cape Fear series pottery is based on the imposition of classificatory definitions derived from small samples and thus may prove less effective as the database expands. Some indication of this may be foreshadowed in the Riegelwood assemblage, in which these two series proved difficult to sort, and in the array of dates for the two series, which overlap to some degree and, if combined, form an unbroken continuum. Furthermore, it should be remembered that the process of sorting the TL-dated sherds presented in this study was aided by the analysis of petrographic data. The determination of the proportion of sand/grit temper, upon which the New River–Cape Fear distinction is based, is apt to be different when relying on macroscopic data alone. Likewise, it is likely that without petrographic data a few of the sherds here classified as Hanover would, on the basis of macroscopic data alone, have been classified as Cape Fear.

Six Hanover series sherds from the Riegelwood site were TL dated. The range of mean dates for this group is A.D. 184–931 (Table 5.6, Figure 5.11). Including all sites from the southern coastal region and Sandhills, there are about 32 dates for Hanover series pottery, ranging in mean age from A.D. 173 to A.D. 1675. As might be expected, given that the Hanover specimens from Riegelwood occupy the early end of the range, most are cord marked. Although the TL dates for Hanover series pottery from Riegelwood are Middle Woodland in age, it is quite clear from dates derived elsewhere on the southern coast that the Hanover series is well represented in the Late Woodland period. If the Riegelwood, Fort Bragg, and Papanow assemblages are taken as representative of the series, it is also apparent that grog was often added in quite small amounts to an otherwise sand-tempered paste.

Summary

The data gathered at Papanow, Pond Trail, and Riegelwood allow us to draw several important conclusions about refining the pottery sequence on the southern coast, not the least of which is the finding that TL dating is effective and likely to be an increasingly important tool in chronology building. Only rarely have contextual parameters of association between radiocarbon-datable charcoal and pottery artifacts been found to be very convincing in southern coastal settings.

Generally speaking, the sequence of temper and surface treatment styles on the southern coast is similar to that on the northern coast. Sand and grit appears as the earliest regional choice for temper, where it is used in combination with parallel cord marking in the New River series from about 1600 B.C. to 800 B.C. This is a significant observation for the southern coast, as the prevailing sequence in use prior to this study did not include any Early Woodland sand-tempered types (South 1976). However, the details of surface treatment and temper variations through time were not as well secured by the Papanow and Riegelwood data as might be wished. A great deal remains to be done in the way of documenting temporal variation in sand-tempered wares from both the southern and northern regions.

Whereas the Middle Woodland Mount Pleasant series on the northern coast is characterized as being tempered with granules or pebbles, such sherds do not appear to be represented in the southern coastal assemblages in a frequency suggesting the existence of the Mount Pleasant series in this region. On the southern coast the preference for coarse-grained temper in the Early Woodland New River series appears to have shifted slowly to one for medium and fine sand temper in the Middle Woodland Cape Fear series as cord marking concomitantly gained in popularity. Moreover, the practice of adding crushed pottery to raw clay to produce the grog-tempered Hanover ware, so common throughout the southern and central coastal area in the Middle Woodland period, is relatively rare on the northern coast.

New in the southern coastal sequence is the limestone-tempered Hamp's Landing series. As Mathis's (1998, 1999) research demonstrated, limestone-tempered sherds had for some time been erroneously assumed to be tempered with shell and misclassified to the now defunct Late Woodland Oak Island type. Although current research on the southern coast has not yet conclusively identified the chronological place of Hamp's Landing, the present study suggests that the use of limestone or marly clay temper emerged in the Early Woodland period. The profusion of surface treatment types in the temper series suggests that when identified the temporal range may be quite long for this series. At least as significant as the identification of this new Early Woodland series on the southern coast is the fact that in displacing the "shell-tempered" Oak Island series a considerable void has been created in the Late Woodland portion of the regional sequence.

Also new to the description of pottery from the southern coast and indeed to the entire coastal region of the Carolinas is the notion of temporal trends in cord-marked overstamping orientation. Although it must be characterized at this time as merely suggestive, the data appear to describe a trend in which parallel cord marking was predominant earlier (ca. 800–200 B.C.), perpendicular overstamped patterns more frequent later (200 B.C.–A.D. 200), and fabric impressing most common after A.D. 200. As shall be described in the following chapter, data from the upper Cape Fear River valley provide further support for this pattern.

6

MacCord's Excavation of McLean Mound and Recent Excavations in the Sandhills

A unique feature of the North Carolina Sandhills and southern Coastal Plain is the presence of sand burial mounds found along the Upper Cape Fear and scattered across the lower Cape Fear and Neuse river valleys (Irwin et al. 1999; see their Figure 1). Woodland period burial mounds have not been found in the Piedmont, west of the Coastal Plain Sandhills, or north of the New River. It appears, however, that they once existed throughout the interior southern Coastal Plain of North Carolina, and at least one mound has been documented on the coast. Interpretation of these mounds is hindered by the fact that most were excavated during the late nineteenth and early twentieth centuries in a manner that would, by today's standards, be considered little more than looting. Enough evidence remains, however, to suggest that these mounds were part of a regional social complex that emerged during the late Middle Woodland period and flourished in the Cape Fear River valley in the early centuries of the Late Woodland period (A.D. 800–1600).

McLean Mound

The McLean Mound site (31CD7) lies about 100 feet above sea level on an ancient levee of the Cape Fear River in Cumberland County (Figure 4.1). The mound is situated about 1 km from the Cape Fear, where it is accompanied by the Breece village site (31CD8). The soil at the mound site is unconsolidated sand and, at the time of excavation, the water table was within a meter of the surface. The mound was explored by amateur excavators during the early twentieth century, when it was described as being about 6 feet high and covered with trees. By the time it was excavated (1960–1962), the mound had been part of a cultivated field for many years and was substantially reduced in height (MacCord 1966). When excavated, the diameter of the mound's base was about 15 × 20 m, several meters larger than it must have been before the land was put into agricultural use, during which time the mound would have been reduced in height and spread out by plowing. MacCord excavated 5-x-5-foot units in 4-inch levels, but the stratigraphy was made exceedingly complex by many superimposed reinterments and very poor preservation.

The disarticulated skeletal remains of 50 individuals were found in the plow zone and the remains of another 268 were found buried within the mound itself, an area about 6 m in diameter. Among the 268 burials were 25 cremations, a primary bundle, and 242 secondary bundles (MacCord 1966:11). Artifacts found with the burials included shell and bone beads, stone and clay pipes (stone pipes were both platform and tubular and a single clay pipe was tubular), triangular projectile points, and pottery.

Although pottery was found in almost all of the burial mounds on the southern Coastal Plain, in most cases the number of sherds recovered has been but a handful. In the McLean Mound excavations, however, about 200 sherds were found and these are compared to descriptions of about 600 sherds from the Buie, or Red Springs, Mound presented in Wetmore's (1978) study. Although these two assemblages cannot be considered representative of all the mounds of the southern coast of North Carolina, they provide some perspective of temporal or geographic trends. The McLean Mound pottery assemblage was reanalyzed for the present study and these data are compared to Wetmore's (1978) results of her analysis of pottery from the Buie (Red Springs) Mound.

The McLean Mound pottery exhibits enough homogeneity in paste, surface treatment, and vessel form to constitute a contemporaneous assemblage. Although some whole cup-sized vessels appear to be intentionally included with burials, many more sherds of incomplete vessels did not appear to be interred with any particular burial but are assumed nevertheless to be contemporary with the period of mound construction and use. Consisting of a few pieces from many vessels possibly interred over several hundred years, pottery from the mound contrasts with that from many Sandhills Woodland sites where pottery assemblages reflecting short-term habitation sites not uncommonly are made up of a few single-vessel clusters. As such, the mound assemblage represents an opportunity to examine a broader range of technological and stylistic variability associated with a site of regional importance, a location for reunions of groups whose social contacts may have encompassed broad geographic regions with enhanced opportunities for trade, intermarriage, and diversification of the ceramic technological styles.

The predominant temper in the McLean Mound pottery assemblage is a combination of quartz sand and grog. Of 202 sherds with identifiable temper inclusions, approximately 75 percent are tempered with some mixture of grog or clay and sand; the remaining 25 percent are tempered with quartz sand of various sizes and angularity. Among 50 sand-tempered sherds, 82 percent include grains in the medium size range, 14 percent of the grains are coarse, and 4 percent are granule sized. Most grains are uncrushed, either subrounded or subangular in shape, although one rim sherd of a fabric-impressed jar is tempered with angular quartz.

Table 6.1. Temper and Surface Treatment Attributes of the McLean Mound Pottery

	Temper					
Surface Treatment	Medium Sand	Coarse Sand	Granule	Clay/ Sand	Grog/ Sand	Total
Smoothed	9			6	2	17
Smoothed-over stamped				3		3
Net impressed	1	2				3
Fabric paddle-edge	12		2	44		58
Fabric impressed	10	5		73	12	100
Burnished	2					2
Total	34	7	2	126	14	183

Fifteen sherds are tempered with grog or crushed pottery. One sand-tempered, net-impressed specimen exhibits voids in the paste, suggesting some marl inclusions.

Fabric impressing is the primary surface treatment, with some notable minority treatments occurring as well. Among 183 specimens with identifiable surface treatments, 86 percent are fabric impressed, 11 percent are smoothed or smoothed-over stamped, 2 percent are net impressed, and 1 percent are burnished (Table 6.1). Among the fabric-impressed specimens, most appear to have been impressed with weft-faced, interlaced, or plaited textile. The structure of most of the fabric suggests rigid warp elements of 3–4 mm in diameter and two-ply cordage weft elements of 1–2 mm in diameter, apparently corresponding with MacCord's (1966:33) dominant "coarser weave." Seven specimens exhibit a weft cordage diameter less than 1 mm and warp diameters of 2–3 mm.

Both S- and Z-twist cordage are represented in the fabric impressions observed on the McLean Mound pottery. About one-third of the fabric-impressed specimens exhibit a variety of impressions created with the narrow (4–5 mm) edge of a fabric- or cord-wrapped or composite paddle. The pattern characterizing this variety of fabric impression is similar to that created by interlaced or plaited fabric, except that the warps are not parallel and integrated into a weft-faced textile but overlap sometimes at nearly perpendicular angles much like overstamped, perpendicular cord-marked wares. This variety of fabric impression is familiar to analysts working in the southern coastal region of North Carolina and has often been illustrated in plates depicting fabric-impressed specimens (South 1976:Figure 9B; Ward and Wilson 1980:Figures 8B, 8C, 9A, 11A; Wetmore 1978:Figure 8A). It is not common, however, in Middle or Late Woodland assemblages from the northern coastal region (viz., in Mount Pleasant, White Oak, Colington, or Cashie fabric-impressed types) and with further study this sort of overstamped fabric impressing may prove to be diagnostic of a southern coastal pottery. The net-impressed specimens in the McLean Mound assemblage are vague, the net structure unclear but suggesting knotted net, perhaps bunched or overstamped. The smoothed and burnished surfaces are found to range from smoothed-over stamped to slightly burnished. It is unclear why stamped pottery would be subsequently smoothed, but it is possible that this reflects a cognitive process wherein stamping was considered to be a step in building the pot and smoothing part of the finishing or decorative process. No specimens exhibit the highly burnished finishes characteristic of the Brunswick series or historic Catawba wares.

Cross tabulation of temper and surface treatment illustrates that both sand and grog/sand series are represented among most surface treatment classes (Table 6.1). Exceptions to this are the three net-impressed and two burnished specimens that are exclusively sand tempered. The net-impressed specimens may represent redeposited Early Woodland New River sherds incidentally included in the mound. Those with burnished surfaces, not usually found in Hanover series, are more likely to be contemporary but possibly represent trade wares or influences from the early Pee Dee tradition.

Comparison of rim sherds suggests a minimum of 33 vessels. These may be grouped into five categories based on three attributes: (1) form, (2) decoration, and (3) temper, with bowls found to be the most frequent form. Seventeen Hanover vessels were small bowls and cups with fabric-impressed surfaces (Figure 6.1). Two of these are miniature pinch pots and two (including one of the miniatures) have a pair of opposing suspension holes just below the lip. Three small, open Hanover bowls are slightly burnished and decorated with a row of split-reed punctations just below the lip (Figure 6.2). This is an unusual surface treatment and decorative feature for the Hanover series, somewhat reminiscent of the later Pee Dee tradition found at the Town Creek mound.

Three sherds representing two bowls are sand tempered, slightly burnished, and decorated with a row of square-stylus punctations below a flattened lip (Figure 6.3). These bowls are also uniquely large in this assemblage, with estimated orifice diameters of 22 and 32 cm. Nine other clay/sand or grog/sand bowls or cups vary only in rim form, having flared or everted rims and rounded or rolled lips (Figure 6.4). Only four jars are assumed to be cooking or storage containers (Figure 6.5). The cups and bowls were likely used as serving vessels and suggest a burial ceremony that ritualized the act of serving.

A wide range of temper types is represented among the jars, including medium sand, granule-sized crushed quartz (angular grains), and clay/sand. All are fabric impressed. Several conical-based fragments were represented in the assemblage, suggesting that the jars were likely of this form. When orifice diameters are com-

Figure 6.1. Hanover Fabric Impressed cups and bowls from the McLean Mound. Note straight rims and rounded or flattened lips. Orifice diameters range from 7 to 17 cm. One vessel (bottom right) is decorated with a series of horizontally incised lines just below the lip.

pared, a bimodal distribution is observed, with one mode having orifices less than 13 cm and the other, orifices greater than 13 cm. These modes suggest the presence of two size categories, cups and bowls.

With regard to the question of chronology, the majority of the pottery from the McLean Mound can be classified as Hanover. Seventy-five percent of the assemblage consists of clay/sand- or grog/sand-tempered, fabric-impressed specimens. The presence of a background of medium sand in the paste (and complete absence of sherds tempered exclusively with clay or grog), however, distinguishes these specimens from Hanover series specimens typical in assemblages from the lower Cape Fear region.

Although the majority of the specimens may be classified as Hanover (tempered with clay or grog), there is some warrant for considering them as a subset of the series, perhaps occupying a position on the margins of the temporal range for this tradition. This raises the question of the relationship of the sand-tempered materials. The sand-tempered, fabric-impressed sherds are classifiable as Middle Woodland Cape Fear series, according to South's (1976) typology for

Figure 6.2. Hanover Plain bowls from the McLean Mound. Note linear series of circular-reed punctations arranged horizontally around the rim just below the lip. Rims are slightly incurvate and lips are rounded or flattened. Orifice diameters range from 12 to 20 cm.

the lower Cape Fear. Indeed, South (1966:60) considers the six fabric-impressed, sand-tempered sherds from the McFayden Mound to be Cape Fear.

Cord marking, however, is the dominant surface treatment in the Cape Fear series and is completely absent from the McLean assemblage. The Hanover series pottery in the sample is composed of similar proportions of fabric-impressed

Figure 6.3. Two sand-tempered plain bowls represented by three rim sherds from the McLean Mound. All specimens are slightly burnished. A square stylus was used to decorate one vessel with a single row of drag-and-jab punctations horizontally arranged about 2.5 cm below the cleanly fashioned, flattened lip. Rims are slightly incurvate, and orifice diameters range from 22 to 32 cm.

and smoothed surface treatment types. Rather than the presence of two tempering traditions denoting two disparate cultural components, the evidence seems to suggest a homologous relationship between the sand-tempered and clay- or grog-tempered wares of minimal, if any, temporal or cultural distance. The three medium and coarse sand–tempered, net-impressed sherds, on the other hand, could be classified as Early Woodland New River series (Loftfield 1976:151–152; Phelps 1983:29–31, Figure 1.6B) and may, in fact, represent a second component in the assemblage, likely in secondary context.

We can conclude, therefore, that the majority of the McLean Mound pottery assemblage (excepting the net-impressed ware) seems to be a late expression of the Hanover tradition. The placement of the clay- or grog-tempered pottery from McLean at the end of the Hanover tradition is logical with regard to the presence of several traits not common to Hanover assemblages elsewhere in the southern coastal region. These include punctate decoration and everted rim forms that are

Figure 6.4. Hanover Fabric Impressed bowls from the McLean Mound. Note rims that include flared, everted, and rolled forms. Orifice diameters range from 9 to 16 cm.

Figure 6.5. Sand-tempered fabric impressed, Mount Pleasant Fabric Impressed, and Hanover Fabric Impressed jars from the McLean Mound. Two with slightly flaring rims, one with a slightly incurvate rim, and one with a straight rim represent variation in vessel form. Orifice diameters range from 28 to 33 cm.

characteristic of later traditions. The circular- and flat-reed punctate bowls suggest some affinity with Pee Dee (Coe 1995:176, 187, Figures 9.18 and 9.35), but other decorative features of Pee Dee pottery (e.g., appliquéd nodes or rosettes and rim notching) are not evident in the McLean assemblage. Circular-reed punctate decorations noted on sand-tempered plain ware from the lower Cape Fear were suspected by South (1976:42) to represent a relationship with Lamar period traditions. Very similar fine sand–tempered burnished sherds with reed punctations were found at the Buck Hall site on the central South Carolina coast, where they were identified as Mississippian Plain (Poplin et al. 1993:180, Figure 65). The reed punctate decorated bowls from the McLean Mound are also similar to those found at the Buie Mound (Wetmore 1978:45, Figure 7D). Despite these similarities, however, the Buie Mound pottery assemblage is otherwise quite different from that of the McLean Mound.

Wetmore (1978:44, Table 3) classified most (79 percent) of the sherds from Buie as sand-tempered burnished plain, with clay- or grog-tempered sherds making up 12 percent of the assemblage. These proportions are reversed at McLean, with 75 percent clay or grog tempered and 24 percent sand tempered. Fabric impressing appears as a minority type (about 10 percent) at the Buie Mound but is the most common surface treatment (86 percent) among the McLean Mound sherds. These several indicators suggest that the McLean Mound assemblage may be somewhat earlier than that of the Buie Mound, although similarly exhibiting some association with the Mississippian Pee Dee and Savannah traditions to the west and south.

Based on these data, Irwin and colleagues (1999:71) postulated that the date secured by MacCord (1966:17) for the McLean Mound, 980 ± 110 B.P. (cal A.D. 815–1270 [p = .95]), did not represent the late portion of the temporal range for interments in the mound, which, judging from the characteristics of the pottery assemblage, may have extended several hundred years after this date. In order to test this hypothesis, three carbon samples from the McLean Mound were subsequently submitted for radiocarbon assay. Two of the three carbon samples were obtained from charcoal from a burial context and a third from soot on a sherd from general mound context (Herbert et al. 2002). The first sample consisted of fine grains of charred plant remains extracted from a sample of sandy soil reportedly removed from the interior of one of the pipes that was associated with a burial. The recovery context of the pipe, the condition of its contents at the time of removal, and the manner in which the material was removed were not recorded. This sample returned a modern date, considered erroneous. The second sample submitted was a single large chunk of wood charcoal reportedly found with a cremation. This sample returned a date of 760 ± 100 B.P. (cal A.D. 1030–1410 [p = .95]) (Beta 145510). The third sample, consisting of soot scraped from the exterior of a clay/sand-tempered, fabric-impressed potsherd found in general mound context, returned an AMS (accelerator mass spectrometry) date of 1250 ± 40 B.P. (cal A.D. 675–880 [p = .95]) (Beta 143709). Taking the most conservative interpretation of the difference between the lower range of error for the youngest date (A.D. 1030) and the upper range of the error for the oldest calibrated date (A.D. 880) yields a period of 150 years, which is rather a long time for a culture group to reuse a ceremonial burial mound from the perspective of the Mississippian culture but not out of the question for a Late Woodland repository of secondary burials. Based on a figure of 40 years per generation, this period represents about four generations of reuse of the mound. Even with this minimum estimate for the period of interment, the span of time and ceremonial context provide ample opportunity for the burial mound to have accumulated an eclectic mix of pottery, perhaps resulting from an exchange network that encompassed a broad geographic area.

Sandhills Sites

Whereas in other areas of the coast prior research had established stylistic pottery types for which the temporal ranges were reasonably well understood, the Sandhills presented a less studied area at the outset of this project. In technical reports of Sandhills sites, pottery had typically been described and classified by analogy to types from adjacent environmental regions. While such associations served to provide a general sense of temporal relationships, they were not supported by absolute dates or studies of contextual provenience and were accompanied by very few descriptive data. Perhaps the most serious impediment to developing a regional ceramic sequence in the Sandhills is that environmental conditions have worked against the formation of stratified or datable deposits. After thermoluminescence (TL) dating was found to be effective at the Papanow, Pond Trail, and Riegelwood sites, the procedure was applied to ceramics from sites on Fort Bragg in order to devise a pottery type sequence for the Sandhills.

Pottery samples were selected from Fort Bragg sites to reflect the diversity of temper and surface treatment attributes observed in the pottery from the Sandhills region. The sample selection process relied exclusively on temper and surface treatment attributes to establish this diversity. The widest ranges of temper types and surface treatments among the sherds that fit size and contextual criteria were included in the sample. Sherd size was critical because smaller sherds provide less datable material and so yield more scatter in results and greater error in age estimates. Sherds for dating were selected only from excavated assemblages where soil samples were taken from an area within a 30-cm radius of the location where the sherd was recovered. A total of 20 samples was selected from excavated assemblages and a thin section was made of each sample.

The analysis considered three types of aplastic constituents as temper (material added to the clay paste by the potter). These three constituents were sand, crushed rock, and grog. Sand can occur naturally in clay deposits from the region and no claim is made that all of the sand observed in the samples was added by the potters. It is assumed, however, that sand grains in the fine and larger Wentworth grain size grades may have affected the performance characteristics of the clay and the ceramic vessels and therefore are more likely to represent a tempering agent. Very fine and silt-sized particles are not assumed to have been purposefully manipulated by the potters and are not considered as temper.

Grog-tempered sherds were also found to have some amount of sand in the paste. Depending on which was the greater proportion, classes were defined for

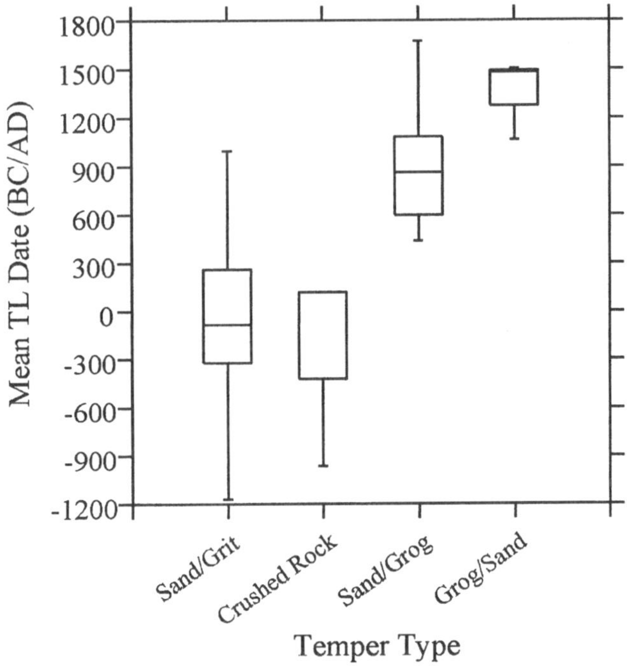

Figure 6.6. Mean TL dates for temper types among the Fort Bragg sample (n = 20).

sand/grog- and grog/sand-tempered sherds. Four temper classes were formed from the three temper types: sand/grit, sand/grog, grog/sand, and crushed rock.

The range of the TL dates for the pottery from Fort Bragg spans 2,846 years, from 1171 B.C. to A.D. 1675. This range of age estimates is correlated with clusters of petrographic attributes revealing four classes of temper: sand/grit, crushed rock, sand/grog, and grog/sand (Figure 6.6, Table 6.2).

The seven sherds classified as sand/grit tempered incorporate quartz sand grains in several sizes from very fine (vf, .0625–.125 mm) through very coarse (vc, 1–2 mm). A box plot of the distribution of the mean TL dates indicates an extensive age range for this group from 1171 B.C. to A.D. 997, but with five of the dates (about 71 percent) falling between 400 B.C. and about A.D. 400 (Figure 6.7). Although ratios of sand size grades do not appear to be temporally patterned, the proportion of the total amount of sand, grit, or crushed-rock temper in the ceramic matrix is temporally patterned. Among sand/grit-tempered sherds, the oldest have the highest proportion of sand, grit, or crushed-rock temper and the youngest sherds the lowest (Figure 6.7).

Three sherds tempered with crushed rock range in age from 963 B.C. to A.D. 121. The mean age (average of the three TL-date means) for this temper group is 224 B.C. As previously described, the crushed-rock temper in these sherds appears to be granite. The range of dates for these sherds also falls within the range of dates for the sand/grit-tempered samples.

Seven sherds tempered with sand and grog range in age from A.D. 435 to A.D. 1675. The principal component of the temper in these sherds is sand. Grog in the coarse and very coarse size range is included in the matrix in proportions between 1 and 5 percent. The classification of three of the samples as sand/grog-tempered sherds was made only after grog was identified in the petrographic analysis.

Three sherds tempered with grog and sand range in age from A.D. 1084 through A.D. 1503. Very coarse and granule-sized grog particles are included as the principal component of the temper in these samples, ranging in proportion from 5 to 9 percent. Medium-sized quartz sand was also included at proportions between 2 and 3 percent.

Four surface treatment classes are represented: net impressed, cord marked, fabric impressed, and check stamped. Five net-impressed sherds range in age from 1171 B.C. to A.D. 405 (Table 6.2, Figure 6.8). Some variation exists in net construction, but most samples appear to be made by knotting multi-ply cordage of about 1-mm diameter with knots spaced about .5 cm apart. Final twist direction was not observable on the net-impressed specimens.

Six sherds are from vessels stamped with a cord-wrapped paddle. The cord-marked sherds range in age from 374 B.C. to A.D. 997. The three oldest samples (New River and Cape Fear series) with parallel cord impressions exhibited S-twist cordage, a Hanover Cord Marked sherd with perpendicular overstamped impressions was marked with Z-twist cordage, and the youngest, a Cape Fear III Cord Marked sherd, exhibited S-twist.

Eight fabric-impressed sherds range in age from A.D. 483 to A.D. 1675. Some variation exists in fabric construction, but most samples appear to be twined-cordage wefts, about 1 mm in diameter, interwoven or possibly twined over rigid warps, 2–4 mm in diameter. This is the most common type of textile impressed on Late Woodland ceramics from the coastal region.

The single check-stamped sherd included in this sample was dated A.D. 706 ± 174. As with temper types, the dates for surface treatment types exhibit a sequential pattern with overlapping ranges (Figure 6.8). The youngest date in the cord-marked class was derived by the SARA (single aliquot/regeneration and added dose) method and could be slightly less reliable than other dates in the class. The very young date for the fine weft fabric-impressed sherd exhibited significant fading and is the least reliable of all the dates.

The 20 TL dates for pottery from Fort Bragg provide a model for the development of a sequence of ceramic classes for the Sandhills region. Trends in tempering techniques and methods of treating vessel surfaces have been presented independently as a means of developing evolutionary histories for each technological tradition. Factors concerning the function of various tempering techniques and

Table 6.2. Temper and Surface Treatment, TL Dates, and Ceramic Series for the Fort Bragg Samples

		Proportion of Temper Constituents (%)[a]				
Sample	Temper Type	Quartz vf–f	Quartz m–vc	Other vf–vc	Quartz/ Other Total	Grog
18	Sand/grog	5	3–5		8–10	1–3
11	Grog/sand	1–3	2	1	4–6	7–9
20	Grog/sand	5–10	3		8–13	2–7
25	Sand/grog	5–10	1–3		6–13	4–5
22	Grog/sand	1	1		2	4
23[b]	Sand/grit	2	3	1–2	6–7	
15	Sand/grog	3–5	3–5		6–10	1
3	Sand/grog	5–10	3		8–13	1–3
28	Sand/grog	5–10	3–5		8–15	2
14	Sand/grog	3–5	1–3		4–8	1–3
2	Sand/grog	5	3–5		8–10	1–3
12	Sand/grit	5	5	1	11	
16	Crushed rock	1	4	11	15	
10	Sand/grit	5	3–5	1–2	9–12	
13	Crushed rock	3–5		11–15	11–15	
19	Sand/grit	5	3–5	4	10–14	
9	Sand/grit	3	3	1	7	
26	Sand/grit	5–107	5	3–5	13–20	
17	Crushed rock		3–5	9–15	12–20	
21	Sand/grit	5–10	3–5	8	16–23	

[a]Key to size-grade abbreviations: vf = very fine; f = fine; m = medium; vc = very coarse. Other minerals include polycrystalline quartz, microline, rock fragments, feldspar, and microperthite.

Surface Treatment	Surface Treatment Characteristics: Secondary	Tertiary	Twist	Ceramic Series	TL Date
Fabric impressed	Rigid warp	Fine weft		Hanover I	A.D. 1675 ± 59
Fabric impressed	Rigid warp	Medium weft	Z	Hanover II	A.D. 1503 ± 156
Fabric impressed	Rigid warp	Medium weft		Hanover II	A.D. 1481 ± 58
Fabric impressed	Rigid warp	Medium weft	S	Hanover I	A.D. 1219 ± 256
Fabric impressed	Broad warp	Medium weft	S	Hanover II	A.D. 1084 ± 124
Cord marked	Overstamped	Perpendicular	S	Cape Fear III	A.D. 997 ± 123
Fabric impressed	Rigid warp	Coarse weft		Hanover I	A.D. 946 ± 233
Fabric impressed	Rigid warp	Fine weft		Hanover I	A.D. 864 ± 160
Check stamped	Square	Rhombohedral		Hanover I	A.D. 706 ± 174
Fabric impressed	Broad warp	Medium weft		Hanover I	A.D. 483 ± 173
Cord marked	Overstamped	Perpendicular	Z	Hanover I	A.D. 435 ± 314
Net impressed	Knotted	Closed		New River	A.D. 405 ± 272
Net impressed	Eroded			Yadkin I	A.D. 121 ± 290
Cord marked	Overstamped	Parallel		Cape Fear I	A.D. 118 ± 229
Net impressed	Knotted	Open		Yadkin I	A.D. 118 ± 233
Cord marked	Overstamped	Parallel	S	Cape Fear I	82 ± 196 B.C.
Cord marked	Overstamped	Parallel	S	Cape Fear I	278 ± 370 B.C.
Cord marked	Overstamped	Parallel	S	New River	374 ± 259 B.C.
Net impressed	Eroded			Yadkin I	963 ± 356 B.C.
Net impressed	Knotted	Closed		New River	1171 ± 541 B.C.

[b]Sample 23 was small and exhibited high scatter in growth curves. The luminescence age was estimated by the SARA method and may be less reliable.

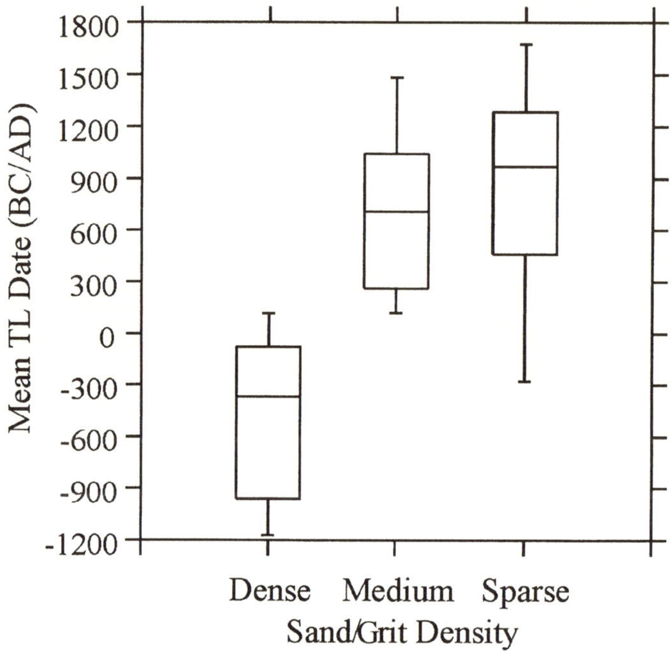

Figure 6.7. Density of sand/grit temper among the TL-dated sample (n = 10) from Fort Bragg. Density is defined as dense (>15 percent), medium (10–15 percent), or sparse (<10 percent).

surface treatment styles and their effects on vessel performance characteristics are, no doubt, potentially important but are not the focus of this study. It remains, however, to examine trends in these two attribute categories simultaneously. As temper and surface treatment are the principal attributes used to distinguish pottery series and types in this region, the following discussion considers trends in the context of what is known of regional ceramic sequences. By doing so, it is shown that Sandhills traditions, as represented in the Fort Bragg sample, are in reasonable accord with series descriptions for pottery from surrounding regions. On the other hand, the Fort Bragg sample also provides a source of data revealing potential trends not observed in the southern Coastal Plain or southern Piedmont that may yet inform research in those regions as additional archaeology provides the means for securing dates for comparable pottery.

A schematic chart illustrating the temporal relationships of the major classes of temper and surface treatment type provides a means of visualizing the trends in these traditions over the Woodland era (Figure 6.9). Sand appears to have been added to clay as a tempering agent from the Early Woodland period up to historic times, although sand occurs mostly in combination with grog after about

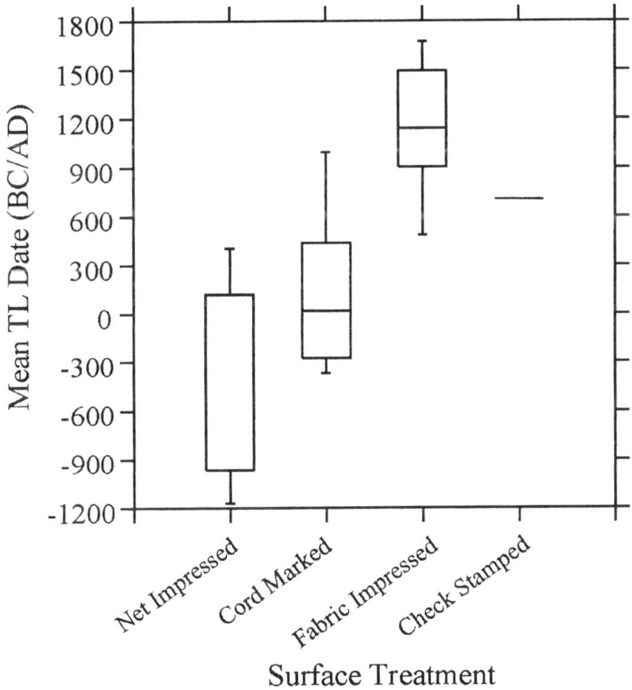

Figure 6.8. Mean TL dates for surface treatment types among the Fort Bragg sample (n = 20).

A.D. 400. Despite the ubiquitous presence of sand, there is no clear evidence that preferences for sand grain sizes are expressed in this sample.

Sherds tempered with quartz sand grains in the very coarse and granule sizes are, so far as this sample shows, most common in the period from about 400 B.C. to A.D. 400, but grains of this size were nevertheless included as temper throughout most of the Woodland era. Although grain size has not proven especially useful as a means of discovering temporal trends in the sand-tempered ware in this study, the amount of sand added as temper, estimated as a proportion of the matrix by comparing thin sections to Rice's (1987:349, Figure 12.2) comparison chart, does appear to be temporally patterned.

Judging from the range of TL dates associated with sherds of various temper densities (Figure 6.7), it appears that the sherds with the highest density (>15 percent) of sand/grit or crushed rock are among the earliest (in this sample, predating A.D. 200). It has also been demonstrated that among the Fort Bragg sample, net-impressed and cord-marked vessels overstamped in parallel fashion are among the earliest, all dating prior to A.D. 400 (Herbert et al. 2002). These findings were used to assign sherds in the larger sample to taxonomic series (Table 6.2).

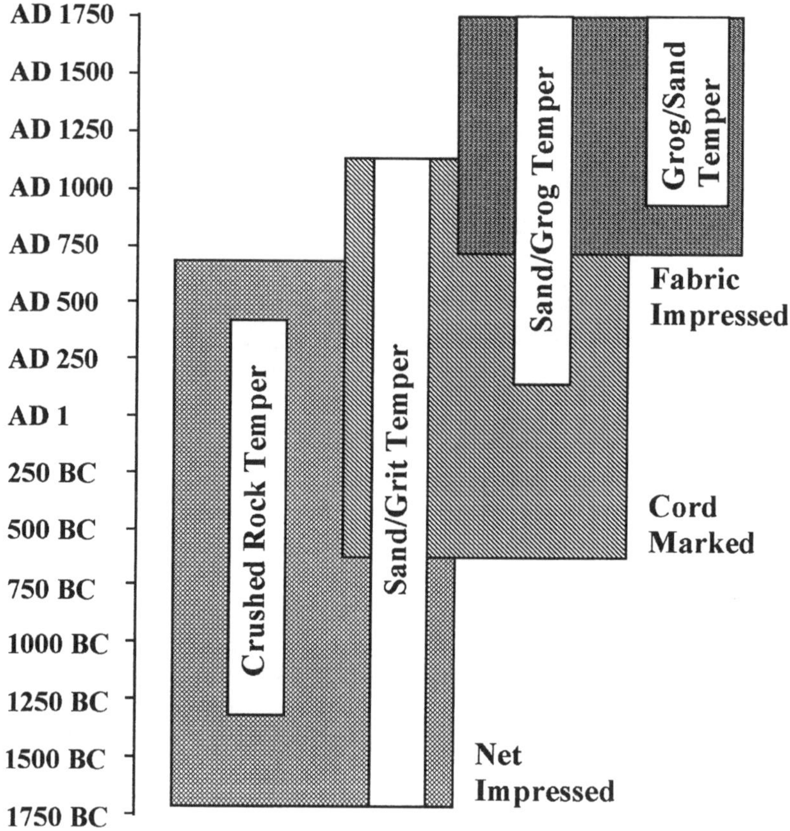

Figure 6.9. Approximate temporal relationships between temper and surface treatment in assemblages from the southern coast. Notice that although both temper and surface treatment practices shift sequentially, the shifts are not simultaneous.

Summary

The sequence model for prehistoric pottery developed in this study is provisional. That is to say, the range of attributes observed in this small sample of TL-dated pottery is not necessarily representative of the richness or diversity of prehistoric pottery types in the Carolina Sandhills or adjacent regions. As additional data are obtained, information will undoubtedly become more complex. Nevertheless, this study does provide pertinent regional information and an example of how TL dating may be used for refining ceramic sequences elsewhere in the Southeast. Identification of subsets within the three broad temper groups (sand/grit, crushed rock, and grog) provides an indication of the complexity that lies ahead. Within the sand/grit group, two series (Early Woodland New River and Middle Woodland Cape Fear) are distinguished by differences in temper density and surface treatment. The crushed-rock group is interpreted as a variety of the Middle Woodland Yadkin series, distinguished by different rock types, but its relationship to the crushed-quartz–tempered variety is unclear. Among the grog-tempered group are the Middle Woodland Hanover I series and the Late Woodland Hanover II series, distinguished by differences in grog density and surface treatment. But these distinctions are as yet based on very limited data observed primarily in thin sections.

The sequence of surface treatment types, including (from earliest to latest) net impressing, cord marking (parallel overstamped), fabric impressing (flexible warp textile), cord marking (perpendicular overstamped), and fabric impressing (rigid warp textile), provides the basis for defining types within the four series (New River, Yadkin, Cape Fear, and Hanover). Future studies, however, may suggest more effective ways of arranging typological classes. It may be preferable, for example, to classify the grog/sand-tempered pottery of the Sandhills as a new series distinct from the Hanover series ware found on the coast. The crushed-rock–tempered ware of the Sandhills may prove to be temporally or geographically distinct from the Yadkin series as more information is obtained on the range of attributes and dates for the Piedmont Yadkin series.

The information presented in Chapters 4, 5, and 6 has focused rather narrowly on the temporal placement of pottery-making traditions in each of three areas of the North Carolina Coastal Plain: (1) the northern and central region, (2) the southern lower coast or lower Cape Fear valley, and (3) the southern upper coast or upper Cape Fear valley. The task of arranging traditions in time has been addressed in part by reexamining several assemblages that were found in stratified deposits and by considering in some detail the radiocarbon and TL data from several key sites. In the chapter that follows, the sequence of ceramic traditions is arranged in a broader context including every published date from the Coastal Plain of North Carolina that can be reasonably associated with pottery.

7
Ceramic Sequence for Eastern North Carolina

Previous chapters have detailed information regarding the pottery types found at several key sites. In this chapter, that information is placed in the broader context of all published chronometric information for pottery from any site on the North Carolina Coastal Plain. The types discussed are those described in the site-assemblage sketches presented in Chapters 4, 5, and 6, with relevant chronometric data presented from several additional sites (Figure 7.1). A comparison of the regional pottery sequences for each of the three environmental provinces (Sandhills, Sea Island, and Embayed sections) is presented (Figure 7.2) and all chronometric data for sites in the North Carolina Coastal Plain are illustrated in the charts presented in Figure 7.3 (the Embayed Section) and Figure 7.4 (the Sea Island Section and Sandhills).

Early Woodland Period Pottery Series (2200–400 b.c.)

Stallings

At present, all fiber-tempered pottery found in coastal North Carolina is classified to the Stallings series, although fiber-tempered pottery has yet to be dated from any North Carolina site. In South Carolina it has been found to range in age from 2500 b.c. to 1100 b.c. (Griffin 1943; Sassaman 1993; Stoltman 1972, 1974) and it is expected that when dating opportunities arise in North Carolina it will be found to date to this period.

Marcey Creek

Soapstone-tempered pottery, originally defined as the Marcey Creek series in the Potomac Basin (Egloff and Potter 1982; Evans 1955; Manson 1948), is thought to date to 1200–800 b.c., although it has yet to be dated at any site in North Carolina.

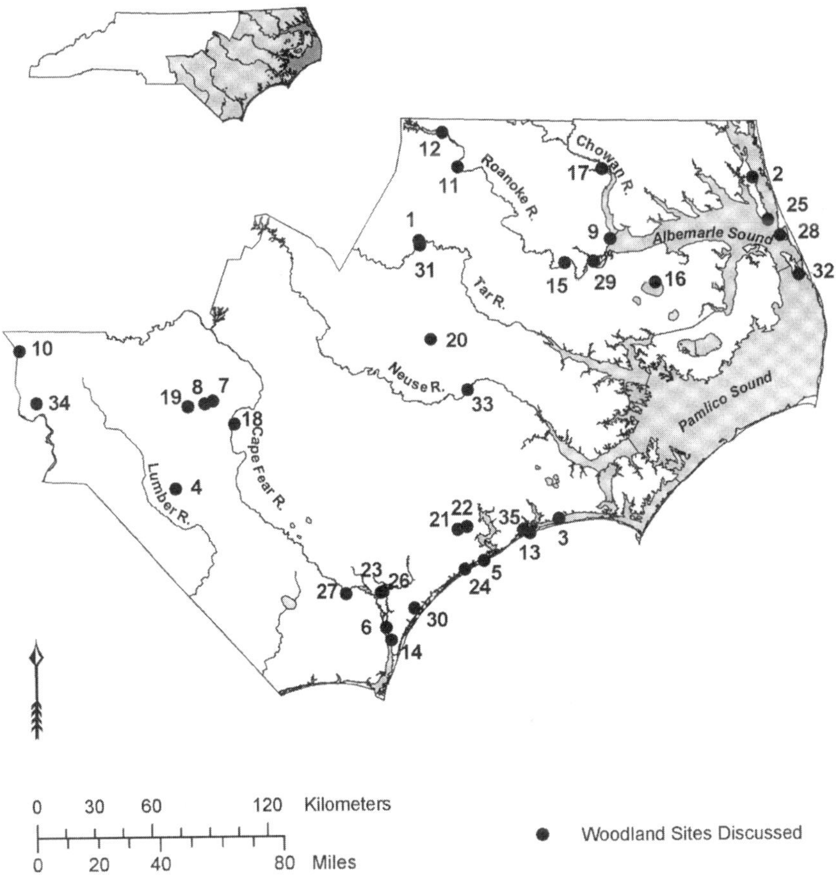

Figure 7.1. Location of sites discussed in the text and tables: (1) Battle Park; (2) Baum; (3) Broad Reach; (4) Buie Mound; (5) Cape Island; (6) Cold Morning; (7) 31CD551; (8) 31CD622; (9) Davenport; (10) Doerschuk; (11) Fishing Creek; (12) Gaston; (13) Hammocks Beach West; (14) Hamp's Landing; (15) Jordan's Landing; (16) Lake Phelps Canoe; (17) Liberty Hill; (18) McLean Mound; (19) 31MR93; (20) Neoheroka Fort; (21) 31ON542; (22) 31ON596; (23) Papanow; (24) Permuda Island; (25) Point Harbor; (26) Pond Trail; (27) Riegelwood; (28) Rush Point; (29) Sans Souci; (30) Sidney Brook; (31) Thorpe; (32) Tillett; (33) Tower Hill; (34) Town Creek; (35) Uniflite.

Croaker Landing

Apparently contemporary with the Marcey Creek series is the clay/grog-tempered Croaker Landing series (Egloff and Potter 1982; Egloff et al. 1988; Evans 1955; Pullins et al. 1996) (Figure 7.2). Croaker Landing specimens are well represented at the Davenport site (Figure 7.1, location 9) on the Chowan River in Bertie County and other sites in the Albemarle Sound area (Byrd 1999) but have yet to be dated at any site in North Carolina.

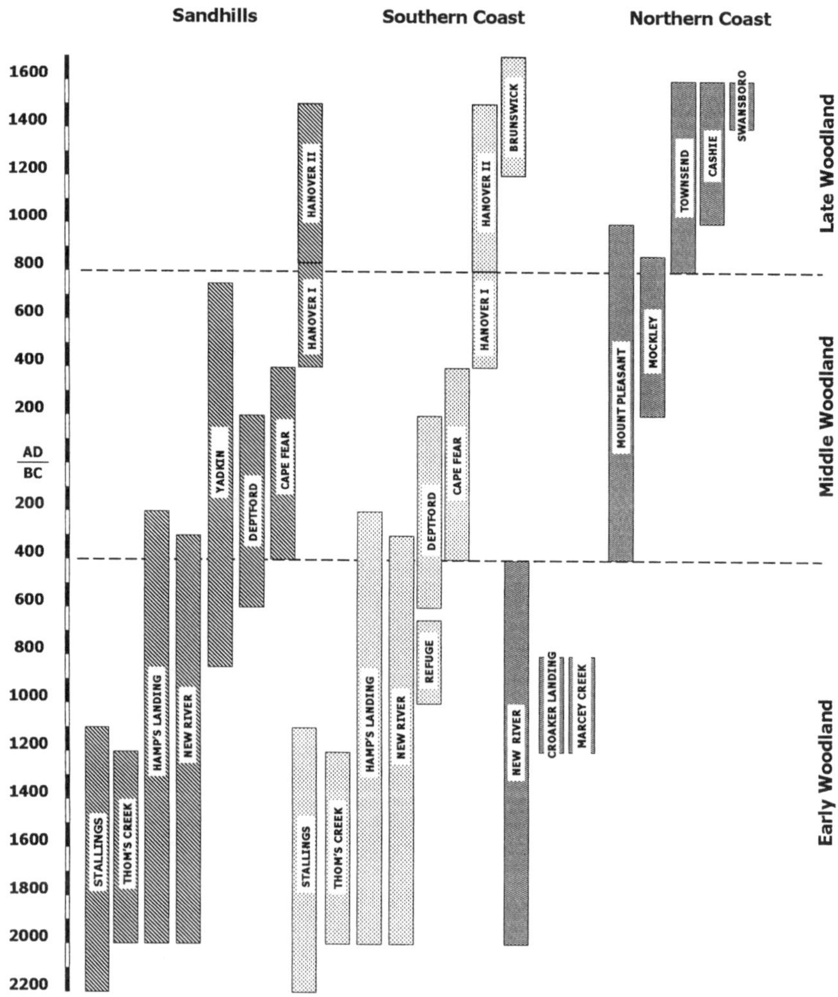

Figure 7.2. Regional ceramic sequences of the Coastal Plain and eastern Piedmont of North Carolina.

Hamp's Landing

Hamp's Landing has been proposed as an Early Woodland or early Middle Woodland type (Hargrove 1993; Hargrove and Eastman 1997, 1998; Herbert and Mathis 1996; Mathis 1999). At the type site (Figure 7.1, location 14), Hamp's Landing series pottery was found in stratigraphic context between, and overlapping with, Thom's Creek and Middle Woodland period Hanover types (Hargrove 1993). Three subsequent radiocarbon dates for Hamp's Landing sherds suggest that this series is earlier than first thought (Figure 7.4).

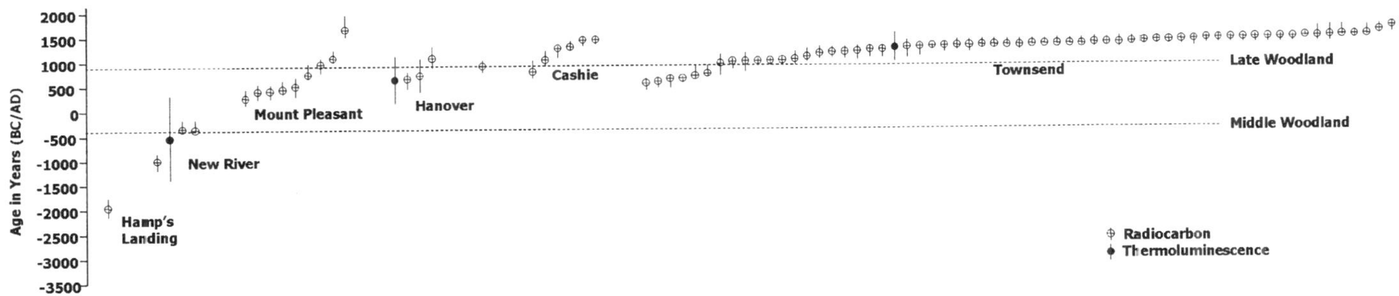

Figure 7.3. Radiocarbon and thermoluminescence dates associated with pottery from sites in the Embayed Section of the Coastal Plain of North Carolina. Error bars are two-sigma ranges.

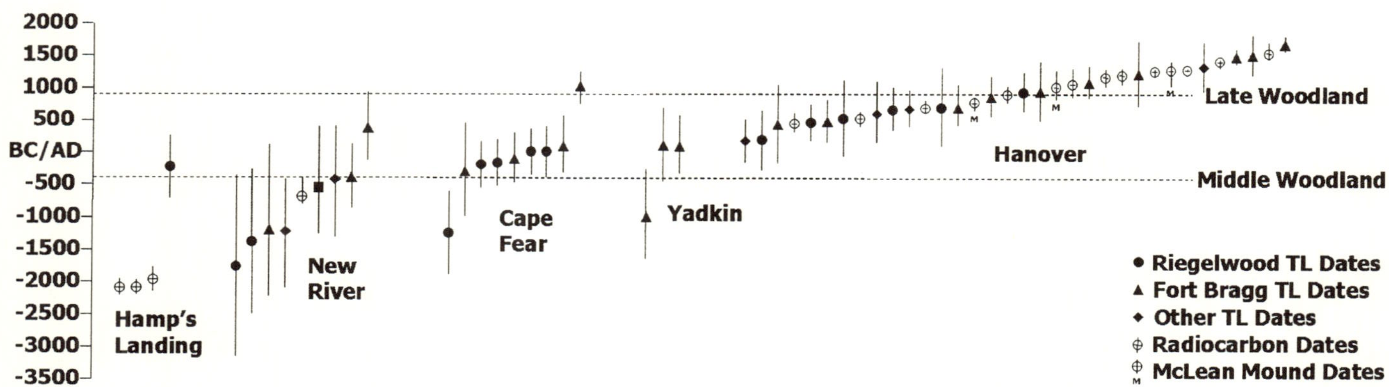

Figure 7.4. Radiocarbon and thermoluminescence dates associated with pottery from sites in the Sea Island and Sandhills sections of the Coastal Plain of North Carolina. Error bars are two-sigma ranges.

A feature containing nearly 66 fragments of a partially reconstructable Hamp's Landing Fabric Impressed vessel was found in a refuse-filled pit at the Cape Island site in Onslow County (Figure 7.1, location 5) and radiocarbon dated to 3610 ± 70 B.P. (2145–1760 cal B.C. [p = .05]) (Jones et al. 1997) (Table 7.1). This was "dismissed as a spurious date" by Jones et al. (1997:38). It is, in fact, very similar to the two ^{14}C dates secured from features containing Hamp's Landing series sherds at the Riegelwood site in Columbus County (Abbott et al. 1999) and seems acceptable if Hamp's Landing is assumed contemporaneous with the Thom's Creek phase.

As mentioned in the discussion of the Riegelwood site (Chapter 5), only one Hamp's Landing Cord Marked sherd submitted for thermoluminescence (TL) dating from that site produced a reliable date (221 ± 249 B.C.). This date is significantly younger than three radiocarbon dates with calibrated intercepts ranging from 2025 B.C. to 1890 B.C. (Figure 7.4). In a close examination of the contexts from which the radiocarbon-dated materials were derived, in each case the association of the date with Hamp's Landing sherds was not beyond reasonable doubt. This places the range of dates thus far associated with Hamp's Landing series sherds on a somewhat less certain footing than would be desired. Also contributing to the dubiousness of the current date range of this series is that sherds tempered with marl or limestone, classifiable as Hamp's Landing, exhibit almost every type of surface treatment. Particularly disconcerting is the presence of check-stamped, perpendicular cord-marked, and rigid fabric-impressed surface treatment styles typically associated with the Middle Woodland. The Early Woodland affiliation for Hamp's Landing should therefore be considered preliminary, as there is some reason to expect Middle Woodland associations as further dating opportunities arise.

Thom's Creek

Early Woodland Thom's Creek series pottery (2000–1200 B.C.), more common on the lower Savannah River and South Carolina coast (Griffin 1945; Phelps 1968; Sassaman 1993; Stoltman 1974; Trinkley 1980, 1989), is also occasionally found in collections from the southern coast of North Carolina (Phelps 1983; South 1976) and as far north as Camp LeJeune on the New River. In general, the Thom's Creek material that is found in assemblages from southern coastal North Carolina consists primarily of plain or reed-punctate varieties thought to be among the earlier (2000–1000 B.C.) surface treatment types in South Carolina (Cable et al. 1998:306, Figure 113; Trinkley 1980, 1990).

There are no dates for Thom's Creek series pottery from the North Carolina coast. The narrow range of surface treatment styles suggests either dilution of the

Table 7.1. Early Woodland Dates Associated with Pottery from Eastern North Carolina

Sample[a]	Site Name	Target Pottery[b]	Minimum (Mean) Maximum[c]
UW-226	Papanow	New River Fabric Impressed	–1285 (–434) 417
UW-?	31ON542	New River Plain	–1410 (–546) 318
UGA-2551	Uniflite	White Oak (possibly misidentified Hamp's Landing)	–781 (–645) –396
B-115425	Riegelwood	New River, Hamp's Landing, and Hanover series	–785 (–750, –695, –540) –410
B-107426b	Fairway	New River Plain and Fabric Impressed	–885 (–767) –534
B-130061	Long Point	New River, Hanover, and Mockley series	–930 (–820) –785
UW-400	31HT347	Yadkin I Smoothed-Over Net Impressed	–1660 (–963) –265
UW-653	Riegelwood	New River Cord Marked (perpendicular cord currently requires classification as Cape Fear)	–2605 (–1000) 605
B-16675	Lake Phelps	Deep Creek Net Impressed	–1205 (–1000) –845
UW-402	31HT392	New River Net Impressed	–2231 (–1171) 111
UW-224	Papanow	New River Cord Marked	–2076 (–1221) –419
UW-658	Riegelwood	Thom's Creek Cord Marked	–1892 (–1247) –602
UW-660	Riegelwood	New River Cord Marked	–2500 (–1385) –270
UW-662	Riegelwood	New River Cord Marked	–3164 (–1765) –366
B-115428	Riegelwood	New River Cord Marked (originally classified as Thom's Creek)	–2195 (–1975) –1770
B-104165	Cape Island	Hamp's Landing Fabric Impressed and Refuge Punctate *variety Allendale*	–2145 (–1955) –1760
B-115427	Riegelwood	Hamp's Landing Simple Stamped	–2210 (–2120, –2085, –2050) –1945
B- 115429	Riegelwood	Hamp's Landing Simple Stamped and Cord Marked	–220 (–2120, –2085, –2050) –1965

Sample[a]	Site Name	Target Pottery[b]	Minimum (Mean) Maximum[c]
B-115426	Riegelwood	New River	–3010 (–2900) –2870
UW-657	Riegelwood	Hamp's Landing Simple Stamped	–8148 (–3056) 2036

[a]UW = University of Washington Luminescence Laboratory (TL dates); UGA = University of Georgia; B = Beta Analytic Radiocarbon Dating Laboratory.

[b]TL dates the pottery itself; radiocarbon dates organic material associated with the pottery.

[c]Minimum, mean, and maximum dates are 2σ calibrated intercepts for 14C samples and mean and 2σ errors for TL samples. Negative ages are calendar years B.C.; positive ages are calendar years A.D.

decorative tradition at the periphery of its geographic range (see Chapter 8) or perhaps the representation of only a portion of the 800-year temporal range.

Refuge

The Refuge series material found on the southern coast of North Carolina primarily consists of the Refuge Punctate *variety Allendale* type, originally defined by Stoltman (1974:276–277) for material from the lower Savannah River, South Carolina. Refuge Punctate *variety Allendale* is thought to date to a relatively short period (1000–800 B.C.), coeval with Thom's Creek, occurring stratigraphically below Refuge Dentate Stamped, thus occupying an early position in the Refuge series (Anderson et al. 1996:224). In the current study, the few specimens exhibiting Allendale type punctations were uniformly characterized by Thom's Creek series paste and vessel attributes.

New River

The first series to be defined for Early Woodland pottery of the North Carolina coast was the sand-tempered New River series (Loftfield 1976). The Deep Creek series was defined by Phelps (1981b, 1983) for very similar material occurring on the northern coast. Phelps (1983:31) proposed three phases within the Deep Creek series (2000–300 B.C.) characterized by trends in the popularity of various surface treatments. The earliest component is characterized by a predominance of cord marking, the middle component by a rise in the popularity of simple stamping, and the latest component by a decline in the popularity of simple stamping. At present there is no evidence that New River and Deep Creek are two distinct pottery types and, for simplicity, they are here combined as the New River series.

New River series sherds have been found to date from about 1750 B.C. to 400 B.C. (Herbert 1999b; Herbert and Mathis 1996; Loftfield 1976). Two ^{14}C dates possibly associated with New River series sherds were secured from the Riegelwood site (Table 7.1) (Abbott et al. 1999; Sanborn and Abbott 1999). The earlier of the two dates is questionable, as it predates the earliest Stallings dates by about 500 years (Herbert 1999b). Two TL dates for New River sherds from the Papanow site and one from site 31ON542 indicate a date range for the series from about 1200 B.C. to 400 B.C. (Herbert 1997, 1999b; Reid and Simpson 1996). Three TL dates for New River pottery obtained from sherds from the Riegelwood site extend the early end of the range to 1765–1247 B.C. On the late end, there is even one date as young as A.D. 405 ± 272, although this is considered to be an outlier (Figure 7.4). Given the dates associated with pottery of this series from sites on the south coast, it seems reasonable to suggest a date range for the series of about 1200–400 B.C.

Most previous analyses of collections from the southern coast did not distinguish between New River and early Cape Fear (e.g., South 1976; Wilde-Ramsing 1978) and, on a sherd-by-sherd basis, the distinction may often be impossible. As a consequence, the frequency of the occurrence of Early Woodland coarse sand–tempered sherds in most collections from the southern region is not known, but it is likely that some of the material previously identified as Middle Woodland is actually Early Woodland. Crawford's (1966) Lenoir series is also considered equivalent to the New River and Deep Creek series (Eastman et al. 1997), and Trinkley (1980, 1990) has classified coarse sand–tempered ware from the northern coast of South Carolina as Deep Creek. It must also be added that the New River series would seem to be related to the Early Woodland Vincent series first described for materials found on Piedmont sites in the Roanoke River valley (Coe 1964).

Middle Woodland Period Pottery Series (400 B.C.–A.D. 800)

Yadkin

Yadkin series pottery has traditionally been considered to be a Middle Woodland series but was not dated at either the Doerschuk site, where it was first defined (Coe 1964), or at the Town Creek site, where additional material prompted revisions to the definition (Coe 1995). At the Haw River site a radiocarbon date of 2190 ± 95 B.P. (405 cal B.C.–A.D. 20 [p = .05]) was associated with Yadkin pottery (Claggett and Cable 1982:248; Eastman 1994a:6). At the E. Davis site, a date for charcoal, 2170 ± 80 B.P. (396 cal B.C.–A.D. 14 [p = .05]), has been associated with pottery thought to be in the Yadkin series (Eastman 1994a:43). In the Sandhills of South Carolina, Yadkin pottery was found in two features at site 38SU83 (Blanton et al. 1986). Feature 11 was a concentration of 156 sherds from one Yadkin Fine Cord Marked vessel. Charcoal removed from the soil around the pottery dated to 2130 ± 70 B.P. (379 cal B.C.–A.D. 56 [p = .05]) (Blanton et al. 1986:59, Table 45; Eastman 1994a:84). One of the sherds from Feature 11 was also TL dated to 1220 ± 120 B.P. (A.D. 541–1011 [p = .05]). A second feature (Feature 17), determined to be a burned tree stump, was ^{14}C dated to 2330 ± 80 B.P. (762–186 cal B.C. [p = .05]). Yadkin Check Stamped, Yadkin Simple Stamped, and Pee Dee Complicated Stamped sherds were recovered from the fill of Feature 17 (Blanton et al. 1986:61, 146–147, Table 45). Most subsequent reviewers (Eastman 1994a, 1994b; Ward and Davis 1999:86) have downplayed contextual problems, accepting the ^{14}C dates as reliably associated with the Yadkin sherds and not accepting the TL date. In fact, Feature 11 exhibited no pit boundaries distinguishable by contrasting soil color, and Feature 17 was determined to be a natural disturbance with both Middle and Late Woodland ceramic components represented. On the other hand, no warrant for excluding a TL date of A.D. 766 ± 120 from the expected range for the Yadkin series is offered other than that it differs from the radiocarbon dates from the same context.

Based on evidence from the Sandhills, the Yadkin series is expanded in this study to include the crushed-rock–tempered, net-impressed, and cord-marked wares. At Fort Bragg, one net-impressed specimen tempered with crushed granitic rock has been TL dated to the Early Woodland, and two specimens have been TL dated to the Middle Woodland period (Table 7.2). Evidence from other sites on Fort Bragg includes vessels tempered with crushed soapstone and possibly chlorite schist, suggesting a relation to the Early Woodland period Marcey Creek series. There may also be some relation to the New Hope feldspar-tempered series defined for materials found in the lower Haw River valley, although at present this is thought to be a Late Woodland tradition (Claggett and Cable 1982; McCormick 1969). Consequently it must be concluded that the grounds for determining the temporal range for Yadkin series pottery are still inadequate. It is possible that sequences may differ regionally, with Yadkin occurring earlier in the Sandhills and later in the eastern Piedmont, but chronometric data are too sparse at this time to make this determination with confidence. In this study, therefore, Yadkin is placed in the earliest portion of the Middle Woodland period, but it is considered possible that the Yadkin tradition extends into the later portion of the Middle Woodland, perhaps informing the Late Woodland Uwharrie tradition of tempering with crushed rock, as suggested by Coe (1964).

Deptford

The sand-tempered Deptford series (Caldwell and Waring 1939) has its origin in the Early Woodland, about 650 B.C. (Anderson et al. 1982; Trinkley 1980, 1990), contemporary with the later portion of the Early Woodland Deep Creek phase. Cable et al. (1998:286–297, 322–324, Table 91) suggest a taxonomic sequence for

Table 7.2. Middle Woodland Dates Associated with Pottery from Eastern North Carolina

Sample[a]	Site Name	Target Pottery[b]	Minimum (Mean) Maximum[c]
B-43628	Tower Hill	Cashie Fabric Impressed and Plain	635 (780) 1005
UGA-2549	Uniflite	White Oak series	655 (725, 735, 765) 895
UGA-3144	Thorpe	Mount Pleasant Cord Marked	645 (725, 735, 765) 960
B-130059	Long Point	None noted	670 (770) 890
UW-449	31MR241	Hanover I Check Stamped	365 (706) 1047
UW-647	Riegelwood	Hanover II Cord Marked	91 (701) 1311
B-107427	Fairway	Hanover Fabric Impressed	610 (695) 815
B-127355	Hammocks Beach West	Hanover Cord Marked and Fabric Impressed; White Oak series	630 (690) 885
UW-222	Pond Trail	Hanover Fabric Impressed	396 (680) 964
UW-651	Riegelwood	Hanover II Cord Marked	338 (675) 1012
B-127367	Hammocks Beach West	None noted	615 (670) 785
B-119389	Hammocks Beach East	None noted	550 (650) 705
B-58941	Broad Reach	Hanover Fabric Impressed	430 (643) 777
B-127358	Hammocks Beach West	White Oak Fabric Impressed; Mockley Cord Marked and Net Impressed	545 (635) 675
UW-645	Riegelwood	Hamp's Landing Punctate *variety Allendale*	–136 (634) 1404
B-11941	Permuda Island	White Oak series	430 (625) 700
UW-?	31ON596	Hanover series	139 (621) 1103
UGA-2547	Uniflite	White Oak series	425 (575) 660
UGA-2548	Uniflite	White Oak series	390 (535) 640
B-7011	Sidney Brook	Hanover series	390 (530) 630
UW-659	Riegelwood	Hanover I Fabric Impressed	–62 (528) 1118

Sample[a]	Site Name	Target Pottery[b]	Minimum (Mean) Maximum[c]
UGA-3435	Tillett	Mount Pleasant series	280 (499) 673
UW-443	31HT344	Hanover I Fabric Impressed	144 (483) 822
B-130904	Long Point	Hamp's Landing, New River, Hanover, and Mockley series	385 (465, 480, 520) 625
UW-649	Riegelwood	Hanover I Cord Marked	172 (462) 752
B-107422	Fairway	Hanover Fabric Impressed	315 (445) 608
UGA-1085	Baum	Mount Pleasant series	340 (440) 615
UW-450	31MR93	Hanover I Cord Marked	–180 (435) 1050
UW-442	31CD622	New River Net Impressed	–128 (405) 938
B-48970	Point Harbor	Mount Pleasant series	240 (400) 535
B-73744	Liberty Hill	Mount Pleasant series	225 (390) 540
UGA-1088	Rush Point	Mount Pleasant series	111 (264) 434
UW-648	Riegelwood	Hanover I Cord Marked	–288 (184) 656
UW-223	Papanow	Hanover Cord Marked	166 (173) 512
B-11942	Permuda Island	None noted	55 (155) 340
UW-399	31HT347	Yadkin Net Impressed	–447 (121) 689
UW-396	31CD551	Cape Fear I Cord Marked	–331 (118) 567
UW-395	31HT269	Yadkin Net Impressed	–337 (118) 573
B-131574	Goose Creek (Bogue)	Hanover and White Oak	–115 (65) 245
UW-655	Riegelwood	Cape Fear Cord Marked	–357 (4) 365
UW-650	Riegelwood	Cape Fear Cord Marked	–399 (5) 409
UW-446	31HT355	Cape Fear I Cord Marked	–466 (–82) 302
UW-661	Riegelwood	Cape Fear Cord Marked	–533 (–168) 197
UW-652	Riegelwood	Cape Fear Cord Marked	–562 (–199) 164
UW-654	Riegelwood	Hamp's Landing Cord Marked	–709 (–221) 267
UW-393	31CD486	Cape Fear I Cord Marked	–1003 (–278) 447

Continued on the next page

Table 7.2. *Continued*

Sample[a]	Site Name	Target Pottery[b]	Minimum (Mean) Maximum[c]
B-73732	Little Cedar Island	Deep Creek series	–421 (–347) –162
B-73743	Liberty Hill	Mount Pleasant series	–400 (–365) –165
UW-394	31HT471	New River Cord Marked	–134 (–374) 882

[a]B = Beta Analytic Radiocarbon Dating Laboratory; UGA = University of Georgia; UW = University of Washington Luminescence Laboratory (TL dates).

[b]TL dates the pottery itself; radiocarbon dates organic material associated with the pottery.

[c]Minimum, mean, and maximum dates are 2σ calibrated intercepts for 14C samples and mean and 2σ errors for TL samples. Negative ages are calendar years B.C.; positive ages are calendar years A.D.

the northern coast of South Carolina that merges the Deptford and Cape Fear series, recognizing three phases, each distinguished by slightly different paste characteristics and relative frequency of surface treatment types (Table 7.3).

The trend toward softer pastes with smaller sand grains at lower proportions observed in coastal South Carolina and the North Carolina Sandhills appears, in general, to have been replicated along the central and northern portions of the coast. Crawford's (1966) data for the middle Neuse River drainage indicate higher relative frequencies of sherds with smaller sand grain sizes in the Tower Hill series, the later of two sand-tempered series from that area. On the central outer coast, Loftfield (1976) identified a fine sand–tempered ware, Adams Creek, as a Late Woodland type based on his seriation model but later suggested that Adams Creek might actually be more accurately placed in the Middle Woodland, contemporary with Mount Pleasant. Initially, Phelps (1983:33) observed "a trend toward larger clastic temper" in the Middle Woodland Mount Pleasant series. Later, he proposed a fine sand–tempered ware, the Middle Town series, for the terminal Middle Woodland period in the central and northern coastal regions (D. Phelps, personal communication 1999).

The trend in surface treatment styles observed in northern South Carolina and in the Sandhills is characterized by a predominance of cord marking in all three phases, decreasing proportions of carved-paddle stamping (check, simple, and complicated), and increasing proportions of fabric impressing at the expense of cord marking. A similar trend toward a higher relative frequency of fabric impressing with a decline in simple stamping and cord marking is noted by Phelps (1983:29–32) through Deep Creek phases I–III (1000–200 B.C.).

Table 7.3. Cape Fear and Associated Phases, Pottery Paste, Temper, and Surface Treatments in Northern South Carolina

			Surface Treatment (%)		
Associated Phases	Estimated Age	Paste and Temper	Cord Marked	Fabric Impressed	Carved-Paddle Stamped
Cape Fear III, Hanover I	A.D. 200–800	Soft to compact paste, sparse fine sand	47	39	14
Cape Fear II, Late Deptford, Deep Creek III	200 B.C.–A.D. 200	Compact paste, moderately abundant medium sand	56	22	22
Cape Fear I, Early Deptford, Deep Creek II	600–200 B.C.	Very hard paste, abundant medium and coarse sand	50	23	27

Note: Adapted from Cable et al. 1998.

Occasionally, sand-tempered, check-stamped sherds are found on southern coastal and Sandhills sites in North Carolina, and these are presumed to be related to the Deptford series. As mentioned, check stamping also is known to occur in relatively low frequency in the Yadkin series. Cable et al. (1998) observed sand-tempered, check- and simple-stamped sherds together with cord- and fabric-impressed types in Horry County, South Carolina, and suggest lumping all of these types under a single Cape Fear I series. Similarly, check and simple stamping is found on grog- or clay-tempered Hanover series sherds in that region (Cable et al. 1998). Check stamping is rare among sand-tempered sherds from southern North Carolina and only occasionally seen in the Hanover series. This suggests that the northern extent of the Middle Woodland carved-paddle stamping tradition is found in the southernmost counties of North Carolina. Considering its association with Deptford materials, carved-paddle stamping also signals the earlier portion of the Cape Fear and Hanover series, coeval with Deptford I and II (ca. 600 B.C.–A.D. 200).

Cape Fear

Also present in the Middle Woodland period in the Sandhills and elsewhere in the southern coastal region is a long-enduring sand-tempering tradition—the Cape Fear series—that appears to be related to a number of series from adjacent areas. The sand/grit-tempered Cape Fear series (where grit denotes particle size greater than 1 mm) appears to have an age range from about 400 B.C. to A.D. 400, based on TL dates from Fort Bragg (see Chapter 6). In the Sandhills and on the southern coast, where the series was first defined by South (1960), cord marking is the predominant surface treatment found in the Cape Fear series. Cable and colleagues (1998) divided the Cape Fear series into three phases corresponding to classes exhibiting varying proportions of sand, sand size, and relative frequency of surface treatment characteristics (Table 7.3). It is possible that such a tripartite division will prove useful in identifying temporal components within the sand-tempered wares from the Sandhills and southern coast, but the distinctions that have been drawn thus far among the three classes are quite subtle, requiring large sample sizes and well-controlled contexts to test (or accurately identify) the presence of one or the other phases.

As such, Cape Fear I coincides with early Deptford and late New River. There appear to be some temporal trends in paste characteristics over the period such that a very hard-pasted ware with abundant medium and coarse sand shifts to a compactly pasted ware with moderately abundant medium sand (Cable et al. 1998). Anderson and colleagues (1982) approach the resolution of Middle Woodland sand-tempered wares into mutually exclusive classes through the use of the type-variety system. Whereas Cable and colleagues interpret the Cape Fear series from Horry County, South Carolina, as part of a Deptford continuum (200 B.C.–A.D. 200), Anderson and colleagues (1982:293–299) identify similar sand-tempered, fabric-impressed ware from Berkeley County, South Carolina, as Cape Fear *variety St. Stephens,* a late Middle Woodland (A.D. 500–700) type. They recognize relatedness among the sand-tempered, fabric-impressed ware found at the Mattasee Lakes sites and South's (1960) Cape Fear series, Phelps's (1981b) Deep Creek and Mount Pleasant series, and Loftfield's (1976) New River series and suggest subsuming all of them as varieties of Cape Fear (Anderson et al. 1982:299).

Mount Pleasant

The Middle Woodland Mount Pleasant ceramic series, found on the northern coast of North Carolina, is thought to be contemporary with the Hanover series of the south coast (Figure 7.3). The latest Mount Pleasant date, 1060 ± 80 B.P. (cal A.D. 903–1292 [p = .05]), was derived from shell found in the midden at Rush Point. Exception is taken to the outlying date, 270 ± 50 B.P. (cal A.D. 1477–1954 [p = .05]), from Feature 1 at site 31WL170 until further assays demonstrate continuity in this series of dates (Table 7.4). The relationship of the Mount Pleasant and Cape Fear series is not well understood. Phelps (1983:35) equated the two, suggesting they form a single series. Haag (1958) described a grit-tempered series, similar or equivalent to Mount Pleasant, for the interior Coastal Plain that may have subsumed specimens classifiable as Cape Fear. Mount Pleasant series sherds also resemble Middle Woodland Vincent series (Coe 1964:101–102) of the Roanoke Rapids area of Piedmont North Carolina and Evans's (1955) Stoney Creek series from the Potomac River valley in Virginia.

Very few Mount Pleasant series sherds were identified in the surface collections used in this study, although this was the principal type recognized from the Bandon site midden. Results of the analysis of sherds from the Bandon midden raise some questions regarding the taxonomy and sequencing of Mount Pleasant series pottery. The Middle Woodland shift from coarse sand to granule tempering that was expected, on the basis of published information, was not found. Instead, the frequency of granule-tempered sherds was greater at the base of the midden, with temper grain size decreasing in the middle and upper levels. This reversal of the expected trend did not appear to be the result of postdepositional disturbance but suggests that systematic analyses of sand-tempered assemblages of Middle Woodland components found on sites are needed to refine definitions and sequences.

Hanover

Following Coe (1952:306) and Haag (1958:108), South (1976:40) concluded that fabric impressing was an earlier technology than cord marking and surmised that the Hanover series was associated with an earlier culture phase than the Cape Fear series. As is demonstrated in the Bandon midden and among dated materials from the southern coast and Sandhills, however, fabric impressing is without question more frequent later in the sequence than cord marking. Based on radiocarbon dates from South and North Carolina, a conservative estimate for the temporal range of the Hanover series is 200 B.C.–A.D. 650 (Figure 7.3). Several recent radiocarbon assays suggest that the Hanover series dates well into the Late Woodland period, possibly as late as A.D. 1400 (T. Hargrove, personal communication 1998; Herbert et al. 2002; Mathis 1999). Irwin and colleagues (1999) have reanalyzed the ceramics from the McLean Mound and found them tempered with sand and grog rather than sand as originally thought, therefore suggesting that these materials are Hanover series rather than Cape Fear. Also, a sample of soot from the surface of a sand/grit-tempered fabric-impressed sherd from the McLean Mound was submitted for radiocarbon dating. The AMS (accelerator mass spectrometry) assay returned a date of 980 ± 110 B.P. (cal A.D. 821–1282 [p = .05]), somewhat earlier than expected for the mound but in the expected range for Hanover series pottery. Some researchers subsume Hanover as a variety of the Wilmington series (Anderson et al. 1982:272; Trinkley 1990:17–18). The grog-tempered Wilmington and St. Catherine's series (Caldwell 1952; DePratter 1979; Waring and Holder 1968) from the Georgia Sea Islands and south coast of South Carolina date from ca. 200 B.C. to A.D. 1150 and, hence, are contemporary with part of the Hanover phase. Although these series include an array of surface treatments not seen on

Table 7.4. Late Woodland Dates Associated with Pottery from Eastern North Carolina

Site	Site Name	Sample[a]	Target Pottery[b]	Minimum (Mean) Maximum[c]
31HY43	Amity	B-31110	Colington Simple Stamped	1530 (1665) 1950
31HT355		UW-445	Hanover I Fabric Impressed	1559 (1675) 1791
31WL170		B-48782	Mount Pleasant series	1490 (1645) 1945
31CR53	Shelly Point	B-69590	Townsend series[d]	1477 (1630) 1697
31HF30b	Liberty Hill	B-8134	White Oak Fabric Impressed	1455 (1530, 1545, 1635) 1665
38HR243	Little River Neck	B-96114	Hanover I series	1431 (1533) 1691
31CD594		UW-397	Hanover II Fabric Impressed	1197 (1503) 1808
44KG3	Deshazo	SI-137	White Oak Fabric Impressed	1325 (1500) 1950
31HT392		UW-447	Hanover II Fabric Impressed	1367 (1481) 1595
31CR53	Shelly Point	B-69588	Fabric impressed	1408 (1476) 1626
31CR14	Piggott	B-73741	Townsend series	1420 (1455) 1635
31ON665	Hammocks Beach West	B-127369	White Oak Fabric Impressed	1382 (1452) 1538
31CR218	Broad Reach	B-58943	Townsend series	1405 (1452) 1645
31HY43	Amity	B-17507	Colington Simple Stamped	1300 (1440) 1650
31HY43	Amity	B-34062	Colington Simple Stamped	1305 (1430) 1630
31CR218	Broad Reach	B-52529	Townsend series	1400 (1430) 1480

	Ellis	B-76688	Cashie series	1326 (1426) 1473
31CR218	Broad Reach	B-58947	Townsend series	1325 (1425) 1460
44WM119	White Oak Point	DIC-1766	Townsend series	1400 (1425) 1460
31BR7	Jordan's Landing	UGA-1086	Cashie series	1295 (1415) 1475
31CR218	Broad Reach	B-58946	White Oak Fabric Impressed	1295 (1405) 1435
31ON665	Hammocks Beach West	B-127364	None noted	1295 (1410) 1445
31ON665	Hammocks Beach West	B-127360	Hanover Fabric Impressed; White Oak Fabric Impressed and Plain	1290 (1410) 1455
31ON665	Hammocks Beach West	B- 127359	Hanover Cord Marked; Mockley Net Impressed; White Oak Fabric Impressed	1305 (1410) 1445
31ON33	Uniflite	UGA-2550	Townsend series	1295 (1410) 1450
31NH331	Eagle Point	B-128620	Hanover series	1300 (1405) 1435
31ON305	Flynt, ossuary	B-30209	Townsend series	1295 (1403) 1443
31BF25	Archbell Point	B-31Bf25	Colington Simple Stamped	1291 (1396) 1462
31ON665	Hammocks Beach West	B-127366	White Oak Fabric Impressed	1285 (1395) 1435
31CK9	Baum	B-73735	Townsend series	1220 (1299, 1375, 1375) 1427
31CK9	Baum	B-73734	Townsend series	1266 (1301, 1372, 1378) 1413
31ON309	Jarretts Point	UGA-5467		1264 (1318, 1368, 1387) 1430

Continued on the next page

Table 7.4. *Continued*

Site	Site Name	Sample[a]	Target Pottery[b]	Minimum (Mean) Maximum[c]
31ON665	Hammocks Beach West	B-127357	White Oak Fabric Impressed	1280 (1310, 1365, 1380) 1415
31BR1	Shipyard Landing	B-4394	Colington Fabric Impressed	1275 (1310, 1365, 1380) 1420
31ON624	Jarman Point	B-112272	Hanover series; Cape Fear series (?)	1275 (1315, 1345, 1390) 1435
31CR218	Broad Reach	B-58944	Townsend series	1285 (1315, 1350, 1390) 1420
44WM119	White Oak Point	DIC-1768	Townsend series; Currioman series	1285 (1315, 1350, 1390) 1425
31ON665	Hammocks Beach West	B-127361	Hanover Fabric Impressed; White Oak Fabric Impressed and Plain	1263 (1334) 1443
31ON624	Jarman Point	B-112271	None noted	1235 (1300) 1425
31DR14	Kitty Hawk Bay	UGA-3847	Townsend series	1213 (1323) 1450
31CR53	Shelly Point	B-69589	Townsend series; Cape Fear series	1245 (1323) 1433
31CK9	Baum	UGA-1089	Townsend series	1224 (1320) 1440
31NH690	Papanow	UW-225	Cape Fear Cord Marked	943 (1319) 1695
44WM119	White Oak Point	DIC-1764	Townsend series	1275 (1305) 1410
38HR243	Little River Neck	B-96112	Hanover Fabric Impressed	1275 (1300) 1410
31ON196	Permuda Island	B-11939	White Oak Fabric Impressed	1275 (1300) 1410
31HY43	Amity	B-30866	Colington	1270 (1300) 1405
31ON190	Cape Island	B-104465	New River Simple Stamped; White Oak Plain	1265 (1300) 1415

31BR1	Shipyard Landing	B-4395	Colington Fabric Impressed	1260 (1300) 1410
31ON665	Hammocks Beach West	B-127363	New River series (?); Hanover Fabric Impressed; White Oak Fabric Impressed	1255 (1300) 1420
31CR218	Broad Reach	B-53075	Hanover series; Townsend series	1218 (1297) 1422
31BR7	Jordan's Landing	B-73742	Cashie series	1210 (1285) 1395
31ON665	Hammocks Beach West	B-127362	Hanover Fabric Impressed; White Oak Fabric Impressed and Plain	1177 (1290) 1395
31ON665	Hammocks Beach West	B-127368	White Oak Fabric Impressed	1210 (1290) 1405
31ON665	Hammocks Beach West	B-127365	Hanover Fabric Impressed; Townsend series	1250 (1290) 1395
31DR38	Hatteras Village	B-77128	Townsend series	1214 (1290) 1404
31CR218	Broad Reach	B-58945	Townsend series	1185 (1280) 1395
31DR33	White Court	UGA-1087	Colington Fabric Impressed	138 (1280) 1387
31NH330		B-	Hanover Fabric Impressed and Simple Stamped; Cape Fear Fabric Impressed	1255 (1280) 1295
31BF58	Midgette Point	B-	Townsend series	1137 (1273) 1338
31CK9	Baum	B-77127	Townsend series	1194 (1271) 1295
31ON190	Cape Island	B-104169		1020 (1270) 1420
31ON235	Pelican Point	B-842464	White Oak Fabric Impressed; Hanover Fabric Impressed; Cape Fear Fabric Impressed	1055 (1260) 1305

Continued on the next page

Table 7.4. *Continued*

Site	Site Name	Sample[a]	Target Pottery[b]	Minimum (Mean) Maximum[c]
38HR243	Little River Neck	B-96113	Hanover I series	1170 (1255) 1290
31ON82	Hammocks Beach	B-11937	White Oak Fabric Impressed	1025 (1250) 1385
31NS3b	Thorpe	UGA-3143	Cashie Simple Stamped and Fabric Impressed	1050 (1250) 1295
31JN2	Long Point	UW-451	Townsend series	957 (1249) 1541
31ON190	Cape Island	B-104167		1085 (1240) 1315
31ON624	Jarman Point	B-112275		175 (1260) 1295
44NB147	Blue Fish Beach	SI-4230	Rappahannock Incised and Fabric Impressed	1035 (1220) 1290
31HT450		UW-448	Hanover I Fabric Impressed	719 (1219) 1721
31ON305	Flynt	B-12815	Onslow series; White Oak Fabric Impressed	1030 (1205) 1280
31ON305	Flynt	B-12816	Townsend series	1030 (1205) 1280
31NH331	Eagle Point	B-122725	Hanover series	1050 (1200) 1295
31ON305	Flynt	B-12353	None noted	1025 (1175) 1260
31ON235	Pelican Point	B-79500	White Oak Fabric Impressed; Hanover Fabric Impressed	990 (1170) 1285
31NH142	Hamp's Landing	B-63184	Hanover series	1020 (1170) 1290
31ON196	Permuda Island	B-11940	White Oak Fabric Impressed; Hanover Fabric Impressed	1010 (1160) 1260

38HR258	Fairway	B-107425	Plain and fabric impressed	1005 (1159) 1289
44PG4	Irwin	SI-138	Rappahannock Fabric Impressed	1040 (1155) 1185
31ON33	Uniflite	UGA-2552	Townsend series; Hanover series	1027 (1154) 1265
31JN2	Long Point	UW-452	Townsend series	947 (1141) 1335
31NH28	Cold Morning	B-1285	Cape Fear series; Hamp's Landing series	980 (1123, 1141, 1152) 1280
31CR53	Shelly Point	B-136918	Townsend series	1012 (1132) 1274
31ON624	Jarman Point	B-112273	Cape Fear series; Hanover series; Townsend series	1000 (1040) 1251
31HT392		UW-398	Hanover II Fabric Impressed	841 (1084) 1327
	Little Cedar Island	B-73731	Mount Pleasant series	982 (1067) 1231
31FR14	Kitty Hawk Bay	UGA-1090	Colington Fabric Impressed	966 (1063) 1237
31CR305	Goose Creek	B-131575	Hanover Cord Marked; Townsend series	848 (1059) 1297
31JN2	Long Point	B-130060	Cape Fear series; Hanover series; Townsend series	995 (1040) 1225
31ON536			Hanover series; Townsend series	1040
44WM119	White Oak Point	SI-4374	Rappahannock Fabric Impressed	980 (1040) 1245
31CD7	McClean Mound	M-1354	Cape Fear series; Hanover series	815 (1025) 1270
31NS3b	Thorpe	UGA-3142	Cashie series	895 (1020) 1195
31CR53	Shelly Point	B-131572	Townsend series	900 (1015) 1170

Continued on the next page

Table 7.4. *Continued*

Site	Site Name	Sample[a]	Target Pottery[b]	Minimum (Mean) Maximum[c]
31HT402		UW-401	Cape Fear III Cord Marked	756 (997) 1238
31CR53	Shelly Point	B-131573	Townsend series	875 (995) 1040
38HR258	Fairway	B-107426a		839 (995) 1087
31ON305	Flynt	B-9381	New River series; Hanover series; Onslow series; Townsend series	880 (990) 1030
31ON665	Hammocks Beach West	B-127356	Hanover Cord Marked and Fabric Impressed; White Oak Fabric Impressed, Plain; Mockley Cord Marked and Net Impressed	875 (980) 1025
31DR35	Tillett	UGA-3433	Townsend series	765 (980) 1150
31ON305	Flynt	B-9382	New River series; Hanover series; Onslow series; Townsend series	815 (970) 1020
31DR15	Rush Point	UGA-3849	Mount Pleasant series	765 (950) 1070
31HT344		UW-444	Hanover I Fabric Impressed	489 (946) 1403
31ON624	Jarman Point	B-112278		865 (975) 1020
31CB114	Riegelwood	UW-656	Hanover II Fabric Impressed	629 (931) 1233
31HF20	Mount Pleasant	UGA-4011	Townsend series	685 (905, 930, 945) 1115
31ON305	Flynt	B-12817	Cape Fear series	765 (895) 1010
38HR258	Fairway	B-107423	Hanover Fabric Impressed	772 (906) 1034

31CR218	Broad Reach	B-58942	Townsend series	888
44HE470	Alvis	UGA-4818	Rappahannock Fabric Impressed	680 (875) 1005
31CD750		UW-441	Hanover I Fabric Impressed	550 (864) 1178
31JN2	Long Point	B-130905	Cape Fear series; Hanover series; Townsend series	690 (815, 840, 855) 970

[a]B = Beta Analytic Radiocarbon Dating Laboratory; UW = University of Washington Luminescence Laboratory (TL dates); SI = Smithsonian Institution; DIC = Dicarb Radioisotope Company; UGA = University of Georgia; M = University of Michigan.

[b]TL dates the pottery itself; radiocarbon dates organic material associated with the pottery.

[c]Minimum, mean, and maximum dates are 2σ calibrated intercepts for 14C samples and mean and 2σ errors for TL samples. Negative ages are calendar years B.C.; positive ages are calendar years A.D.

[d]Sherds here classified as Townsend series are those lacking attributes clearly distinguishing them as either Colington or White Oak types. The assignment of Colington or White Oak classification reflects the original reported information, often based on geographic context, not morphological attributes.

Hanover ceramics from North Carolina (e.g., simple stamping, check stamping, and linear check stamping), the tempering technique and geographic proximity suggest some relatedness.

Based on TL dates and petrographic analysis of pottery from the Sandhills, two temporal phases for the grog-tempered Hanover series have been proposed (Herbert et al. 2002). A late Middle Woodland phase, Hanover I (A.D. 400–800), is characterized by pottery tempered principally with sand to which a minor amount of finely crushed grog was added. Surface treatments in this variety include cord marking, check stamping, and fabric impressing. A Late Woodland variety, Hanover II (A.D. 800–1500), is tempered mostly with grog with a small amount of sand included in the paste and is represented by mostly fabric-impressed sherds.

Mockley

The Mockley series, defined by Robert Stephenson and colleagues (1963:105–109), dates to the latter half of the Middle Woodland period. Dates for Mockley series pottery range from about A.D. 200 to A.D. 880 (Artusy 1976:9; Barka and McCary 1977:43; Gardner and McNett 1971; Opperman 1980:4; Potter 1982:121; Waselkov 1982). In the coastal North Carolina region, Mockley ware is characterized as having thick vessel walls, coarse shell temper, cord-marked or net-impressed surfaces, and simple jar forms with direct rims, wide mouths, and semiconical or rounded bottoms (Potter 1982:124). Potter (1982:124) suggested that among Mockley materials from the Northern Neck of Virginia, cord marking was more common in the earlier part of the phase and net impressing more common in the later part. This sequence appears to be reversed in southern Maryland (Herbert 1995:20) and on the coast of North Carolina, where net impressing is the more common of the two surface treatment styles early in the sequence, with cord marking more popular in the later part of the period, persisting into the earliest portion of the Late Woodland (A.D. 800–900).

Late Woodland Period Pottery Series (A.D. 800–1600)

One of the most significant recent developments in understanding the Late Woodland in the southern coastal region has been the recognition of potential for confusion regarding the distinction between shell-tempered Late Woodland ware (formerly Oak Island series) and Early Woodland limestone-tempered Hamp's Landing series sherds. A recent reappraisal suggested that previously analyzed "shell-tempered" assemblages from several southern coastal sites may have included a number of limestone- or marl-tempered specimens (Herbert and Mathis 1996). A subsequent study designed to assess this problem by reanalyzing a portion of the collection that South (1960) used to define the Oak Island series found that among a sample of 112 sherds (45 percent of South's original collection) none could be positively identified as shell tempered (Mathis 1999).

As researchers began to realize that much of what had been identified as Late Woodland shell-tempered Oak Island was actually Early Woodland Hamp's Landing series, some of the perplexity regarding surface treatments vanished. Net-impressed and cord-marked surface treatments occurring in the Late Woodland period—problematic with regard to our current understanding of the sequence of surface treatment traditions for the coast—made much more sense in an Early Woodland context. Mockley-like pottery with cord-marked and net-impressed surface treatments has been found at the Long Point site in the central coastal area (Shumate and Evans-Shumate 2000). Similar material has been found in the area north of the Albemarle and from a few sites on the central coast, where it occurs in relatively low frequency. These ceramics are classified as Mockley in the current study.

The undoing of Oak Island also has ramifications for interpretation of the age of the Cold Morning ossuary. Two pottery types, Cape Fear Fabric Impressed and Hamp's Landing Plain, are associated with the Cold Morning ossuary burials, dated 1000 ± 80 B.P. (cal A.D. 778–1163 [p = .05]) (Eastman 1994a:10; Ward and Wilson 1980). The sherds found in the Cold Morning ossuary, originally classified as Oak Island, have been reclassified as Hamp's Landing (Mathis 1999). The provenience reported for these specimens does not allow discrimination of temporal priority for one or the other series (see Ward and Wilson 1980:27). Present data suggest that it is the sand-tempered component in the ossuary that dates to the early Late Woodland period.

Hanover II

A second development that holds promise for the Late Woodland chronology on the southern coast pertains to filling of the gap left by the retirement of the shell-tempered Oak Island series. The pottery from the McLean and Buie mounds furnishes a line of evidence regarding Late Woodland pottery series. Seventy-five percent of the McLean Mound pottery is fabric impressed and tempered with sand and grog (Herbert 1999b; Irwin et al. 1999). The presence of medium sand along with clay or grog, and the complete absence of sherds tempered exclusively with clay or grog without sand, distinguishes these specimens as a late variety of the Hanover series. Sand-tempered, smoothed, and fabric-impressed ware is also observed in the McLean Mound assemblage. Although the sand-tempered material is classified as Middle Woodland Cape Fear, the total absence of cord marking—the dominant surface treatment in the Cape Fear series—is notable, suggesting either an unusually late position in the Cape Fear sequence or the existence of a Late Woodland sand-tempered series that has not yet been defined. In combination, these data suggest that both the sand-tempered and clay- or grog-tempered wares represent an early Late Woodland tradition, ca. A.D. 700–1200 (Table 7.4). The Buie Mound pottery assemblage includes mostly (79 percent) sand-tempered, burnished plain ware with some (12 percent) clay- or grog-tempered sherds (Wetmore 1978:44, Table 3). Fabric impressing is the minority type (about 10 percent) at the Buie Mound but occurs on 86 percent of the McLean Mound sherds. This suggests that the McLean Mound assemblage may be somewhat earlier than the Buie Mound assemblage (Irwin et al. 1999).

Chronometric data from Fort Bragg indicate that grog-tempered pottery appeared in the region by at least A.D. 400 and through the ensuing centuries displaced sand-and-grit tempering (Herbert 2000; Herbert et al. 2002; see also Chapter 5). This is evident as a declining relative frequency of sand/grit-tempered sherds and decreasing proportions of sand included in the paste of grog-tempered vessels. By A.D. 1000, the temper is predominantly grog, with only a background (1–3 percent) of medium sand in the paste. Also during the transition from the Middle to Late Woodland (A.D. 400–800), cord marking is displaced by fabric impressing. For convenience, the period from A.D. 400 to A.D. 800 may be referred to as the Hanover I phase and the period following A.D. 800 the Hanover II phase.

Townsend

The Late Woodland period in tidewater North Carolina is considered synonymous with shell-tempered ceramics. The Colington series was defined by Phelps (1983) for shell-tempered ware found along the coast in the northern region, and the White Oak series was defined by Loftfield (1976) for shell-tempered ware found in the central coastal region. Both areas were the traditional territory of the Carolina Algonquians and are consequently related to the Townsend series in coastal Virginia and southern Maryland (Egloff and Potter 1982:107–108; Griffith 1980; Potter 1993:114–119; Stephenson et al. 1963; Wright 1973). Few significant differences appear to exist between the pottery defined as White Oak and that defined as Colington, but some differences do exist, especially as relates to surface treatments and rim form (Herbert and Mathis 1996; Marshall 1999).

As originally conceived, Colington and White Oak are contemporary shell-tempered series that include fabric-impressed and plain or smoothed types; however, simple stamping and incised decorations have not been confirmed in White Oak assemblages, while these surface treatment types are common in the Colington series. Burnishing is occasionally seen in the White Oak series while not found in the Colington series. A recent study also suggests that statistically significant differences exist in the length and frequency of paddle-edge impressions left on the interior of vessel necks among the sample measured (Marshall 1999). While there is some suggestion that there may be some regional differences, the contemporaneity and overall similarity of these wares has led to the combination of these types into one broad ceramic series referred to as the Townsend series composed of Colington and White Oak types.

There are at this time a sufficient number of radiocarbon dates for anthropogenic features with associated pottery to conclude that the shell-tempered Townsend series dates to the period from about A.D. 800 to at least A.D. 1600 (Table 7.4, Figure 7.3). There is some suggestion that Colington Simple Stamped was more frequent later in the sequence, with Colington and White Oak Fabric Impressed types occurring throughout the Late Woodland period.

Recent research at the Cape Creek site adds radiocarbon data to the Townsend and Hanover phases. From the top of Zone IIIB within the midden in Square M-E2, a radiocarbon date of A.D. 1250–1445 (cal, p = .95) was obtained for wood charcoal found in association with Townsend series pottery (these chronometric data were provided by D. S. Phelps [personal communication 2000], who is analyzing materials recently excavated from the Cape Creek site; as his analysis is still under way and the information unpublished at the time of this writing, these dates are not recalibrated or included in the summary charts for radiometric data for the northern coast). A second date of A.D. 870–1140 (cal, p = .95) was obtained from wood charcoal associated with Colington pottery in Feature 5A, Square M-A10. This date is considered by Phelps to represent an early date for Townsend at the site. Three dates were obtained from Cape Creek that were thought to be associated with Hanover series pottery. The youngest, A.D. 670–970 (cal, p = .95), was for charcoal obtained from Feature 5B, Square M-A8. A second date, A.D. 555–775 (cal, p = .95), was obtained from the tip of the shell midden and a third, A.D. 510–775 (cal, p = .95), from the bottom of the shell midden.

Cashie

The Cashie phase and pottery series were first described by Phelps (1983) and revised (Phelps and Heath 1998) on the basis of data recovered from the Jordan's Landing (31BR7), Neoheroka Fort (31GR4), Sans Souci (31BR5), Thorpe (31NS3), Battle Park (31NS19), and Fishing Creek (31HX61) sites. The Cashie series, dating from ca. A.D. 800 to A.D. 1715, is considered contemporary with the Townsend series and similarly includes fabric-impressed, simple-stamped, incised, and plain types. Cashie is tempered with granule- and pebble-sized quartz particles, occasionally crushed, which often protrude simultaneously through the interior and exterior surfaces of the vessel walls. In addition, Phelps and Heath (1998) note that "perhaps as significant as any observed exterior treatment of Cashie vessels, is the dominant addition of an interior finishing treatment that is regionally unique to the series . . . floated and/or slipped interiors."

Cashie simple-stamped ware is thought also to be equivalent to Gaston simple-stamped ware (Coe 1964) from the Roanoke Rapids area and, in Virginia, to the Branchville series (Binford 1965) and the Sturgeon Head series (Smith 1971) in the Meherrin and Nottoway river basins. Minority surface treatment types found in the Gaston and related series (e.g., cord marked, cob marked, and check stamped) have not been observed in the Cashie series. The earliest dates associated with Cashie pottery are from the Thorpe site, a seasonally occupied site near the Tar River fall line, and are 1000 ± 70 B.P. (cal A.D. 895–1195 [p = .05]) and 800 ± 65 B.P. (cal A.D. 1050–1295 [p = .05]) (Table 7.4). The Jordan's Landing site, a permanently occupied, palisaded village on the Roanoke River, produced two radiocarbon dates from a feature context, 670 ± 60 B.P. (cal A.D. 1260–1408 [p = .05]) and 525 ± 70 B.P. (cal A.D. 1297–1610 [p = .05]) (Byrd and Heath 1997). With the additional date obtained from the Ellis site, 500 ± 50 B.P. (cal A.D. 1326–1473 [p = .05]), the range of calibrated intercepts for radiocarbon dates associated with Cashie series pottery is A.D. 1022–1418.

The extensive and unique ceramic assemblage from the Neoheroka Fort site and the Contentnea Creek survey (Byrd 1996; Byrd and Heath 1997) provides an exceptional example of pottery from the final decades of the Cashie phase. The fort, built by the Tuscarora to defend their homeland in the Tuscarora War of 1713, was occupied but one winter when it was besieged by Barnwell's colonial militia, its defenders destroyed, and all structures burned to the ground. This briefly occupied and precisely dated site provides a uniquely encapsulated sample of Cashie phase material culture. The Neoheroka Fort assemblage, along with those from the several other sites mentioned, has allowed Phelps and Heath (1998) to discriminate two periods within the Cashie pottery series, made up of four vessel forms. Vessel forms include large conical-based jars, differing only in degree of rim constriction; small, thin-walled jars; bowls (including deep, flat-based, shallow simple, hemispherical, and double-ended "pouring" types); and dippers.

Large and small jars are primarily simple stamped, while bowls and pouring vessels are mostly fabric impressed. Decorations, usually restricted to the rim and neck, generally consist of punctated patterns including solid and hollow circles, solid semicircles, and ovoid shapes. Incising is also common, especially on the small jar forms. Paste, temper, and construction methods do not change significantly between Cashie I (A.D. 800–1650) and Cashie II (A.D. 1650–1715). No new surface treatments or vessel forms were added; rather, what had been predominant variants disappear, leaving a less rich array of vessel types in the Colonial period.

Swansboro

The Swansboro series is thought to date to the latest portion of the Late Woodland period and the Contact period. This ware may be related to the Yeocomico series found on the Virginia coast (Potter 1982; Waselkov 1982) and to the Warekeck series (Binford 1965), a colonoware found on sites in southeastern Virginia (principally Southampton County). Taxonomically, it is not included in the Townsend series, but it appears to be a late manifestation of the shell-tempering tradition, and future researchers may choose to classify it as a component type in the Townsend series.

Brunswick

Brunswick is a proto-Historic and Historic period (A.D. 1400–1700) series. The series was first defined by South (1960) to describe Colono-Indian ware found at Brunswick Town and Bath, North Carolina, that included burnished and plain types. In this analysis the series is expanded to three types, burnished, corncob marked, and brushed, expanding the potential temporal range to include the centuries just prior to European contact.

Summary

Having reviewed the chronological arrangement of pottery types from the coast, it is useful to think again about the nature of this information as reflecting the social behaviors that lie behind the technological traditions. In an ideal world, each pottery type represents a specific suite of behaviors that had to have been replicated with some measure of fidelity in order to reproduce the combination of traits used by archaeologists to classify each sherd or vessel. One striking feature of the chronometric data (summarized in Figure 7.2) is the length of the periods that types occupy; most series span periods of more than 500 years. The social and cultural implications of this striking feature are explored in Chapter 9.

The foregoing review of the chronological data brings broad patterns into perspective and allows us to contrast sequences between areas. For example, on the southern coast we see that the Stallings, Thom's Creek, Hamp's Landing, and New River series traditions coexisted from the very earliest period (about 2000 B.C.), suggesting that this region was culturally diverse during this period. In contrast, on the northern coast, the New River (including Deep Creek) series appears to stand alone for a thousand years before the appearance of Croaker Landing and Marcey Creek. This apparent discrepancy may be due in part to a lack of chronological data for Croaker Landing and Marcey Creek that when found may suggest greater time depth for these stylistic horizons. Conversely, this pattern may reflect an actual lag in the diversification of Early Woodland period social groups in the northern region.

Contrasting the sequence of Late Woodland series from the northern and southern coasts we find that whereas on the north coast there are three coeval series (Townsend, Cashie, and Swansboro), on the southern coast only the Hanover series is represented, and that by very few dates. Although the relative deficit of Late Woodland pottery on the southern coast may reflect a sampling bias, it suggests that social conditions in the unembayed southern coastal region were quite different from those on the central and northern Carolina coast. In an era when villages and plant husbandry were becoming more common elsewhere on the Coastal Plain, very little evidence of village life has yet been found on the southern coast or in the Sandhills.

The following chapter explores the historical continuities reflected in the spatial distribution of technological traditions by assessing the regional distribution of the pottery types discussed in this chapter.

8

The Spatial Distribution of Types

Inasmuch as pottery series, types, and varieties correspond to sociocultural phenomena that occupy specific periods of time, they are also spatially patterned. It is relatively common for archaeologists to use ethnohistoric information about the geographic arrangement of linguistic or ethnic groups to interpret the spatial distribution of pottery types. It is less common, however, to see this logic worked in reverse, to identify social boundaries (e.g., Algonquian or Tuscarora tribal areas) based on regional ceramic distributions. Although this study proceeds under the logic of the latter approach, the vast majority of the ceramic data presented here relate to remote periods of prehistory for which no ethnohistoric information about any particular linguistic or ethnic group exists and, as will be demonstrated in Chapter 9, no necessary relationship exists between pottery type distributions and ethnic or linguistic boundaries. Neither does the geographic scale of the data lend itself particularly well to identifying band territories, a process requiring a finer grained sampling strategy (e.g., see Sampson 1988). Rather, the purpose to which these data are most appropriate, and the goal of this part of the study, is to explore continuities in the spatial distribution of pottery traits that reflect socially shared technological traditions. To that end, traditions are discussed in approximate order of their age. In some cases the ceramic stylistic areas and boundaries may in fact relate to ancient social territories. In most, however, it appears that prehistoric technological traditions or styles encompassed many potential tribal regions and persisted over vast stretches of time. Certainly, the geographic ranges of most of the ceramic traditions observed here comprise much larger areas than a single band's territory. Likewise, the temporal ranges for traditions reflect styles that persist through the lifetimes of 20 or more generations of potters. Interpretation of temporal and spatial patterns, whether these were a result of the position or displacement of populations or the ebb and flow of information and custom, is explored in Chapter 9.

A few additional comments regarding the patterns illustrated in the following sequence of pottery type distribution maps might be appropriate. When reviewing these maps, the reader is encouraged to keep in mind the overall distribution of the sample from which they were derived (see Figure 3.2). Haag's collection comprises mostly coastal sites. Consequently, mapped distributions whose western boundaries terminate in the lower Coastal Plain (well east of the fall line) may reflect the extent of the data in this study rather than the actual westernmost extent of the pottery type distribution (although in many instances the westernmost extent of mapped distributions may prove to be relatively accurate). The data from Fort Bragg in the Sandhills clearly demonstrate the potential of upper Coastal Plain sites to document the western boundaries of coastal pottery traditions up to the Piedmont fall line and beyond. In fact, there are areas within the coastal zone that are far less well represented than others in Haag's collection. For instance, there are numerous sites representing the Pamlico Basin and no sites at all representing the lower Neuse Valley. This bias is no doubt due to the fact that much of the area adjacent to the Neuse on the north side is Light Ground Pocosin, unsuitable for agriculture. Similarly, there would have been few plowed fields to collect just south of the Neuse, where much of the region is encompassed by the Croatan National Forest.

Regarding the analysis of the spatial data, readers may recall from the discussion of methods in Chapter 3 that the distribution maps were constructed in two ways: one illustrating the frequency or raw count of pottery specimens from each series and another illustrating the relative frequency (proportion) of pottery types calculated as a percentage among types in each period (early, middle, and late). As discussed, the use of proportions serves to lessen the effect that the duration of site occupancy (an unknown factor) might have on sherd frequency. Basic statistics are included in the figure captions to provide data for each type. Map symbols mark the site location, and symbol size reflects the count or the relative frequency of sherds classified to a given series or type.

Early Woodland Traditions

Stallings Series

Fiber-tempered sherds from this region are typically considered to be in the Stallings tradition or related to the Stallings phase (2500–1100 B.C.) and are therefore classified as Stallings series ware. The Stallings ware in this study includes 53 sherds classified as having fiber as the principal tempering agent and 13 having fiber in combination with medium and coarse quartz sand. In addition, a small number (13) from Brunswick and Beaufort counties were observed to have principally sand temper with some fiber in the paste. As the fiber in these specimens appeared to be potentially incidental, they were not classified as Stallings. This determination was judgmental, of course, but it was felt that the classification of these sherds as fiber tempered pushed the class definition too far. Most of the sherds that fell into the incidental-fiber category were classified as New River series based on temper and surface characteristics, but one sherd from site 31BW227 tempered with marl and fiber was classified as Hamp's Landing. Three sand-and-fiber–tempered (sand/fiber-tempered) examples from site 31HK191 also push the definition, as their surfaces are treated with parallel cord marking. These are thought to represent the Early Woodland period, but their numbers are far too thin to warrant interpreting them as witness to a broad-scale transition from fiber to sand or marl tempering. One sand/fiber-tempered sherd from site 31HK204 has check-stamped surface treatment. This surface treatment type is typically associated with the Deptford phase, which has its inception in the Early Woodland period but extends well into the Middle Woodland.

The greatest number of sites with fiber-tempered ware were found in Hoke County (n = 4), in the Sandhills (Figure 8.1). Site 31HK154 yielded 46 fiber-tempered sherds, the majority ware at that site, although all sherds were very small and perhaps belonged to a single vessel. One site each in Columbus and New Hanover counties falls into this group, with a single sherd found in Beaufort County.

The fact that many fiber-tempered sherds were found in the Sandhills suggests that the distribution in southern North Carolina may mirror the distribution in South Carolina, where Stallings series pottery is frequently found at sites on the interior Coastal Plain as well as on the coast. The distribution observed in this study supports the contention that the fiber-tempering tradition is related to the Stallings Island culture emanating from the Savannah River area of South Carolina. To the collection used in this study may be added some 38 sites with fiber-tempered plain ware from surveys conducted in the coastal region (Loftfield 1979; Phelps 1975, 1976, 1983; South 1976; Wilde-Ramsing 1978). These site locations greatly expand the distribution of fiber-tempered pottery, indicating that while the preponderance of sites with Stallings plain ware are found below the Neuse, sites with fiber-tempered sherds are found as far north as Gates County (Figure 8.1). Adding these sites illustrates that the boundary is not an abrupt but a very diffuse margin. Most North Carolina sites have yielded only a few fiber-tempered sherds, suggesting that single vessels were moving from the core area to the periphery by down-the-line exchange or by occasional small group forays.

Marcey Creek Series

Soapstone-tempered Marcey Creek series sherds were found at two sites, 31CK1 and 31DR16 (Figure 8.2). Sherd assemblages at both of these sites were quite variable and suggested the presence of significant Early Woodland components. Typi-

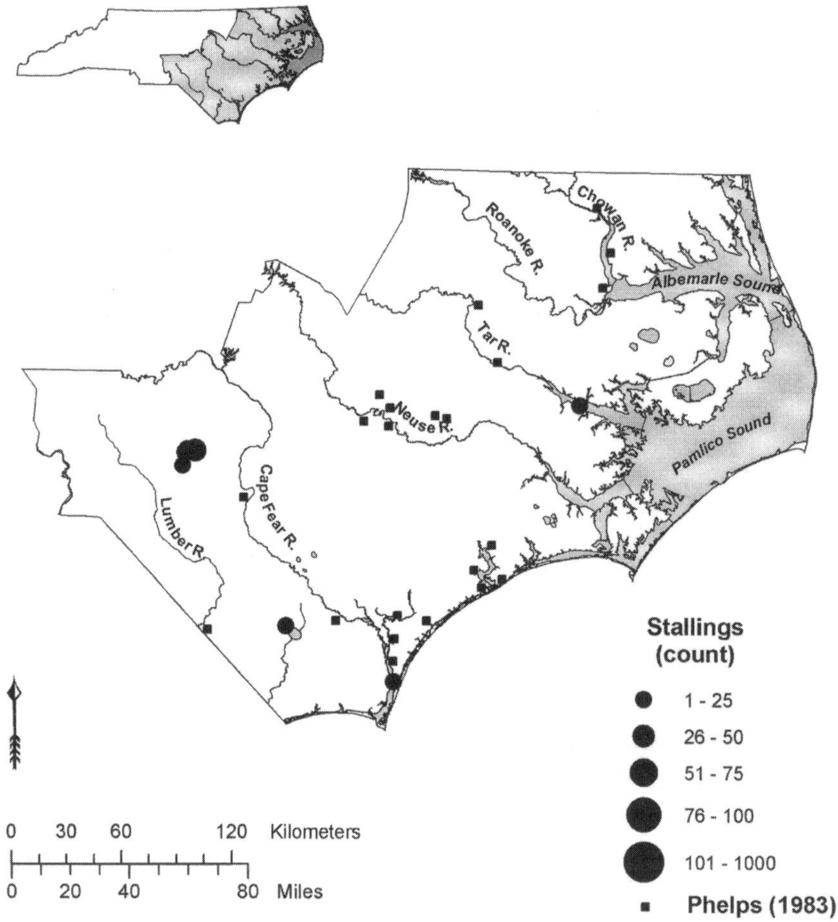

Figure 8.1. Distribution and frequency (count) of Stallings series (count = 7; min. = 1; max. = 46; sum = 66; mean = 9; std. dev. = 15).

cally soapstone-tempered sherds classified as Early Woodland Marcey Creek series (1200–800 B.C.) are found in the Potomac River basin (Egloff and Potter 1982; Evans 1955; Manson 1948). As was seen with the distribution of fiber-tempered sherds, the distribution of soapstone-tempered sherds from the current study may be expanded considerably from other sources.

South (1976:40, 46, Table 1), for example, found a single sherd in his survey of a site in New Hanover County (31NH4). Also in New Hanover County, Wilde-Ramsing (1978:50) reported finding five steatite-tempered sherds, although the site locations are not specified. In the Neuse drainage, Phelps's survey of the Stoney Creek watershed in Wayne County yielded four sites, each with a sherd or two of soapstone-tempered ware (Phelps 1981c:120, Table III). Phelps also reported find-

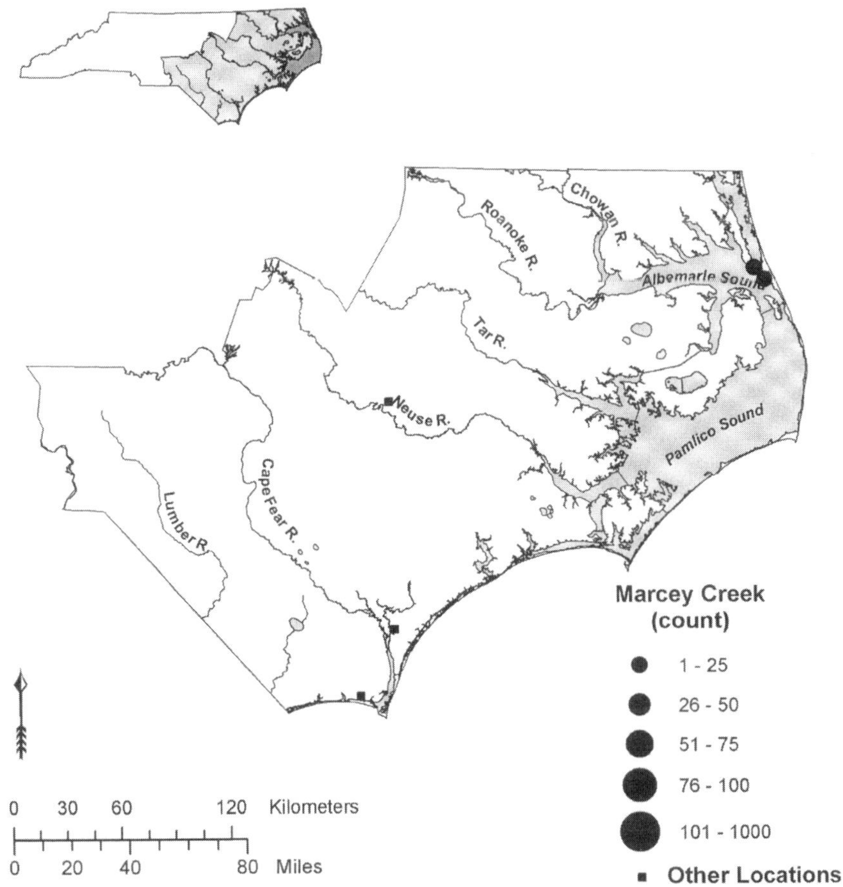

Figure 8.2. Distribution and frequency (count) of Marcey Creek series (count = 2; min. = 1; max. = 2; sum = 3; mean = 2; std. dev. = 1).

ing four steatite-tempered sherds from three sites in Edgecombe County (Phelps 1981b:97, Table 2).

These findings testify to the fact that Marcey Creek–like sherds may occasionally be found in the Neuse Basin and on southern coastal sites. The fact that no soapstone-tempered sherds were recognized by Loftfield (1976) in his survey of Onslow County sites or in Crawford's (1966) survey of a section of the Neuse in Pitt, Lenoir, and Wayne counties suggests that soapstone-tempered sherds are rather rare outside of the extreme northern coastal area. Obviously, the presence anywhere on the coast of soapstone is a clear indication of communication with the interior, as soapstone is a metamorphic lithic material not found in any primary context on the Coastal Plain.

Hamp's Landing Series

As has been described, the identification of marl-tempered pottery is a relatively recent phenomenon on the Carolina coast (Adams and Trinkley 1993; Hargrove 1993; Hargrove and Eastman 1997, 1998). Earlier studies are suspected of having misidentified marl-tempered pottery as shell tempered (Mathis 1998, 1999). The potential for confusing the two is understandable as most of the limestone and marl found in the coastal deposits is fossiliferous. Since Hargrove's (1993) marl-tempered Hamp's Landing series first appeared in print, a handful of dates now suggest marl tempering to be an Early Woodland tradition that may have persisted into the earliest portion of the Middle Woodland period. The data used in this study are not adequate to comment on the distribution of marl-tempered pottery into the interior Coastal Plain, but the northernmost boundary appears to be in the lower Pamlico and Pungo river basins (Figure 8.3).

The geographic range of marl-tempered Hamp's Landing series sherds, as reflected in the Haag collection, is greater than might be expected given the limited area in which they have been recognized and reported thus far in the literature. Prior to this study, marl-tempered sherds had only been found in Horry County, South Carolina, and Columbus, New Hanover, and Onslow counties, North Carolina (Abbott et al. 1999; Adams and Trinkley 1993; Hargrove 1993; Jones et al. 1997; Sanborn and Abbott 1999; Terrell et al. 2000). This may be due, in part, to the difficulty of distinguishing marl from shell temper and the fact that the series is relatively new.

At present, little is known about the specific locations of exposed calcareous deposits that may have been used by prehistoric potters, but it is evident that the distribution of marl-tempered sherds mirrors the distribution of marl. There appears to be no justification at present for assuming that the marl-tempering tradition originated outside of southern and central coastal North Carolina. Based on raw counts, the tradition appears to be centered in the lower Cape Fear valley, but with a surprisingly strong presence in the lower Pamlico drainage. If the idea for tempering with marl spread, radiating as it were from some hypothetical epicenter, its expanding geographic range might be assumed to result in younger expressions of the tradition on the boundaries of the distribution. Sherd frequency at sites with Hamp's Landing components suggests an even distribution, with some indication of higher frequencies on a few sites in the lower Cape Fear valley—presumably the core area for this series.

Following this line of reasoning, we might note that Hamp's Landing Cord Marked (parallel cord marking thought to be an Early Woodland trait) is restricted to the southern coast (Figure 8.4). Marl-tempered sherds with other surface treatment styles, however, are not so geographically restricted. If parallel cord marking is indeed an Early Woodland trait, then the restriction of Hamp's Land-

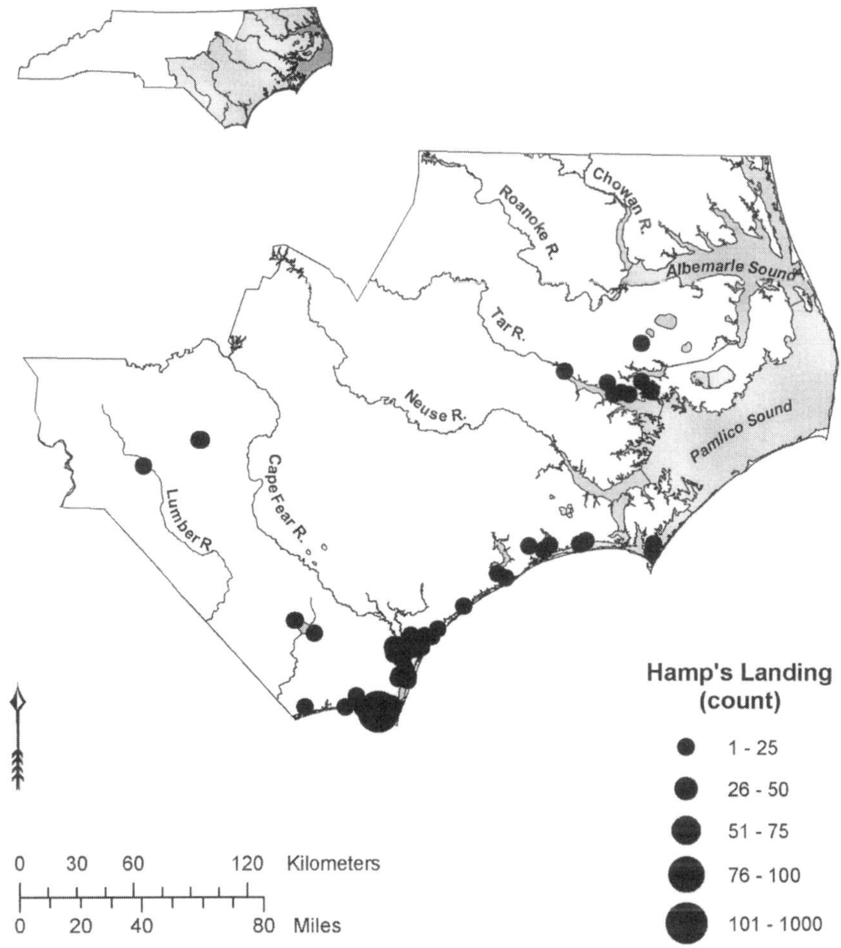

Figure 8.3. Distribution and frequency (count) of Hamp's Landing series (count = 56; min. = 1; max. = 153; sum = 679; mean = 12; std. dev. = 21).

ing Cord Marked to the southern coast suggests that the marl-tempered material found in the Pamlico Basin may in fact relate to a later Middle Woodland component.

Hamp's Landing Fabric Impressed was found in the lower Cape Fear and Pamlico river basins, with little found on the coastal margin between these rivers (Figure 8.5). The frequency of Hamp's Landing Fabric Impressed appears to be greater in the lower Pamlico Basin than in the Cape Fear. This is contrasted with the distribution of Hamp's Landing Cord Marked, which was found to be most frequent in sites from the lower Cape Fear and central coastal margin (lower New and White Oak river basins) but not found at all in the Pamlico Basin. This evi-

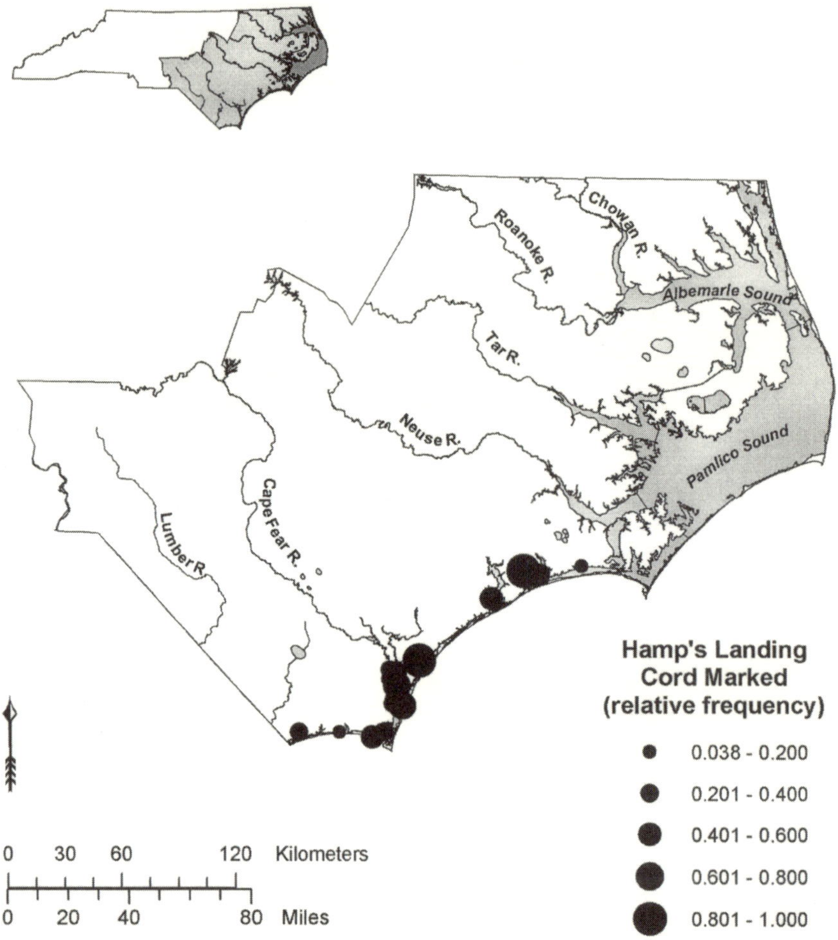

Figure 8.4. Distribution and relative frequency of Hamp's Landing Cord Marked type (count = 26; min. = 1; max. = 97; sum = 230; mean = 9; std. dev. = 18).

dence, that parallel cord marking and flexible warp fabric impressing have different geographic distributions, suggests the possibility that these traditions may be of slightly different age.

Hamp's Landing and New River Simple Stamped were found to be common in the Pamlico Valley, occasionally along the southern and central coasts and in the northern Sandhills, but rarely on the Outer Banks and coastline of Albemarle Sound (Figure 8.6). Hamp's Landing Simple Stamped occurs in low proportions on sites along the lower Cape Fear (two sites in New Hanover County and two in Brunswick County), on one site in Pender County, and on two sites on the Pamlico River in Beaufort County.

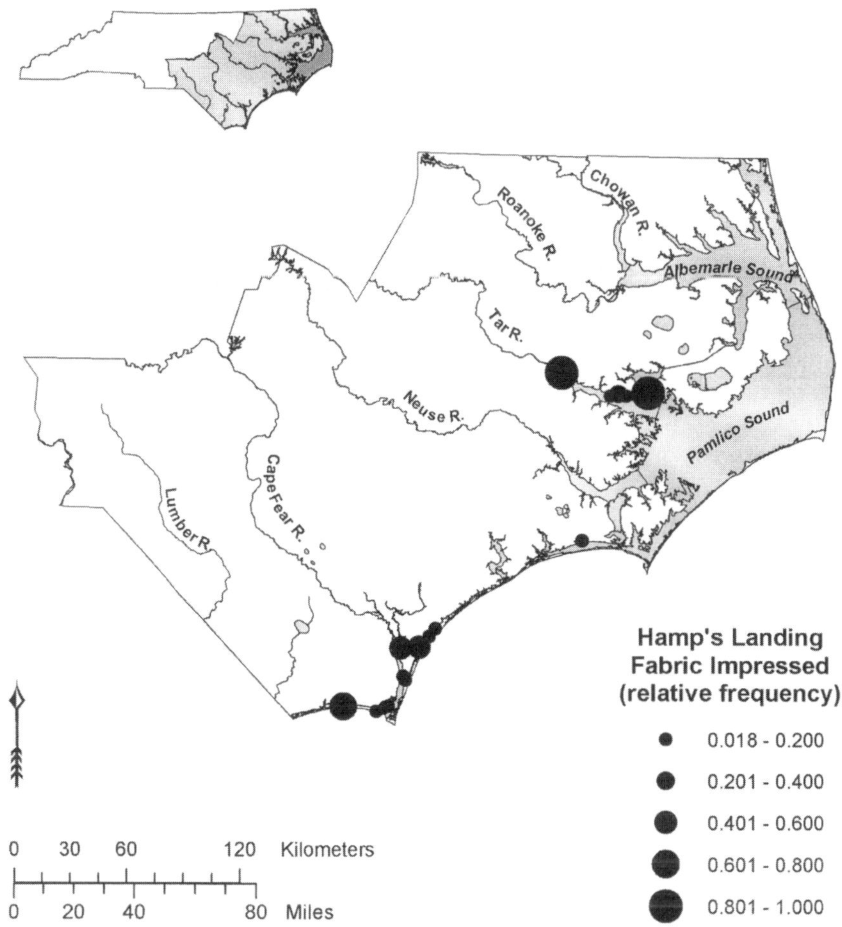

Figure 8.5. Distribution and relative frequency of Hamp's Landing Fabric Impressed type (count = 18; min. = 1; max. = 11; sum = 51; mean = 3; std. dev. = 3).

Hamp's Landing Paddle-Edge Stamped was found at only two sites near the mouth of the Cape Fear River in Brunswick County. The balance of the Early Woodland data for this surface treatment type is made up of New River Paddle-Edge Stamped sherds.

Thom's Creek Punctate Type

The distribution of Early Woodland punctate wares is limited to sites in the lower Cape Fear valley on the coast of Brunswick County and near Lake Wacamaw, Columbus County. This group is composed primarily of Thom's Creek Punctate

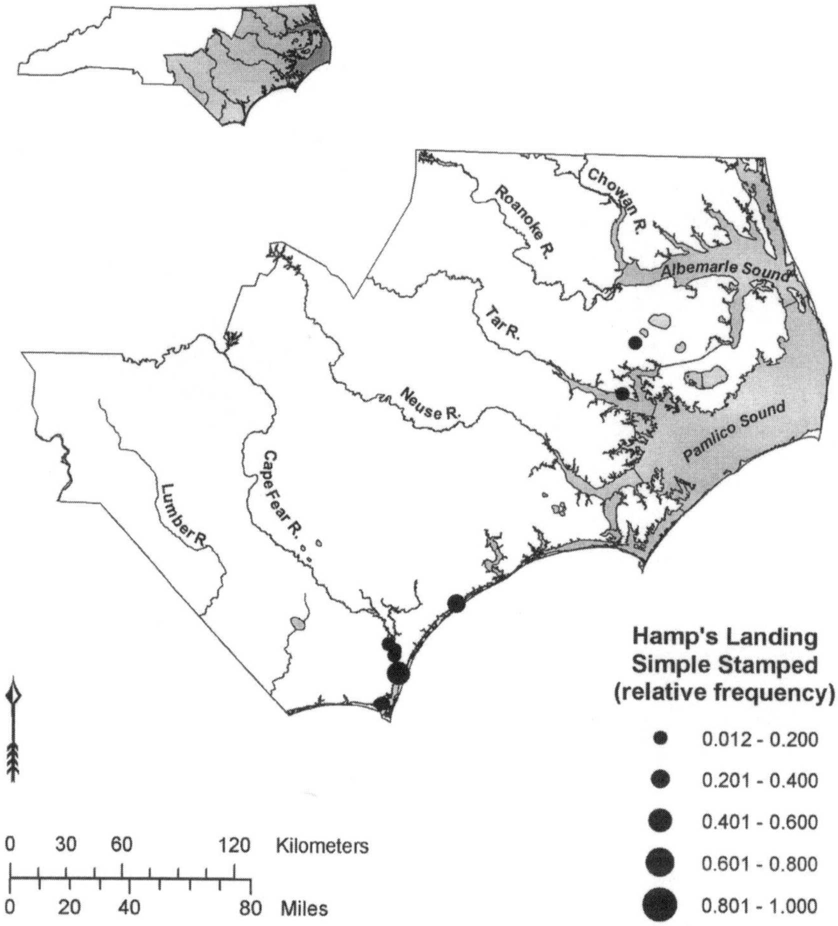

Figure 8.6. Distribution and relative frequency of Hamp's Landing Simple Stamped type (count = 9; min. = 1; max. = 10; sum = 30; mean = 3; std. dev. = 3).

(Figure 8.7) and Refuge Punctate *variety Allendale* (Figure 8.8). The Thom's Creek Punctate found in the Haag assemblages was mostly the separate-reed punctate variety (see Anderson et al. 1996:253–254).

Refuge Punctate *variety Allendale* Type

The surface treatment diagnostic of the Refuge Punctate *variety Allendale* type (Anderson et al. 1996:224–225) has been described as "closely spaced, randomly oriented punctations that must have been made by a composite instrument rather than one impression at a time—a handful of straw or twigs?" (Stoltman 1974:276).

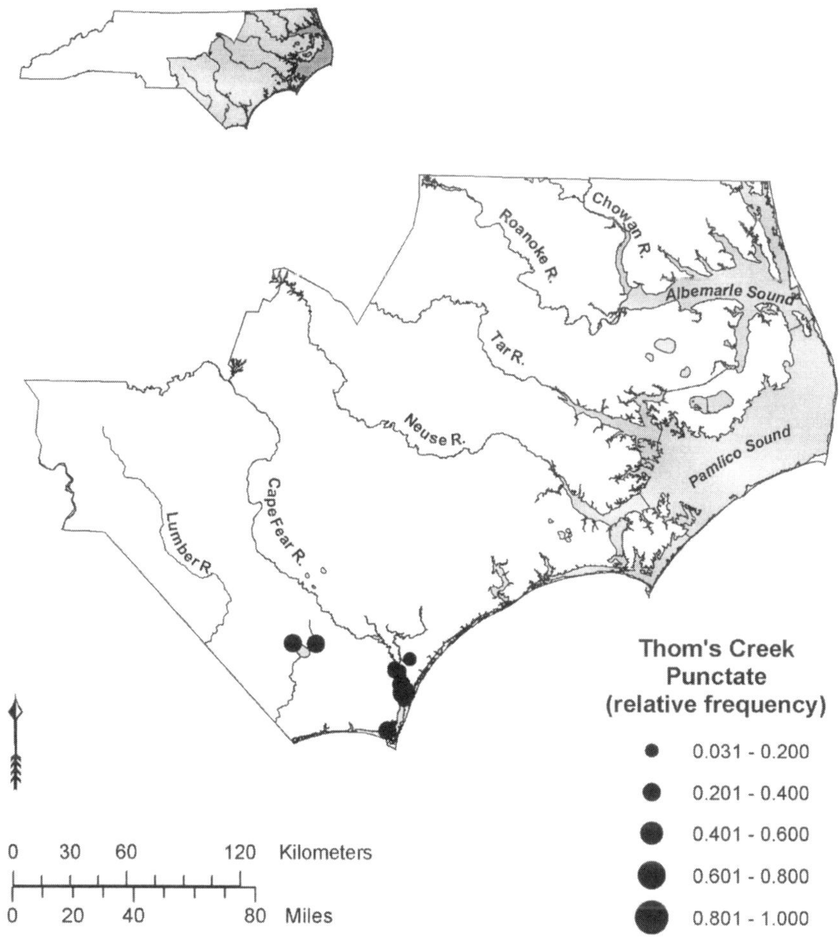

Figure 8.7. Distribution and relative frequency of Thom's Creek Punctate type (count = 13; min. = 1; max. = 31; sum = 66; mean = 5; std. dev. = 8).

Examples of this type of surface treatment from the southern North Carolina coast may in fact be made by rouletting the surface of a leather-hard vessel with a pine cone. The Refuge Punctate *variety Allendale* and the Thom's Creek Punctate components of the distribution are very similar (Figures 8.7 and 8.8). Although no examples of either punctate ware were found farther north than the Cape Fear in this study, these types are known from sites on the lower New and White Oak rivers, at Hammocks Beach, and at the Broad Reach site (M. Mathis, personal communication 2001). The range, therefore, extends north to at least Bogue Sound in Carteret County.

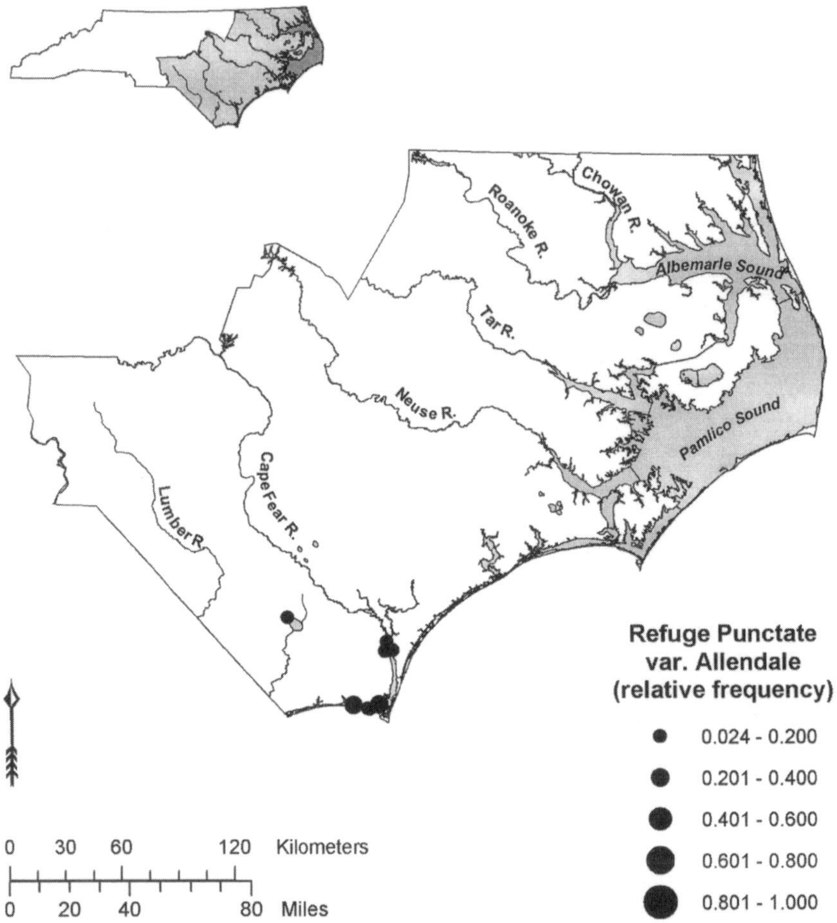

Figure 8.8. Distribution and relative frequency of Refuge Punctate *variety Allendale* type (count = 11; min. = 1; max. = 21; sum = 62; mean = 6; std. dev. = 6).

New River Series

New River series sherds exhibit coastwide distribution, with subtle differences in the distribution of surface treatment types that may reflect shifting social boundaries. New River Net Impressed illustrates the overall distribution but proportions (and raw counts) suggest a strong presence on the lower Currituck Peninsula and in the lower Pamlico River basin, with relatively low proportions on the southern coast (Figure 8.9). New River Cord Marked is also found over the entire study area (Figure 8.10), but this type is nearly absent from Early Woodland assemblages on the Currituck Peninsula, with relatively high proportions in the Cape Fear River

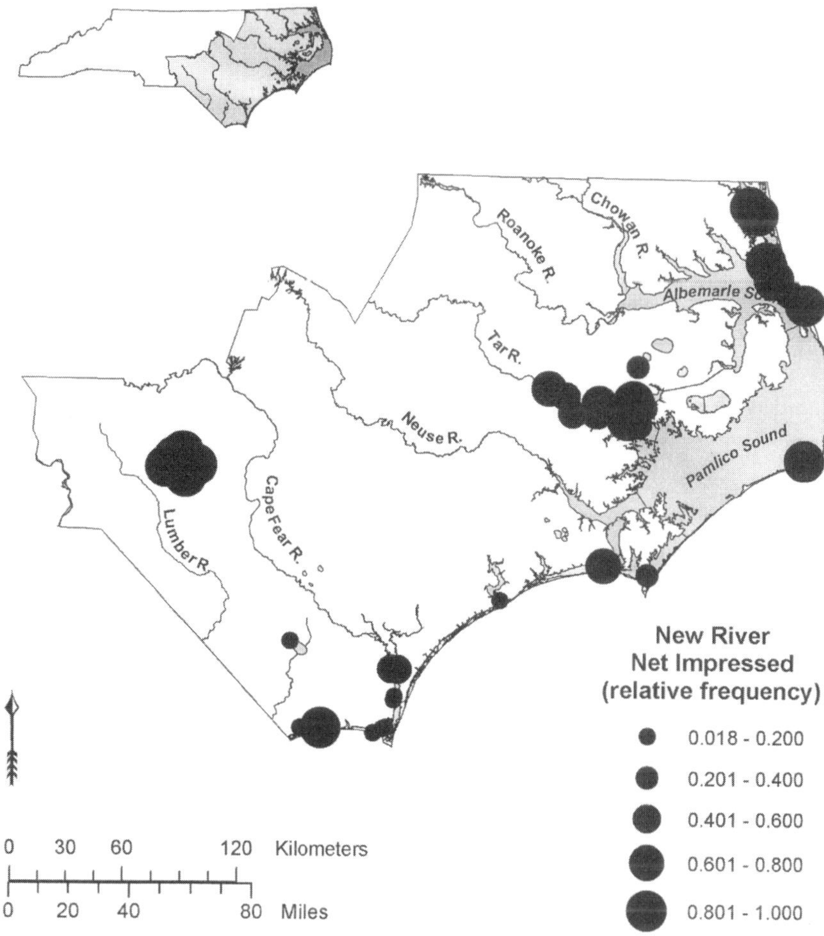

Figure 8.9. Distribution and relative frequency of New River Net Impressed type (count = 50; min. = 1; max. = 67; sum = 447; mean = 9; std. dev. = 14).

basin. Recalling that the tradition of net impressing precedes cord marking, this temporal shift in New River series distributions suggests changing social dynamics, possibly reflecting interaction with groups to the south. It is perhaps no accident that the region with the greatest representation of Thom's Creek and Refuge series, the lower Cape Fear River valley, is also the area with the lowest proportions of the contemporary New River Net Impressed type. This pattern suggests that the interaction of groups making Thom's Creek and Refuge pottery displaced the makers of New River pottery to more northerly locations. This interpretation is strengthened by the fact that proportions of New River Cord Marked and Fabric Impressed types swell on southern coastal sites in the subsequent period, when

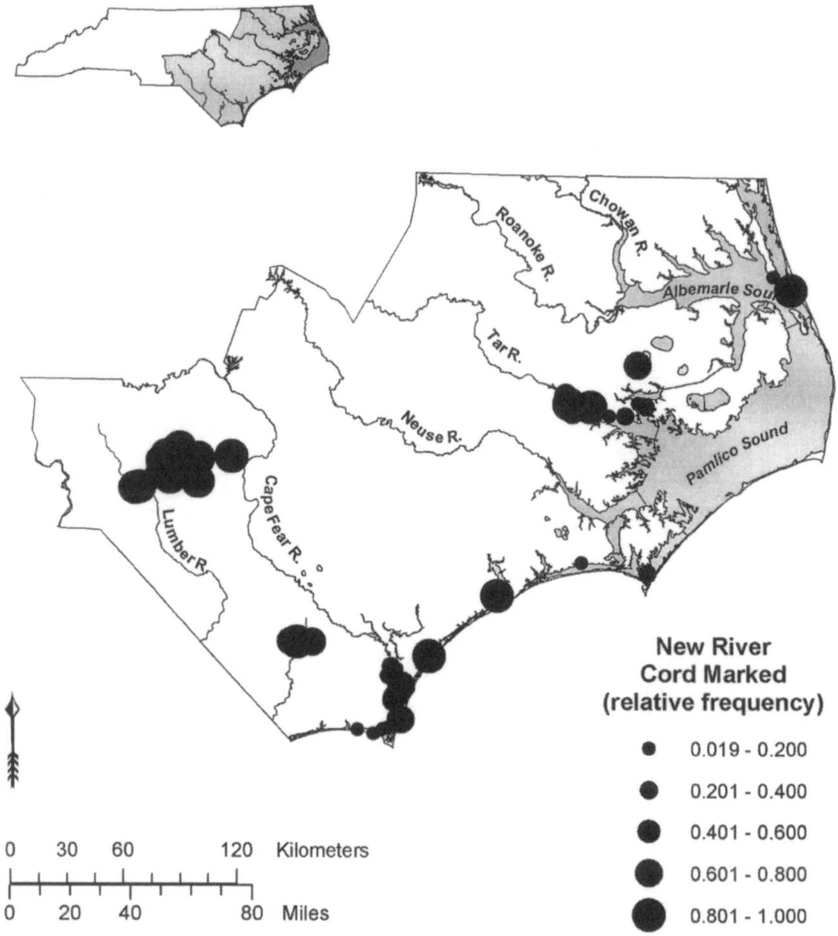

Figure 8.10. Distribution and relative frequency of New River Cord Marked type (count = 67; min. = 1; max. = 37; sum = 359; mean = 5; std. dev. = 7).

Thom's Creek and Refuge disappear from the Cape Fear Valley. The spatial distribution of New River Fabric Impressed (flexible warp textile impressed) suggests a weak boundary at or just north of the Pamlico River, with only a few sites occurring north of this in Currituck County (Figure 8.11). The proportion of flexible warp fabric impressions in assemblages from the Currituck County sites is less than 20 percent. Many sites in the northern Sandhills and on the southern coast, in contrast, have proportions greater than 60 percent. This results in part from the smaller size of site samples in the Loftfield collection, but nevertheless signals higher proportions along the southern coast.

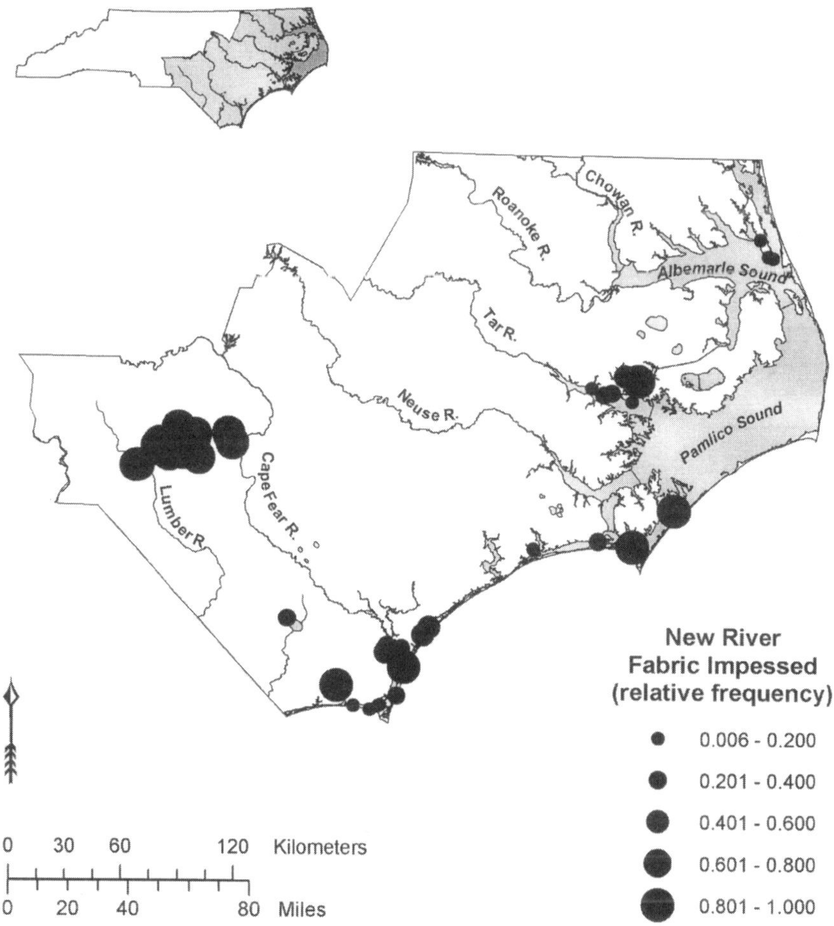

Figure 8.11. Distribution and relative frequency of New River Fabric Impressed type (count = 65; min. = 1; max. = 42; sum = 316; mean = 5; std. dev. = 8).

New River Simple Stamped is a minority type within this series, exhibiting its greatest concentration on the Pamlico River with 12 sites (59 sherds) scattered relatively evenly from the upper to lower portions of the embayed lower reaches of the river, over a 40-mile transect (Figure 8.12). Sites with a few sand-tempered, simple-stamped sherds were also found in the lower Cape Fear valley, in the Sandhills, and on the Outer Banks (31DR26). An especially large number of sand-tempered, simple-stamped sherds was also found in the assemblage from 31CK1 in Currituck County. As the simple-stamped type is considered to be earlier in the New River sequence, more nearly contemporary with net impressing, higher proportions of

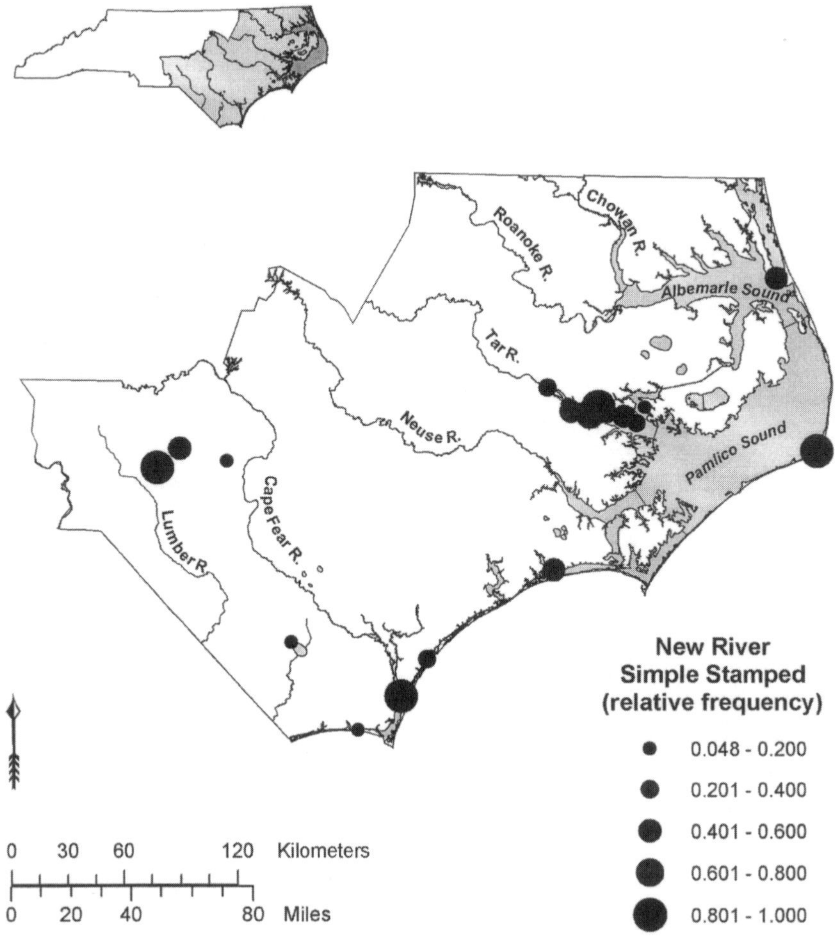

Figure 8.12. Distribution and relative frequency of New River Simple Stamped type (count = 23; min. = 1; max. = 51; sum = 143; mean = 6; std. dev. = 10).

simple-stamped ware on the northern coast seem to make sense if Thom's Creek and Refuge makers were displacing New River groups in the early part of the sequence.

Paddle-edge stamped types were defined for both the Hamp's Landing and the New River series. The distribution of New River Paddle-Edge Stamped includes Brunswick County, the northern Sandhills, and the Cape Fear valley (Figure 8.13). Two sites with proportions less than 20 percent occur on the lower Pamlico River. The suggested boundary for this trait among Early Woodland ware is just northeast of the Cape Fear River in New Hanover County.

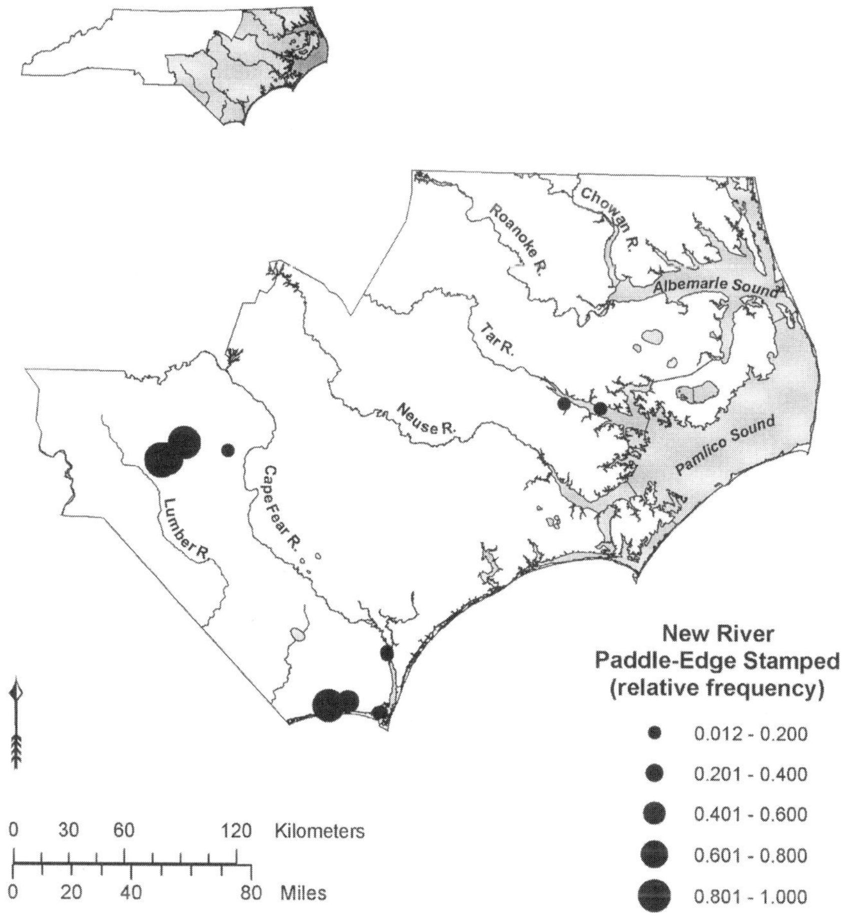

Figure 8.13. Distribution and relative frequency of New River Paddle-Edge Stamped type (count = 17; min. = 1; max. = 16; sum = 53; mean = 3; std. dev. = 4).

Middle Woodland Traditions

There are five pottery series included in this discussion of Middle Woodland period traditions (400 B.C.–A.D. 800): Yadkin, Cape Fear, Mount Pleasant, Hanover, and Mockley. To some extent, each series is characterized by a different temper constituent, although most share temper characteristics with a series dating to another period. Yadkin is tempered with crushed rock, including quartz and occasionally metamorphic rock. The Cape Fear series shares the characteristic of sand tempering with Early Woodland New River and Late Woodland Brunswick types, although surface treatments of these three classes are mutually exclusive. Mount Pleasant is identified by rounded or subrounded granule- and pebble-sized quartz. Angular quartz of the same size is interpreted as crushed quartz, which characterizes the Yadkin and Onslow series and is assumed to represent a distinct process of temper preparation. The Hanover series is tempered with grog, which serves to distinguish it from every other series except the Early Woodland Croaker Landing series (not recognized in the collections analyzed for this study). The Middle Woodland Mockley series is shell tempered and differs from its Late Woodland shell-tempered descendant, Townsend, by comprising only net- and cord-marked types.

Yadkin and Onslow Series

The geographic distribution of sherds tempered with crushed rock occupies two distinct regions: the first represented by 63 sites in the Sandhills and the second by two sites (31CR2 and 31CR11) on Bogue Sound in Carteret County (Figure 8.14). The presence of crushed-quartz tempering on the coast is also evident from six Onslow County sites reported by Loftfield (1976) and from the Long Point site on the lower White Oak River in Jones County (Shumate and Evans-Shumate 2000:28–30). The technique of preparing temper by crushing rock is associated with the Early and Middle Woodland Yadkin series (prior to A.D. 400) in the Sandhills and with the Onslow series on the Coastal Plain.

Loftfield (1976:166) defined the Onslow series on the central coast on the basis of a group of specimens that exhibited "paste tempered with crushed quartz which showed sharp angular edges of newly crushed stone . . . The temper was gravel size and was very much in evidence in the broken edges of the sherds." In the seriation model that Loftfield constructed for central coastal ware groups, the Onslow series appeared to follow the Middle Woodland Carteret (Hanover) series in time, placing it at the beginning of the Late Woodland period (Loftfield 1976:187). As the validity of a seriation model based on surface-collected assemblages is questionable, and as no radiocarbon dates have been associated with this ware, the evidence on which to base the placement of the Onslow sherds in the Late Woodland period is considered slim at best.

It might be argued that Onslow sherds should be classified as Cashie series, assuming sources in the inland Tuscarora villages. Indeed, among the 60 crushed-quartz–tempered Onslow series sherds from sites 31ON31 and 31ON37, 47 (78 percent) were simple stamped, suggesting possible affinity with Cashie, which is primarily a simple-stamped ware. In the Lenoir County survey, Crawford (1966) also mentioned that crushed-quartz tempering was more common in the simple-stamped wares in his collection.

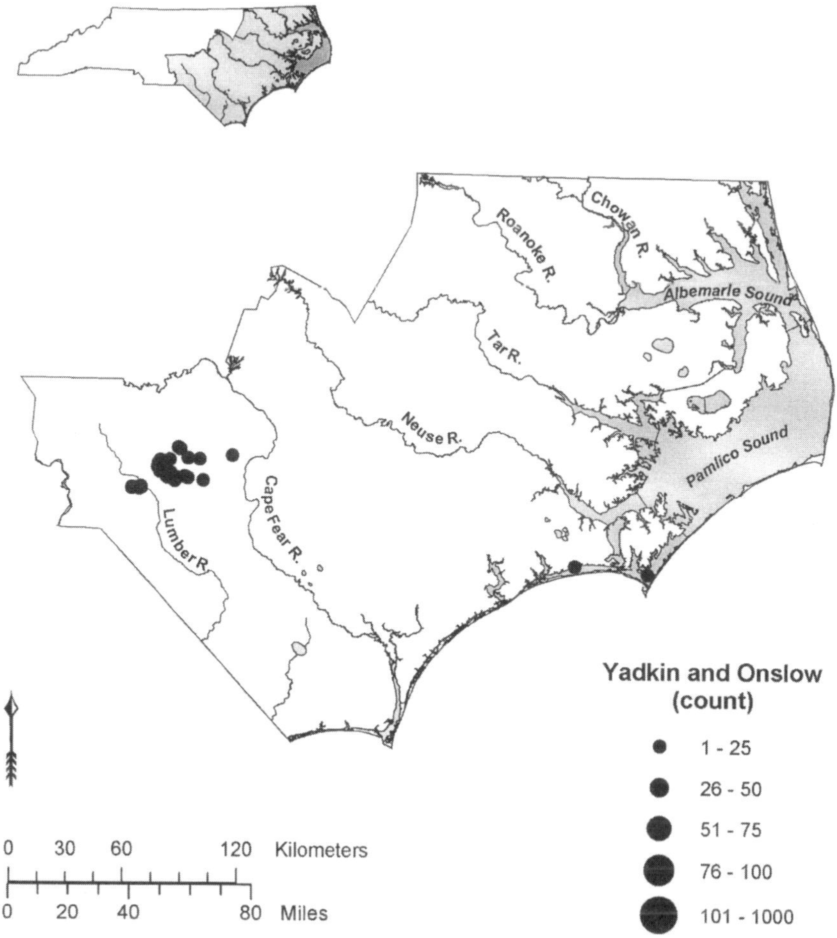

Figure 8.14. Distribution and frequency (count) of crushed-rock–tempered Yadkin (Sandhills) and Onslow (coastal) series (count = 41; min. = 1; max. = 26; sum = 149; mean = 4; std. dev. = 5).

Although this seems to suggest that Loftfield's (1976) Onslow Thong Impressed and Crawford's Lenoir or Tower Hill Simple Stamped may represent one series, Cashie is not known to be tempered with crushed quartz. Furthermore, Loftfield's description of Onslow Thong Impressed is that surfaces appeared to have been "malleated with a thong-wrapped paddle the thongs of which were flat with a cross section either square or rectangular in appearance . . . averag[ing] 1 mm in width with very little deviation from that width" (Loftfield 1976:168). Cashie Simple Stamped exhibits impressions that are rounded in cross section, not square or rectilinear.

In light of these observations, it must be concluded that there is simply not enough evidence to place the very limited amount of crushed-quartz–tempered Onslow series pottery found along the coast in Carteret, Jones, and Onslow counties in the Late Woodland period. The classification of these sherds to the Onslow series seems reasonable but of very little benefit at present in terms of understanding their relationship to other series on the coast.

Among 193 Yadkin series sherds observed in the Sandhills collection, surface treatment styles (distinguishable on 159 specimens) included fabric impressed, cord marked, and plain. Fabric-impressed sherds were most frequent, and among these the flexible warp variety was most common (60 percent). Yadkin Fabric Impressed sherds exhibit the same distribution as the crushed-rock–tempered sherds in general.

Cape Fear Series

The distribution of Cape Fear Cord Marked sherds indicates that this type is present in assemblages from every part of the coast (Figure 8.15). Sites with sand-tempered, perpendicular cord-marked sherds are found in Currituck County and the Outer Banks, along the central coast, and especially in the Pamlico drainage, in addition to being found in the lower Cape Fear valley and Sandhills. Proportions within site assemblages from every part of the coast are often over 60 percent.

Cape Fear Fabric Impressed sherds are also distributed widely over the study area (Figure 8.16). However, proportional values and raw count data suggest an area of particular intensity in the central part of the coast, particularly in the lower Pamlico River valley and the central coastal counties. This is a very surprising fact, since the Cape Fear series was defined from sherds in assemblages from sites on the lower Cape Fear River, and sand-tempered, fabric-impressed sherds have not figured prominently in prior descriptions of assemblages from the central coastal region.

There are several possible explanations for this concentration of sand-tempered, fabric-impressed sherds in the central outer coast. If we look only at Middle Woodland types, sand-tempered, fabric-impressed sherds and cord-marked sherds account for almost 30 percent, and distributions among these two types appear to be quite distinctive. Cape Fear Cord Marked sherds occur in higher proportions on sites in the *upper* portion of the embayed Pamlico River, in the inner or mainland portion of Currituck County, and in relatively high proportions in the lower Cape Fear valley, and on Fort Bragg. Cape Fear Cord Marked sherds do not often appear on the central coast in Carteret County and when present are in low proportions. Cape Fear Fabric Impressed sherds, on the other hand, occur in very high proportion on sites in the *lower* embayed portion of the Pamlico, in high proportion at sites on the Outer Banks in Currituck and Dare counties, and on sites in Carteret

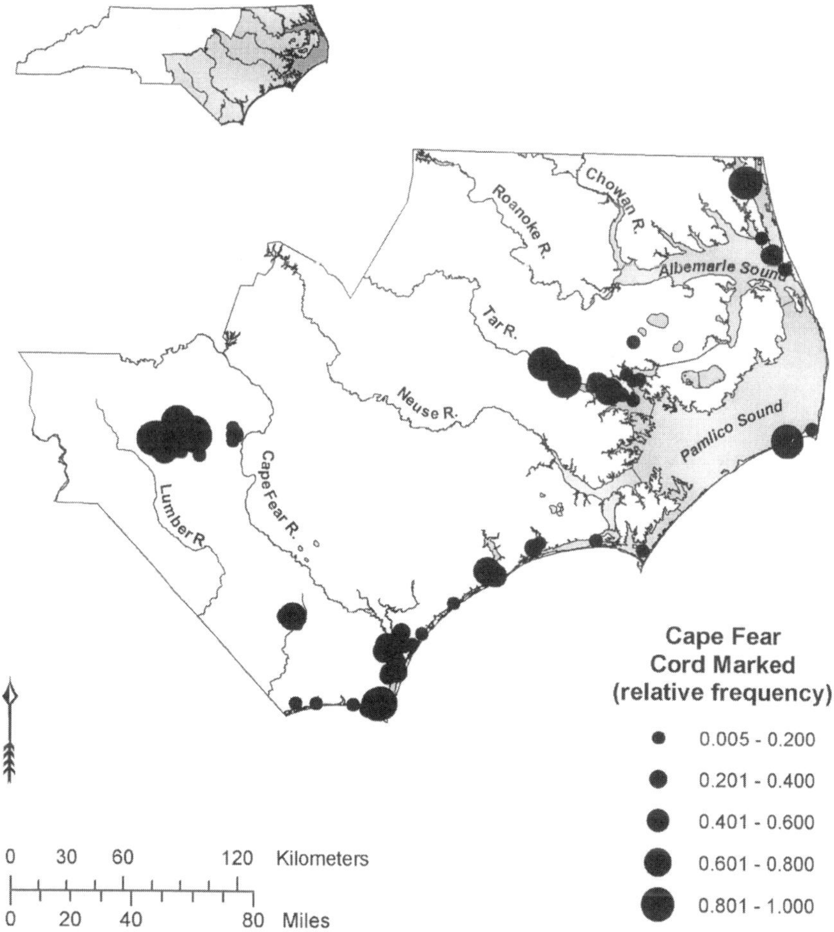

Figure 8.15. Distribution and relative frequency of Cape Fear Cord Marked type (count = 85; min. = 1; max. = 54; sum = 549; mean = 6; std. dev. = 9).

and Onslow counties, occurring in much lower proportion on sites in the Cape Fear drainage in New Hanover and Brunswick counties.

Considering the probable temporal relationship of these two types, the difference in distribution between Cape Fear Cord Marked and Fabric Impressed types seems to reflect a shift from sites focused primarily in the southern part of the coast and interior margins of the sounds, early in the sequence, to sites focused on the lower Pamlico, Outer Banks, and coastal margins in the central coastal region later in the sequence. Although we have no chronometric data to bring to bear on this, the sequence of surface treatment types elsewhere on the coast suggests that the fabric-impressed component is the later of the two.

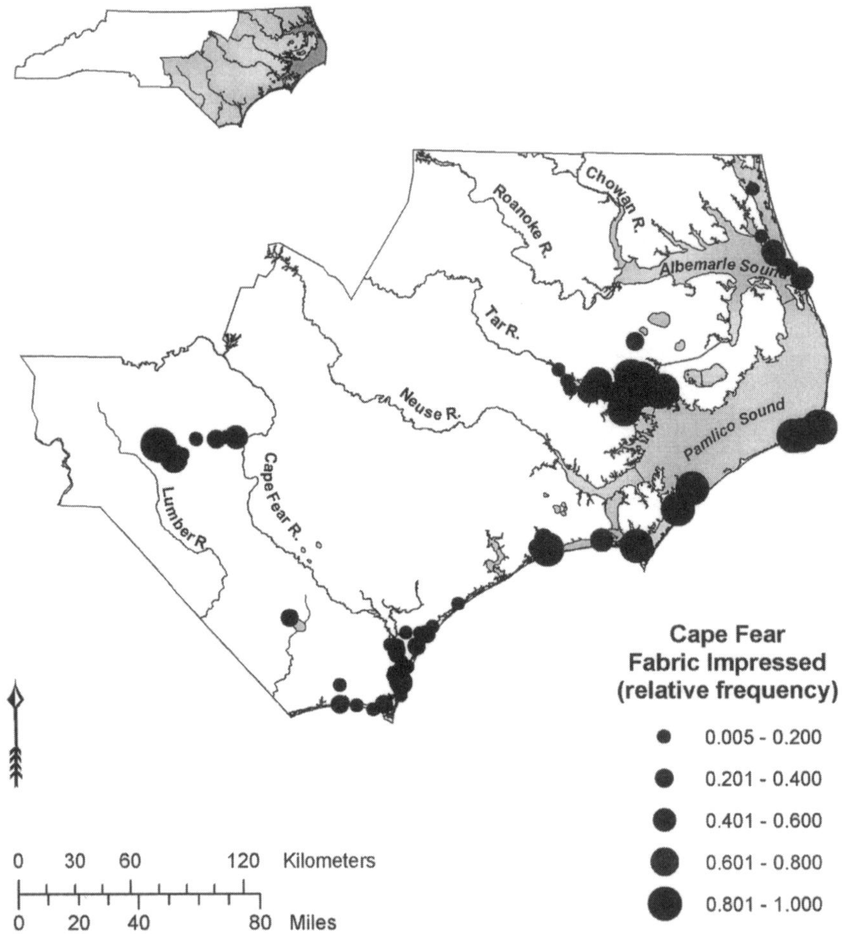

Figure 8.16. Distribution and relative frequency of Cape Fear Fabric Impressed type (count = 92; min. = 1; max. = 144; sum = 1,413; mean = 15; std. dev. = 27).

Mount Pleasant Series

The distribution based on counts indicates that sites with Mount Pleasant series sherds occur across the entire study area (Figure 8.17). The frequency of sites, however, appears to be greatest in the Pamlico River basin (17 sites). Not only site frequency but also the frequency of granule/pebble-tempered sherds are typically higher on the lower Pamlico. A few sites with Mount Pleasant were found as far north as Currituck County, with four sites on Colington Island (including 31DR16 with 208 examples). Four sites were also found in the Hatteras area of the Outer Banks, two sites on the mainland side of the Core Sound in Carteret

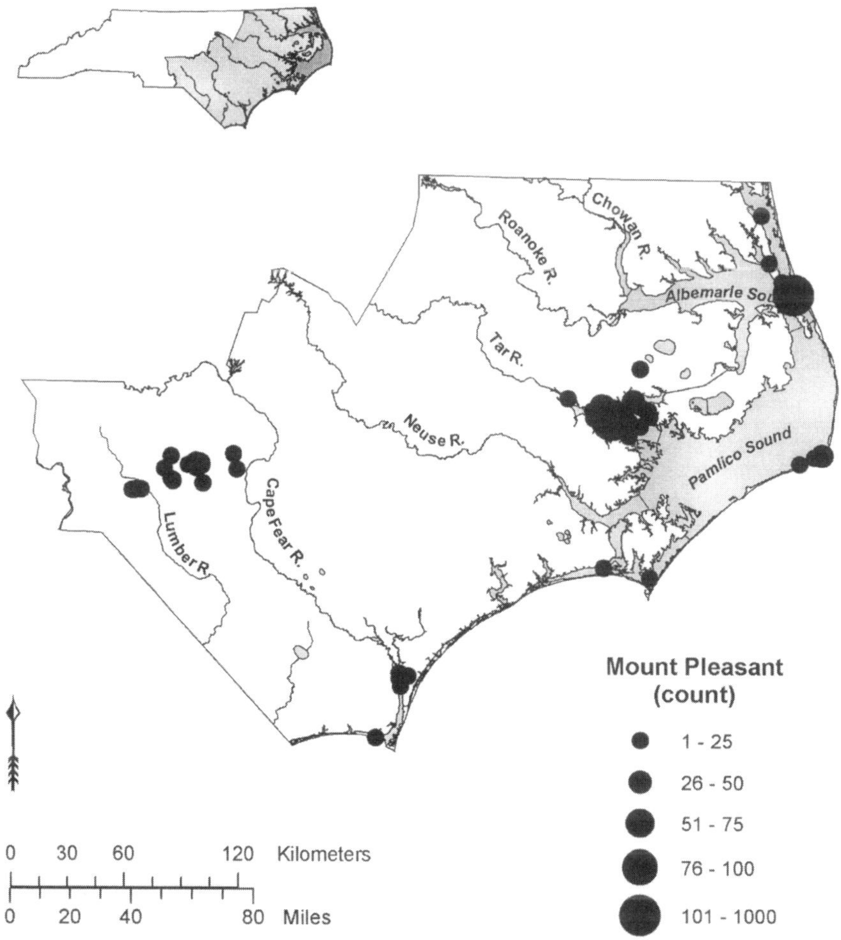

Figure 8.17. Distribution and frequency (count) of granule/pebble-tempered Mount Pleasant series (count = 61; min. = 1; max. = 207; sum = 945; mean = 15; std. dev. = 34).

County, five sites on the lower Cape Fear River, and quite a number of sites (18) with a very low frequency of sherds were scattered across the Sandhills.

The density and frequency of sites on the Pamlico suggest a possible trajectory of dissemination of Mount Pleasant from the Pamlico Basin north and south. An alternative explanation is suggested by the absence of sites with granule/pebble-tempered sherds on the central coast. This gap suggests the possibility that the series may be more frequently represented at sites in the interior northern and central Coastal Plain—areas not sampled in this study.

Mount Pleasant Fabric Impressed and Mount Pleasant Plain types are distributed in essentially the same way as granule/pebble-tempered ware as a whole. Al-

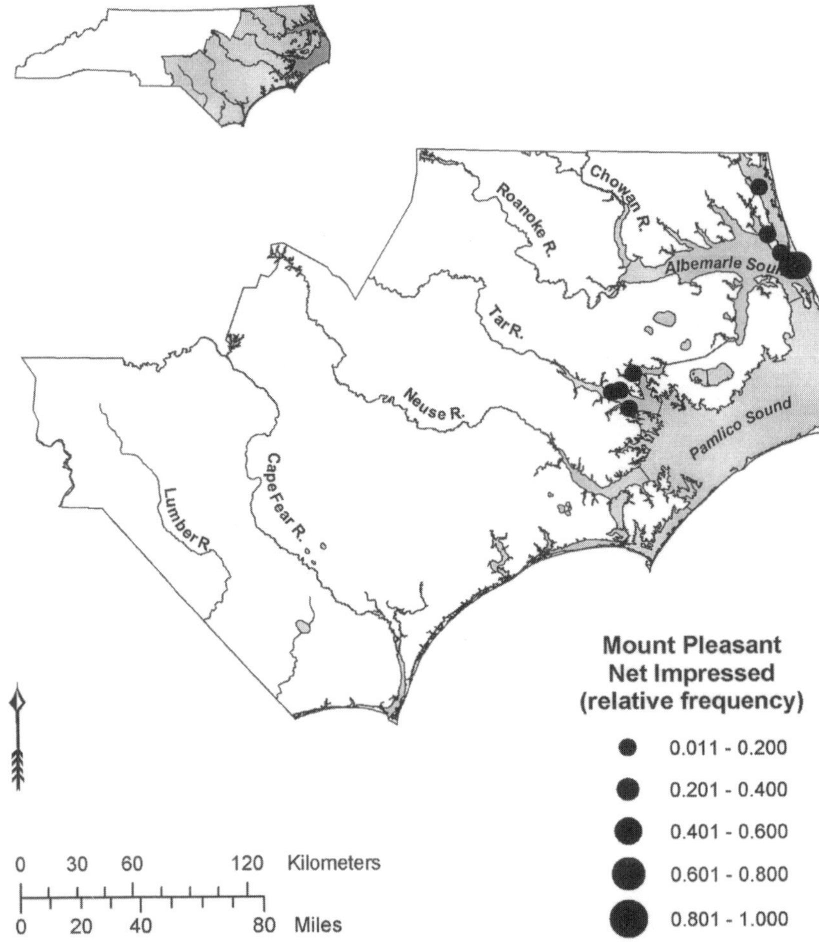

Figure 8.18. Distribution and relative frequency of Mount Pleasant Net Impressed type (count = 9; min. = 1; max. = 10; sum = 38; mean = 4; std. dev. = 4).

though the Mount Pleasant series definition advanced by Phelps included no net-impressed type, granule/pebble-tempered, net-impressed sherds are included in the series definition for this study and are found on sites in the lower Pamlico and Pungo rivers, on Currituck Sound, and on Colington Island (Figure 8.18). No granule/pebble-tempered, net-impressed ware was found on the Outer Banks, on the central coast, in the Cape Fear Valley, or in the Sandhills.

Mount Pleasant Cord Marked is similarly absent from sites on the lower Cape Fear River and central coast (Carteret County). This pattern is also evident in the distribution of Mount Pleasant Simple Stamped (another type not included in the original definition of the series) (Figure 8.19). Granule/pebble-tempered, net-

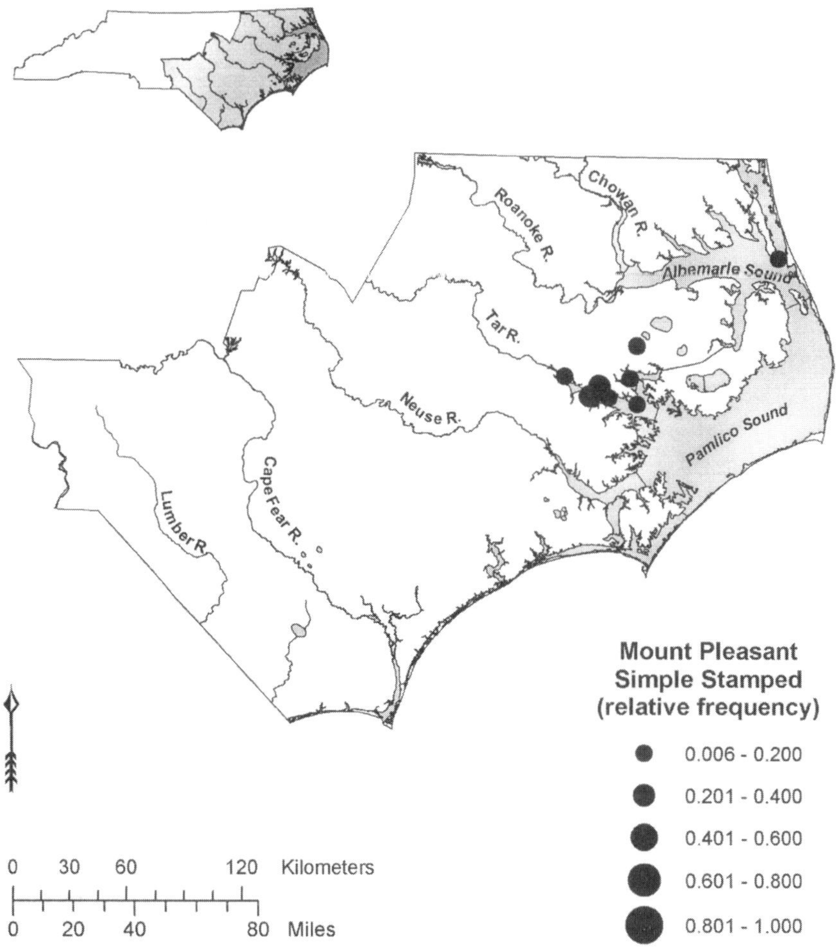

Figure 8.19. Distribution and relative frequency of Mount Pleasant Simple Stamped type (count = 10; min. = 1; max. = 56; sum = 96; mean = 10; std. dev. = 16).

impressed, and simple-stamped types occupy a smaller, more northerly range than the fabric-impressed, cord-marked, and plain types of the Mount Pleasant series.

It is evident from stratigraphic and chronological data that net impressing is early in the coastal sequence. Simple stamping also is known to occur in the Early Woodland New River series. This suggests that the differences in distribution of net-impressed wares may be a function of their early position in the sequence. The similarity of the geographic ranges for Mount Pleasant Net Impressed and Simple Stamped types suggests that they occupy nearly contemporary positions in the sequence regardless of their taxonomic distinction.

Ultimately, insufficient chronological data limits our ability to determine with certainty that net-impressed and simple-stamped components are in fact part of the Middle Woodland Mount Pleasant series. The patterns described for the Bandon site midden (Chapter 4) seem to suggest an early context for at least the net-impressed type. Unfortunately, the question of whether granule/pebble-tempered, fabric-impressed, cord-marked, and plain wares found outside the northern coastal area are in fact Mount Pleasant appears to be unanswerable with these data.

Bearing in mind that the net-impressed and simple-stamped types fall within the range of variation that Phelps (1983) described for the Deep Creek series, a logical conclusion (considering their uniquely restricted geographic distribution) might be to include them as a temper variation of the New River series.

Hanover Series

The definition of clay and grog tempering and their use in identifying Middle Woodland Hanover series sherds are discussed in foregoing chapters. Important distinctions may exist between grog (crushed potsherds) and clay (crushed fired clay) temper, although in many cases making the distinction between the two is difficult. For an initial look at spatial modeling, the most inclusive definition (encompassing both clay and grog) yields a distribution encompassing every portion of the study area (Figure 8.20). Judging from the frequency along the coast, it appears that sites on the Currituck Sound may represent, or be near, the northernmost boundary of the Hanover series distribution.

Collections made along the western scarp of the Dismal Swamp of Virginia consist mostly of ceramics that tend to be early, as the swamp began to fill in about 500 B.C. The majority of the clay-tempered pottery from that area is of the Early Woodland Croaker Landing series, thick walled with plain (smoothed) surfaces and lug handles. Some sherds of this description are lightly cord marked and overstamped, but none appear clearly fabric impressed (K. Egloff, personal communication 2001). As Middle Woodland clay- and grog-tempered Wilmington and St. Catherine's series wares are common on the South Carolina coast, and as the distribution is continuous into southern North Carolina, it can be assumed that the trajectory of dissemination of this tradition, at least on the northern coast of North Carolina, is from south to north.

At the Doerschuk site in Montgomery County, clay temper was included with crushed quartz in sherds classified as Yadkin series (Coe 1964:30). This may represent the westernmost influence of the coastal clay/grog-tempering tradition. The presence of clay/grog-tempered ware west of Fort Bragg in Moore, Richmond, and Harnett counties is not known but, judging from the regularity of its occurrence on sites at Fort Bragg (62 percent of the 227-site Fort Bragg database used in this study includes some clay/grog-tempered sherds), it would not be surprising to find it there. Along the central coast, Loftfield (1976) identified sherds of the

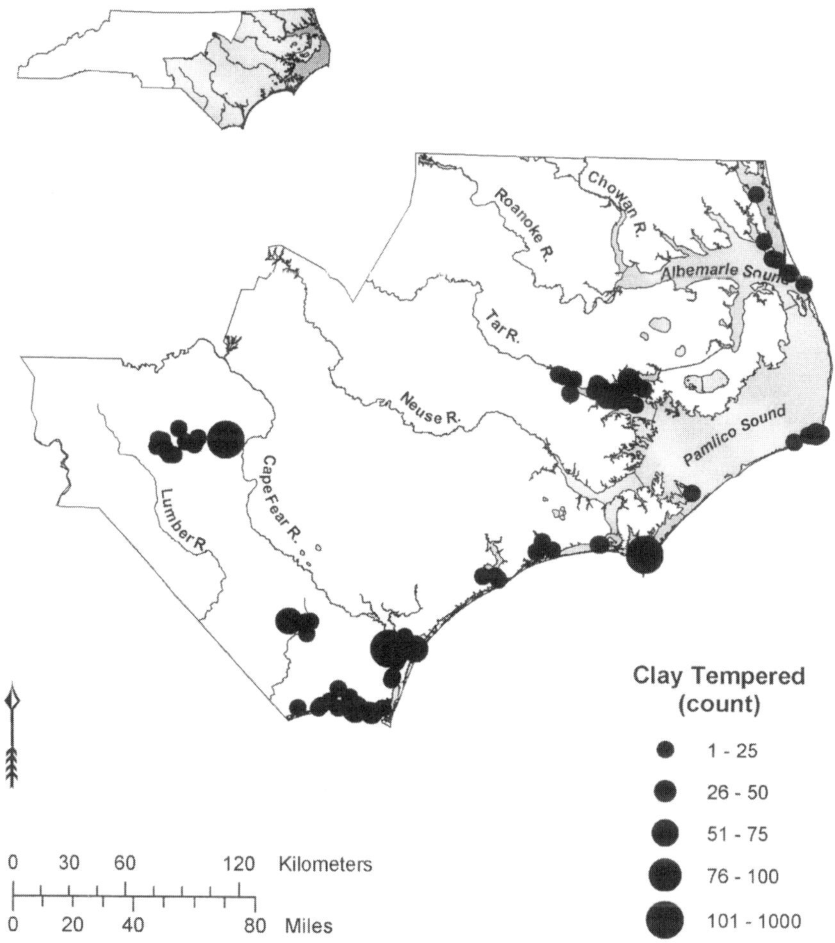

Figure 8.20. Distribution and frequency (count) of clay-tempered ware (count = 224; min. = 1; max. = 222; sum = 3,035; mean = 14; std. dev. = 27).

Carteret series (also clay/grog tempered) on several sites in the New River Basin. Crawford's (1966) survey of the Neuse River valley in portions of Craven, Pitt, Lenoir, and Wayne counties attests to the presence of clay/grog-tempered ware (Crawford's Grifton series) in the interior central region.

As described in Chapter 3, the distinction between clay lumps and grog (crushed sherds) was made in this analysis only when the identification of crushed sherds seemed conclusive. Among a total of 2,251 clay- or grog-tempered sherds in the Sandhills and Coastal Plain collections, grog was positively identified in only 17 percent (390), the remaining 83 percent (1,861) being clay tempered. Sand was identified as a secondary tempering agent in 35–47 percent of both groups.

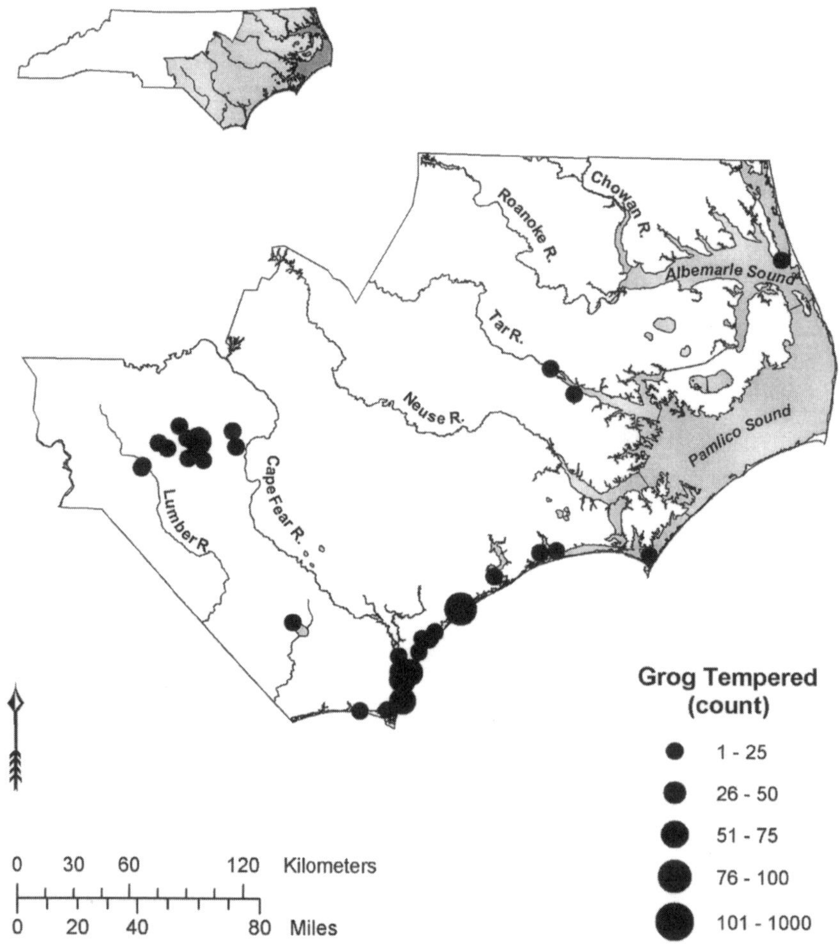

Figure 8.21. Distribution and frequency (count) of grog-tempered ware (count = 45; min. = 1; max. = 97; sum = 620; mean = 14; std. dev. = 24).

With this distinction in mind, there appear to be considerable differences in the spatial distribution of these two subgroups of temper. Based on raw frequency, the distribution of clay-tempered sherds is similar to the distribution of all sites; clay-tempered sherds are well represented in every region of the study area (Figure 8.20).

By comparison, grog-tempered sherds were found predominantly in the lower Cape Fear basin, coincidently the region where the Hanover series was first defined by South (1960) as "sherd-tempered" ware (Figure 8.21). Although there were a few grog-tempered sherds found on one site (31CK1) on the Currituck Sound, one site on the Pamlico River, and three sites in the Sandhills, these numbers stand in distinct contrast to the number of sites with clay-tempered sherds in these same areas.

The differences in the proportions of clay-tempered vs. grog-tempered sherds that make up assemblages from sites in the lower Cape Fear valley, as opposed to sites located elsewhere in the study area, are intriguing. Whether the distribution indicates differences in temper-preparation traditions or simply the characteristics of coastal clays awaits further experimentation.

Hanover series sherds accounted for one of the largest groups in the study. Numerous surface treatment types were identified on grog- or clay-tempered sherds. The proportion of fabric-impressed sherds (57 percent) and cord marking (27 percent) among the grog- and clay-tempered ware resembles that reported from South's (1976) survey of Hanover series sherds from New Hanover and Brunswick counties (about 1:3 cord marked to fabric impressed).

Among the grog- and clay-tempered sherds in the Haag and Loftfield collections were many surface treatment types not usually associated with the Hanover series. South (1976:15) identified only cord-marked and fabric-impressed surfaces among the Hanover sherds in his collection. Check-stamped wares in this region are typically assumed to be associated with the Deptford series, although grog-tempered, check-stamped sherds have been observed in low frequency in assemblages from the central coast of South Carolina, where they have been classified as Wilmington Check Stamped (Anderson et al. 1982:276). Other surface treatment types among the clay- and grog-tempered sherds include net impressing, punctation, and simple stamping. Although the very low frequency of these examples does not warrant a wholesale reconsideration of the Hanover series, their presence suggests that the tradition of tempering with grog or clay may have begun in the Early Woodland period (pre–400 B.C.). As dated examples of grog-tempered ware from Fort Bragg and elsewhere on the coast have indicated, this tradition may also have continued well into the Late Woodland period (post–A.D. 900).

The distributions of Hanover Fabric Impressed (Figure 8.22) and Hanover Cord Marked (Figure 8.23) sherds are very similar as they are found in higher frequencies on sites in the Sandhills and on the central and southern coasts than in the northern part of the coast. The geographic distribution of Hanover Net Impressed and Hanover Plain (smoothed) sherds is similar to those of Hanover Fabric Impressed and Cord Marked types, but assemblage percentages indicate low proportions (<20 percent) of net-impressed and plain types at most sites.

Hanover Paddle-Edge Marked sherds occur in relatively high percentages at several sites restricted to the lower Cape Fear River valley and on Fort Bragg (Figure 8.24). This distribution suggests an association with the Refuge series found principally on the South Carolina coast. A similar pattern is observed among Hanover Check Stamped sherds, although they are restricted to sites on Fort Bragg. Hanover Simple Stamped sherds are found on five sites, two on Fort Bragg and

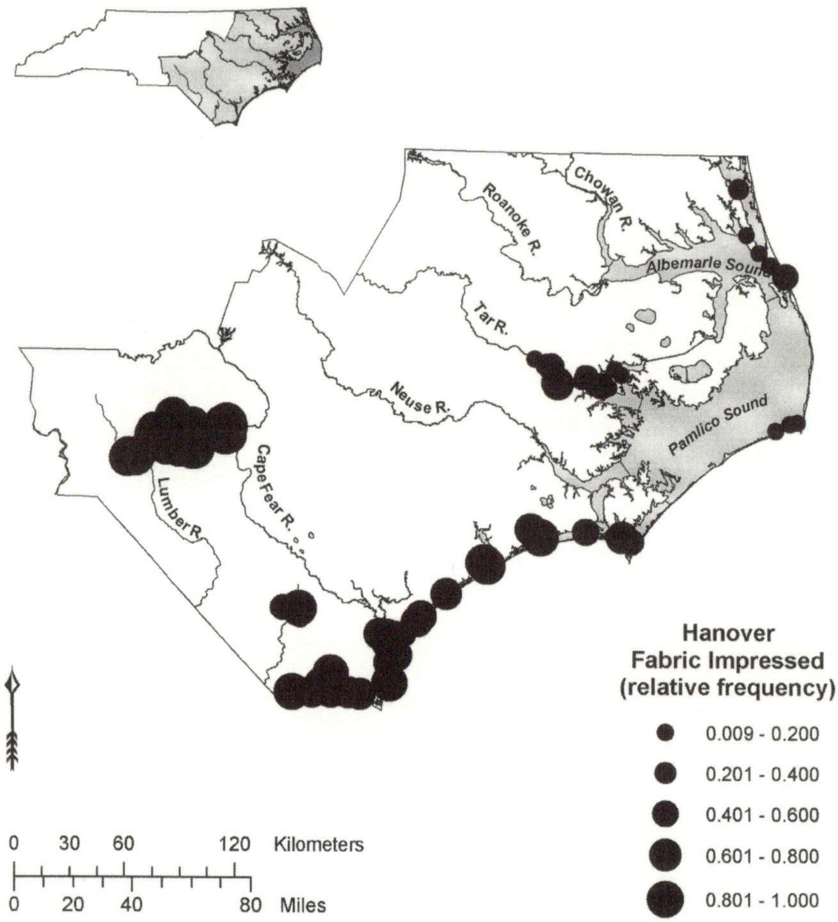

Figure 8.22. Distribution and relative frequency of Hanover Fabric Impressed type (count = 180; min. = 1; max. = 145; sum = 1,791; mean = 10; std. dev. = 18).

one each in Brunswick, Beaufort, and Currituck counties. These surface treatment types are possibly related to the Deptford series and, as with paddle-edge stamped, probably represent the early portion of the Hanover series.

Mockley Series

Raw frequencies at sites where Mockley ware is found on the Carolina coast are typically less than 25 sherds. For both the Mockley Net Impressed (Figure 8.25) and Mockley Cord Marked (Figure 8.26) types, sites are clustered on the mainland side of the Currituck Sound and on the Pungo River.

In addition to sites on the Pungo and Currituck, one site on the mainland

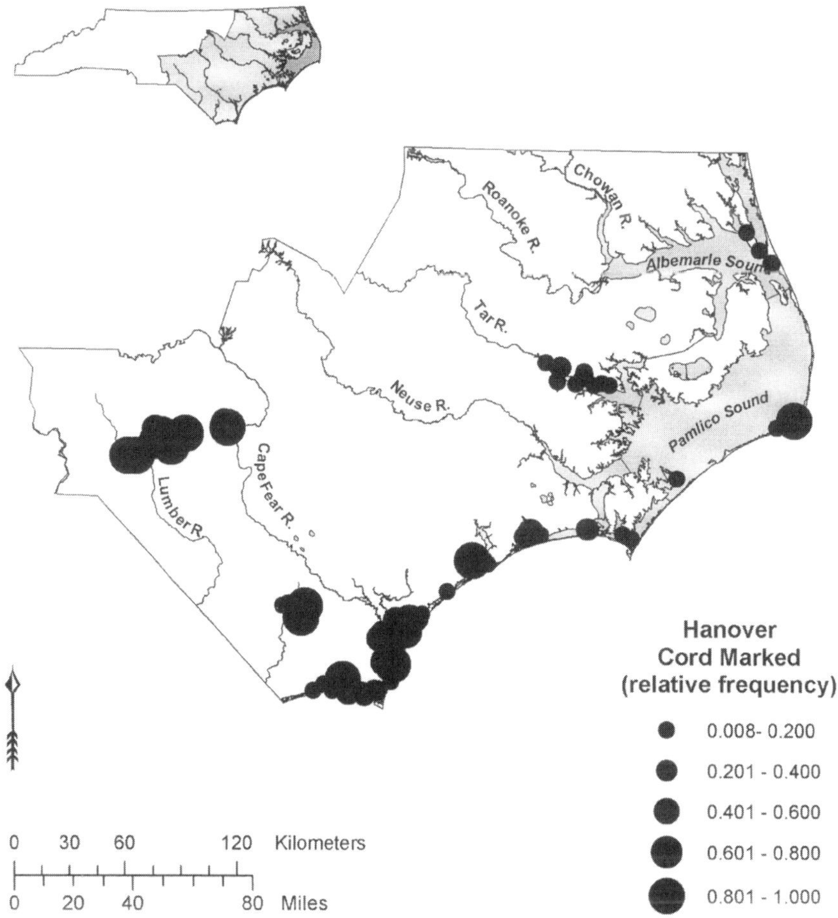

Figure 8.23. Distribution and relative frequency of Hanover Cord Marked type (count = 93; min. = 1; max. = 42; sum = 664; mean = 7; std. dev. = 9).

side of the Core Sound in Carteret County (31CR2) yielded two Mockley Cord Marked and one Mockley Net Impressed sherd. One occurrence of Mockley Cord Marked ware was noted at site 31NH61 on the upper reaches of the embayed portion of the Cape Fear River in New Hanover County. Mockley sherds have also been found at several sites on or near the White Oak River, including the Long Point site (Shumate and Evans-Shumate 2000), the Hammocks Beach West site (Daniel 1999:126–127), and the Broad Reach site (M. Mathis, personal communication 2001).

In the Early Woodland period a ceramic (social) boundary appeared to exist just north of the Cape Fear Valley, where Thom's Creek and Refuge traditions seemed to displace New River to more northerly locations. In the Middle Wood-

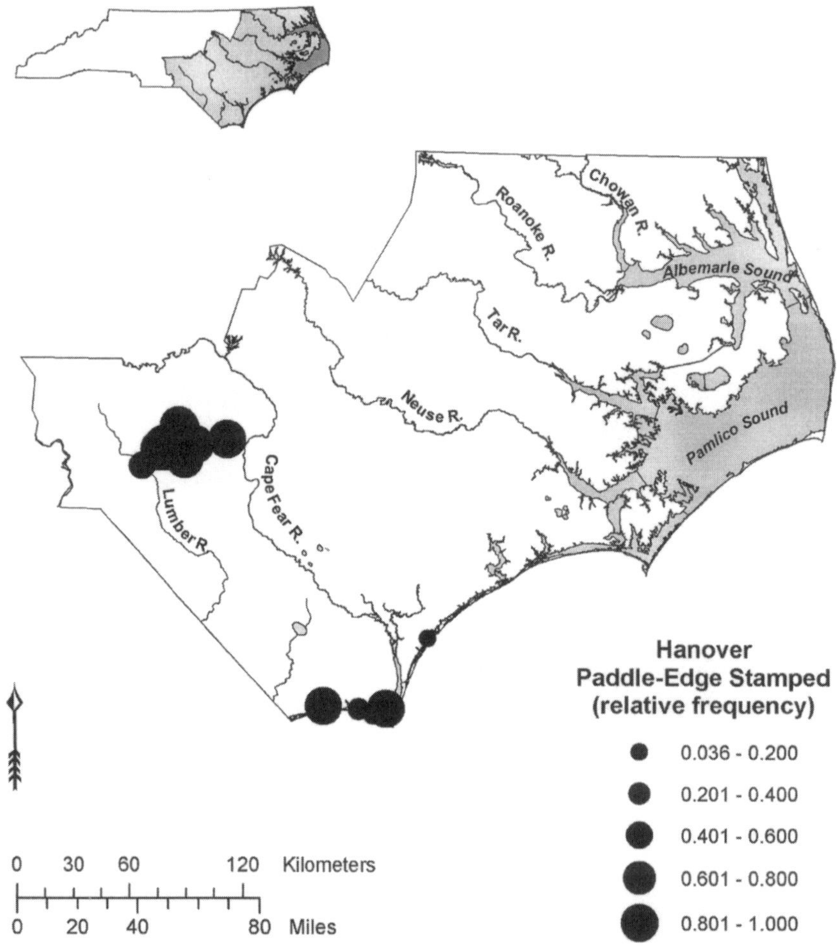

Figure 8.24. Distribution and relative frequency of Hanover Paddle-Edge Stamped type (count = 30; min. = 1; max. = 143; sum = 266; mean = 9; std. dev. = 25).

land period, the pattern seems to have been reversed. In the region north of the New River, we find that the area with fewest Hanover sherds very nearly matches the area where we find Mockley. Knowing as we do that Mockley occupies the most prominent place in the Middle Woodland pottery sequence along the Virginia coast and in the Chesapeake, there is little doubt that its presence in northern North Carolina represents a southern migration in the Middle Woodland period. Although we have no dates for Mockley on the Carolina coast, there is no question that this southern spread occurred when the makers of Hanover were occupying the coast. As we will see, this boundary appears to have become quite firm in the subsequent period, with presumably Algonquian makers of shell-tempered

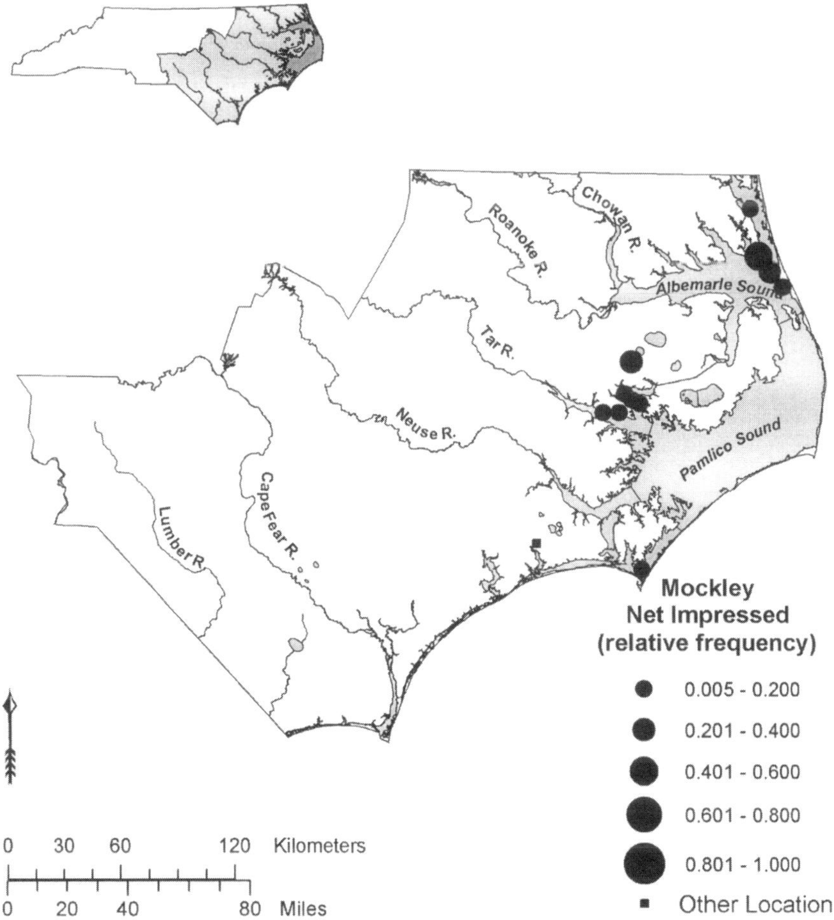

Figure 8.25. Distribution and relative frequency of Mockley Net Impressed type (count = 13; min. = 1; max. = 59; sum = 99; mean = 6; std. dev. = 15).

pottery well entrenched in the embayed tidewater region north of the New River, while the makers of grog-tempered Hanover were confined to the southern coast. Exploring the nature of the interaction among these culture groups will be an interesting subject for future archaeological research.

Late Woodland Traditions

At present, there are four pottery series identified for the Late Woodland period (A.D. 800–1600) Coastal Plain region of North Carolina, a relatively small number when the size of the geographic area and length of the period are taken

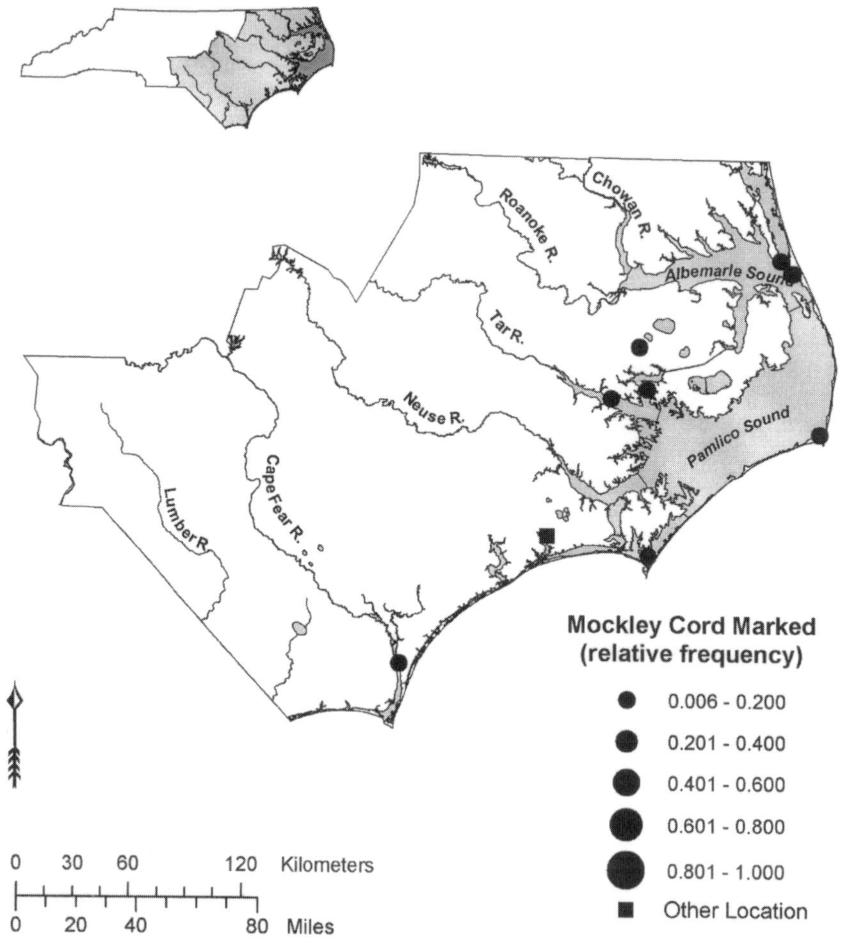

Figure 8.26. Distribution and relative frequency of Mockley Cord Marked type (count = 9; min. = 1; max. = 6; sum = 21; mean = 2; std. dev. = 1).

into consideration. In part, this apparent meagerness is due to gaps in the archaeological data (not necessarily the archaeological record itself) that reflect recent reevaluations. In the central and northern areas of the outer or lower coast, the shell-tempered Townsend series predominates in the Pamlico and Albemarle sounds region. Inland, the grit-tempered Cashie series characterizes the central and northern Coastal Plain. In the Sea Island Section of the southern coast, the shell-tempered Oak Island series, once considered to be the southern equivalent of the northern shell-tempering tradition, has recently been overturned, as the temper in the original type collection was found to be crushed limestone and dates have begun to place the limestone-tempered series in Early and early Middle Woodland contexts (Mathis 1999). In the Sandhills there are, as yet, no convincing candidates for a series dating exclusively to the Late Woodland period. The grog-tempering tradition of the Hanover series appears to have persisted into the Late Woodland, with some modifications to the method of preparing the paste. Quite late in the period two additional series are recognized. The Brunswick series, found mostly in the lower Cape Fear basin, is tempered with fine sand, or appears temperless, and consists primarily of a burnished type with some evidence for brushed and cob-marked types observed much less frequently. Also very late in the period the Swansboro series, tempered with finely crushed shell and typically burnished, is found along the central coast. There continues to emerge some tantalizing suggestion of a sand-tempered Late Woodland series along the central coast but, as described below, evidence is thus far inadequate for the task of defining a new series or confirming and refining the previously defined Adams Creek series (Loftfield 1979).

The use of crushed-shell temper is the most widely spread tradition of Late Woodland pottery making on the Coastal Plain of North Carolina and is characteristic of the Townsend and Swansboro series. The Haag collection is completely adequate to describe the north–south boundaries of the shell-tempered series within North Carolina, although it lacks coverage of the upper reaches of many rivers and streams in the tidewater and upper Coastal Plain regions. Such is not the case for the grit-tempered Cashie series. The Cashie tradition is thought to have been located in the area stretching from the upper reaches of the tidal embayment of the Chowan, Roanoke, Pamlico, and Neuse rivers to the Piedmont–Coastal Plain boundary. Haag sampled very few sites in this region and no Cashie sherds were positively identified in the analysis of the Haag collection. This discussion of coastal pottery traditions therefore is restricted to the shell-tempered Townsend and Swansboro series and the fine sand–tempered Brunswick series.

The Middle Woodland Mockley series, Late Woodland Townsend series, and terminal Late Woodland Swansboro series are expressions of the coastal shell-tempering tradition that are distinguished principally by different surface treatment styles. Mockley series wares are net impressed or cord marked, Townsend is recognized by fabric impressing and simple stamping, and Swansboro by burnishing. There is also some suggestion that the manner of preparing the temper may have differed among some of these series. Mockley is often characterized as being crudely made with large chunks of crushed oyster shell as the predominant temper. Townsend series wares are also tempered primarily with poorly sorted, very coarse (1–2 mm) and granule-sized (>2 mm) pieces of shell mixed in moderate and high proportion. The size, sorting, and proportion of shell temper, therefore, do not appear to be significantly different between the Middle Woodland Mockley and the Late Woodland Townsend series. The Swansboro series, however, is tempered with well-sorted, finely crushed shell, often including more mussel shell

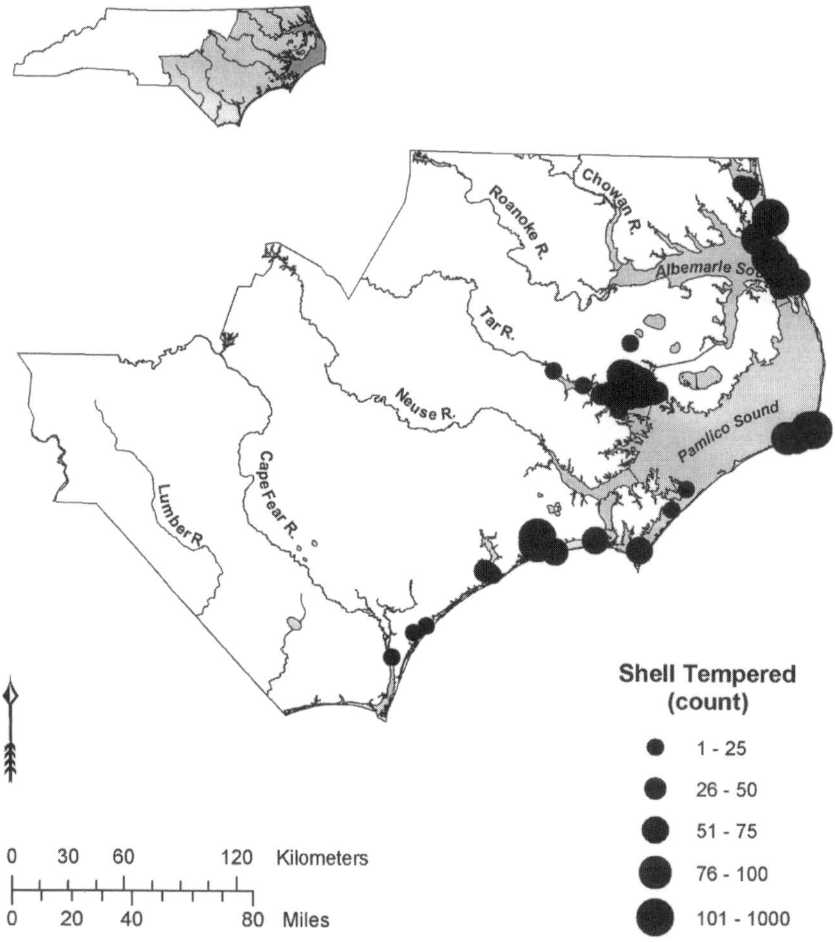

Figure 8.27. Distribution and frequency (count) of shell-tempered ware (count = 56; min. = 1; max. = 313; sum = 3,223; mean = 58; std. dev. = 74).

than seen in the Mockley or Townsend series. Swansboro ware is burnished and typically thin (<8 mm) and it may be that the difference between this ware and the White Oak and Colington wares is one of function.

Townsend Series

The overall distribution of shell-tempered ware appears to be restricted to the tidewater region primarily north of New Hanover County (Figure 8.27). The fact that shell-tempered Townsend and Rappahannock wares are the predominant Late Woodland pottery in Tidewater Virginia and the circum-Chesapeake region attests to the strength of the shell-tempering tradition during this period in the region north of the northern limits of this study collection. The complete lack of shell-tempered ware from sites in Brunswick County and the absence of similar pottery on the South Carolina coast provide equally conclusive evidence that the tradition is rarely found south of the New River.

In this study, all shell-tempered, fabric-impressed sherds are classified as Townsend Fabric Impressed (Townsend Fabric Impressed comprises both the Colington Fabric Impressed and White Oak Fabric Impressed types, indistinguishable in the surface-collected assemblages analyzed here) and all shell-tempered, simple-stamped sherds as Colington Simple Stamped. Evidence suggests that the two types exhibit different spatial distributions. As illustrated in Figure 8.27, the frequency of shell-tempered sherds was greatest in the Albemarle Sound region and least in the Cape Fear Basin. This trend of higher overall frequency of shell-tempered ware on the north coast (Albemarle Sound) and lower frequency on the central coast (Bogue Sound) is reversed if one observes only fabric-impressed wares (Figure 8.28).

Townsend Fabric Impressed. The apparent trend in frequency of fabric-impressed, shell-tempered ware (higher in the southern region and lower in the north) is more clearly expressed when sherd frequencies are standardized by the number of site assemblages analyzed in each region (Table 8.1). Standardized frequencies, calculated as the average number of sherds of each type per region, indicate that the overall proportion of fabric-impressed sherds is slightly higher in the Bogue Sound region than in the Albemarle region. Despite a greater number of sites, there is a lower proportion of fabric-impressed sherds in the Pamlico than in the other two regions. Possible reasons for this are explored in discussions that follow. It might also be noted, however, that there is a tendency for a higher density of fine and medium varieties of fabric impressing among shell-tempered sherds from sites in the Bogue region and a higher density of the coarse variety in the Albemarle region.

The distribution of Townsend Fabric Impressed mirrors the overall distribution of shell-tempered ware (Figure 8.28). Sites with Townsend Fabric Impressed pottery are found from the northern reaches of Currituck Sound to the New River Basin, with a single site in New Hanover County. This type typically makes up over 60 percent of the Late Woodland pottery on sites where it is found. White Oak Smoothed (plain ware) was found to have a very similar distribution, although with many fewer sites and lower proportions.

Colington Simple Stamped. The pattern observed in shell-tempered, simple-stamped ware is reversed in comparison to fabric-impressed sherds (Figure 8.29). Perhaps the most important indicator of this is the fact that no shell-tempered, simple-stamped sherds have been found in the Bogue region. It should be noted that Loftfield (1976:187) did observe shell-tempered, simple-stamped sherds from sites in Onslow County, but they appear to have occurred in very low proportions.

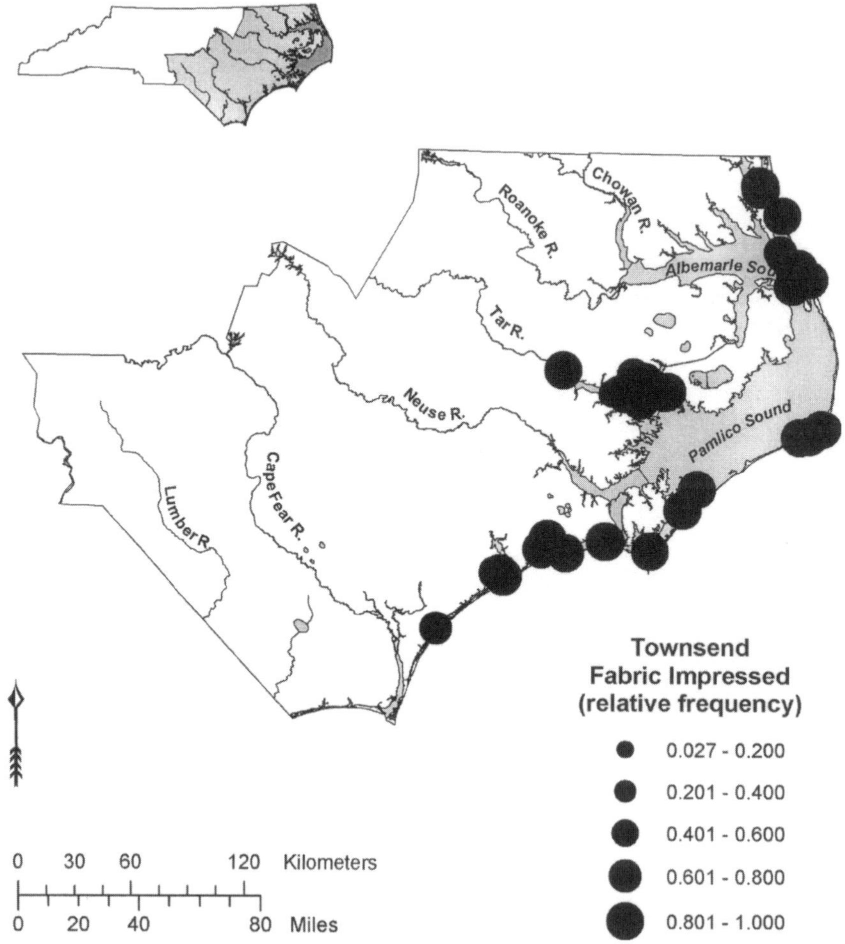

Figure 8.28. Distribution and relative frequency of Townsend Fabric Impressed type (count = 48; min. = 1; max. = 166; sum = 1,457; mean = 30; std. dev. = 39).

Among simple-stamped sherds in the Pamlico and Albemarle regions, very similar overall densities are observed. Among varieties of simple stamping, however, the broad sort is found in higher density on sites in the Albemarle, and the narrow variety is found in higher density on sites in the Pamlico. Colington Simple Stamped was found on sites mainly in the Albemarle and Pamlico Sound area. One small, shell-tempered, simple-stamped sherd was found at site 31NH265 near Ogden in New Hanover County.

Swansboro Burnished. Swansboro Burnished sherds were identified by shell tempering in combination with burnished surfaces. Most Swansboro series sherds

Table 8.1. Shell-Tempered Fabric-Impressed Varieties in Three Coastal Regions

	Geographic Region[a]		
Fabric Impressed Variety	Albemarle (n = 15)	Pamlico (n = 35)	Bogue (n = 23)
Fine weft	27 (1.80)[b]	39 (1.11)	62 (2.17)
Medium weft	92 (6.13)	187 (5.34)	281 (12.22)
Coarse weft	97 (6.47)	14 (0.40)	62 (2.70)
Flexible warp	3 (0.20)	13 (0.37)	8 (0.35)
Total	219 (14.40)	253 (7.23)	413 (17.96)

[a]Regional samples are composed of site assemblages grouped by county in the following manner: Albemarle region, Currituck (n = 7) and Dare (n = 8); Pamlico region, Beaufort (n = 29) and Hyde (n = 6); Bogue region, Carteret (n = 14) and Onslow (n = 9).

[b]Values in parentheses are frequencies standardized by the number of sites; e.g., 27 fine weft sherds from 15 sites in the Albemarle region represent an average of 1.8 fine weft sherds per site.

were tempered with fine shell; however, a few were tempered with medium shell and one was tempered with coarse shell. In all, Swansboro series were found on seven sites including one (31NH650) in New Hanover County. Most were found on the central coast (New River, White Oak River, Bogue Sound), and two sites on the Outer Banks (31DR1 and 31DR25) yielded Swansboro series sherds (Figure 8.30).

Brunswick Series

The Brunswick series was first described by South (1960) to characterize an assemblage of locally made burnished vessels found at Brunswick Town in context with European ceramics dating to the mid-eighteenth century. Brunswick series vessels are described as temperless or occasionally tempered with fine sand. Vessel walls are typically thin (averaging about 6 mm), and surfaces are either burnished or plain. Most unusual are the vessel forms in the two assemblages found by South, one at Brunswick Town and the other at Bath, that indicate early contact with European colonists. Vessel shapes suggest that these were modeled after Delft, Oriental Porcelain, English White Salt-Glazed Stoneware, and Creamware.

Two fine sand–tempered or temperless burnished sherds were noted in the Haag collection, one each from Brunswick and New Hanover counties. Although burnished, neither of these sherds provides evidence of vessel form suggesting likeness to European forms. Also found in the Haag collection were four sherds of

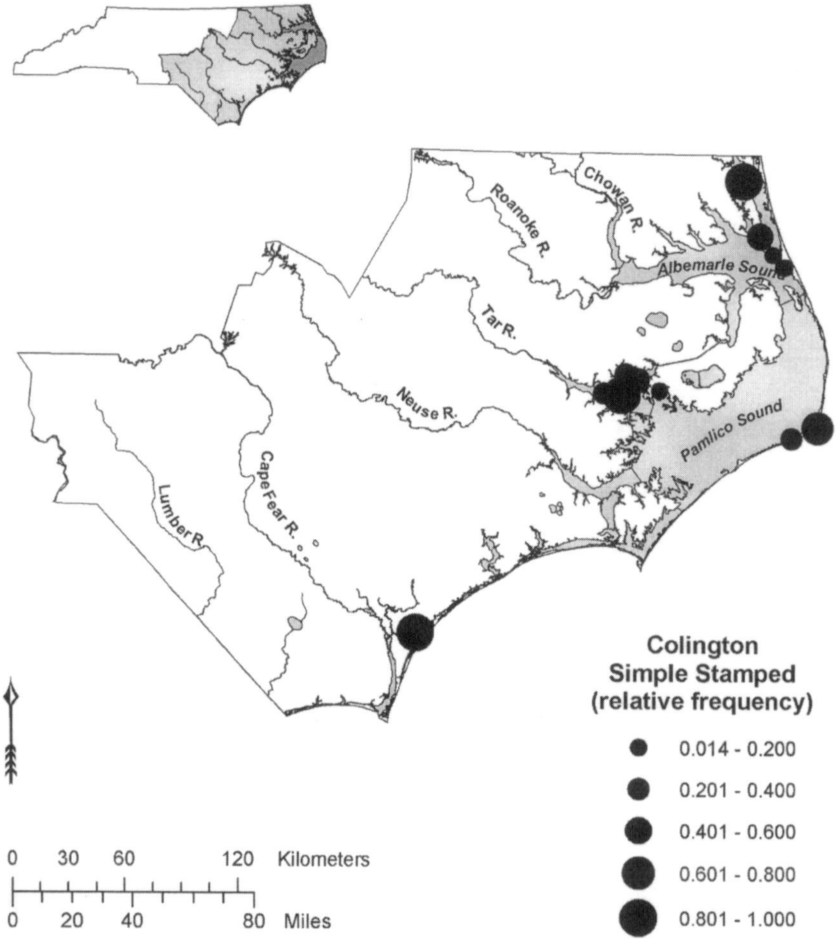

Figure 8.29. Distribution and relative frequency of Colington Simple Stamped type (count = 20; min. = 1; max. = 58; sum = 126; mean = 6; std. dev. = 12).

similar temper, whose surfaces were either corncob impressed or brushed. As there are no formally defined corncob-impressed or brushed types for the coastal region of North Carolina, and these few, small-body sherds do not provide enough data to support such a definition, they are presented here with the Brunswick sherds as examples of Late Woodland or Contact period wares.

Although these few sherds cannot be confidently classified to any particular series, they exhibit certain resemblances to brushed, burnished, and corncob-marked types from neighboring regions. Ceramics associated with the Late Woodland period Dan River and Hillsboro focuses from the North Carolina Piedmont include corncob-marked and well-smoothed types (Coe 1952:310–311).

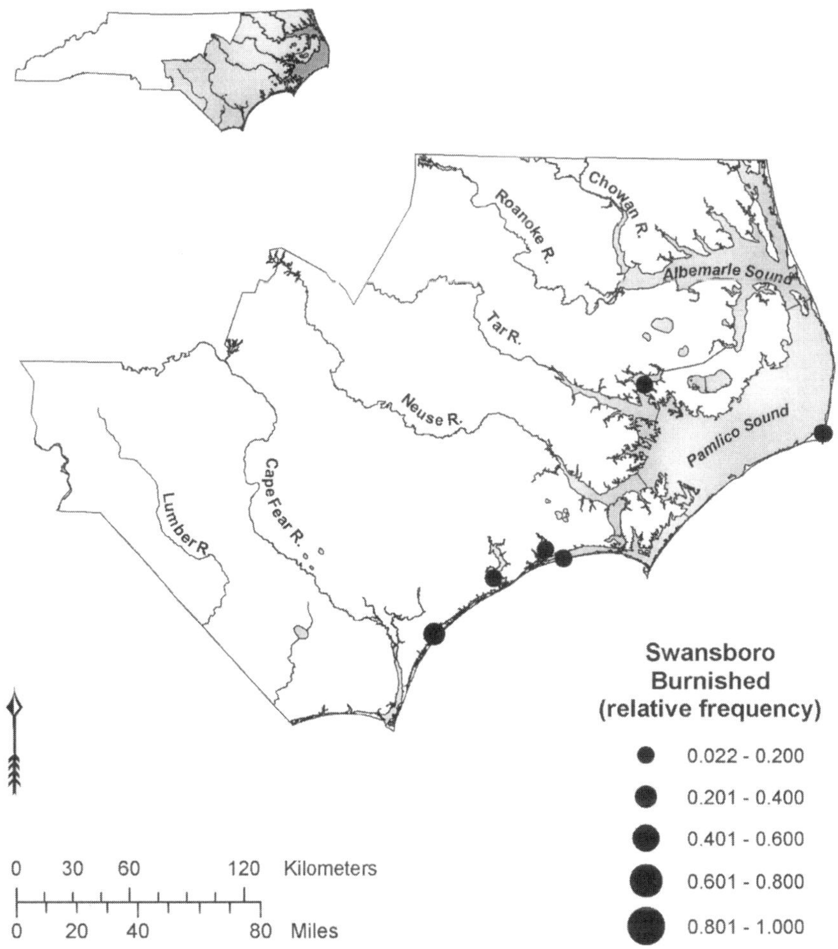

Figure 8.30. Distribution and relative frequency of Swansboro Burnished type (count = 7; min. = 1; max. = 15; sum = 25; mean = 4; std. dev. = 5).

Summary

At the most general level it seems clear that the principal source of information about pottery making in the Early Woodland period on the North Carolina coast reflected the ideas and practices of the Native potters of the South Carolina coast. The Stallings, Thom's Creek, Refuge, and Deptford series had their core areas in the South Carolina or Georgia Coastal Plain. Indigenous Early Woodland traditions, including Hamp's Landing and New River, appear to have emerged in the Cape Fear Valley or central coast and flourished into Middle Woodland times. On the northern coast the regions of distribution of the Croaker Landing and Marcey

Creek series extend into the Virginia Coastal Plain, showing affinity with this region. By Middle Woodland times, these northern and southern influences seem to have abated as the Hanover, Mount Pleasant, and Cape Fear series reflect indigenous traditions that are widely distributed across the North Carolina coast. Northern influences are again seen in the Late Woodland Townsend series, which is unquestionably related to traditions at home in the circum-Chesapeake region. The practice of burnishing, the hallmark of the Swansboro and Brunswick series, may be a local derivation but is certainly related to the much more widely spread practice of making fine sand–tempered burnished ware, so characteristic of Contact and Colonial period pottery over much of the Eastern Woodlands.

The following chapter explores the potential cultural sources of the temporal and spatial patterns that have been discussed up to this point, modeling environmental, technological, and social influences on pottery-making traditions and applying these models to develop explanations.

9
Ceramic Boundaries and Social Spaces

The foregoing chapters have assessed the temporal and spatial patterning of coastal North Carolina pottery types using key sites and collections. Little has been said, however, concerning the context in which the pots were actually made and used. This chapter attempts to interpret the temporal and spatial patterns in ceramic technology, applying relevant theory to construct reasonable explanatory models.

Implications for Coastal Carolina

Turning once more to the temporal and spatial patterns described in the foregoing chapters, we may consider them as case studies of the manifestation of ceramic traits expressed in the context of specific environmental constraints, technological parameters, and social practices. The temporal and spatial contexts for each major ceramic series may be used to explore broad-scale patterns.

Length of Traditional Periods

Looking first at the temporal scale of pottery series, or tempering traditions, we see that series typically occupy periods of 800 to 1,400 years. Ignoring for the moment changes in vessel building technology and decorative finishes that might arise within the period occupied by a single tempering practice, it is useful to explore the implications of the long duration of these traditions. If we assume that a new generation of potters is learning the craft from their cognatic or affinal kin every 25 years or so, in a period of 800 to 1,400 years we can expect there to be 30 to 50 generations of potters.

Among the five major temper types, fiber, sand/grit, crushed rock, crushed pottery, and crushed shell, we find that they emerge more or less sequentially, with each technology replicated for 30 to 50 generations. During the period that each series is replicated, we do not observe simultaneous alternative tempering techniques arising from innovations and declining like branches of an evolutionary tree. Certainly, there are times in which two temper series seem to coexist in a region, and there are even examples of technologies that seem to have very limited historical expression. The Currituck Beaker ceramic technology is a possible example (Painter 1977), but in this case, so very little is known about this archaeological phenomenon that it is impossible to be sure of its temporal range.

Perhaps the performance-related properties of tempering materials are so specific that they constrain innovations such that within the narrow range of possibilities innovation does not arise very often. One problem with this notion is that there are many effective tempering techniques found globally that did not find expression during the Woodland era in the Middle Atlantic: hair, bark, dung, ash, mica, and crushed bone, for example, are effective tempering agents used with success in other parts of the world. Another problem with the notion that the temper types observed have very specific performance-related criteria that constrain deviation in a functional sense is that several of the aplastic materials used as temper are, from a mechanical perspective, rather poor choices. Calcium carbonates such as limestone, marl, and shell are subject to lime spalling that can destroy or weaken a pot (Rice 1987:97–98; Rye 1981:32–33). Quartz grains also expand up to 2 percent at 573°C (temperatures of 900°C are commonly reached in open fires), when they undergo an inversion that changes crystalline structure, resulting in expansion (Rice 1987:94–96). This would seem to argue against the use of large quartz granules or smaller grains in high proportion, since such use would be apt to weaken the vessel. In the case of grog, however, the temper has expansion properties that are identical to the clay and so this would seem to be the ideal tempering agent. In fact, grog tempering emerges in the Middle Woodland period around A.D. 200 and persists well into the Late Woodland, perhaps as late as A.D. 1100, then declines and disappears. Following the decline in the use of grog, pottery in various areas of the coast is tempered with shell (the Townsend series) and quartz sand (the Cashie and possibly Adams Creek series). The fact that the trend in tempering in this case appears to move from a mechanically more effective solution to a mechanically less effective solution would seem to contradict the notion that it is mechanical properties that are constraining or driving changes in tempering traditions.

This apparent contradiction in the adaptionist logic of the development of ceramic technology is no contradiction at all if the standard view of technological evolution as increasingly sophisticated mechanical solutions to adaptive problems is abandoned (Pfaffenberger 1992). There is, however, an abiding sense that in the *chaîne opératoire* of pottery making, tempering is a rather highly specified process; preparing and adding temper is not a casual matter but follows a particular set of guidelines specifying the type, size, and proportion of aplastic agents added in certain proportions to the clay.

Although a wide variety of environmental and social conditions may play important roles in how long a particular technological style is practiced, we have arrived at a few conclusions that we can be relatively certain obtained in this prehistoric case. First, tempering traditions consisted of a set of behaviors or operations that in most instances were very specific, involving several steps that had to be replicated faithfully and in sequence in order to produce the product observed in the archaeological record. Second, these traditions typically persisted over several hundred years, with very few short-lived traditions emerging and declining simultaneously. Given such long periods of time, it is unlikely, although not impossible, that a particular temper style or pottery series represents the product of a single culture group that identified itself, or was identified by others, as a distinctive ethnic group. Equally unlikely is the notion that a single *understanding* of the mechanical properties of a particular technique was passed down over 30 to 50 generations of potters as an explanation for the necessity of using just such a set of behaviors and no others.

Size of Traditional Regions

The spatial scale on which ceramic styles are manifested in this study is similarly grand. For example, in foregoing chapters we saw that fiber-tempered Stallings occupied a region about 450 miles across, stretching along the coast from northern central Georgia to northern North Carolina. The Middle Woodland grog-tempering tradition (including the Hanover and Wilmington series) extended over a region of similar proportions. The Middle Woodland shell-tempered Mockley tradition encompassed the entire circum-Chesapeake region extending south to central North Carolina. This region is very nearly replicated in Late Woodland times by the Townsend series. Although these stylistic regions certainly changed over time, it is useful to begin by limiting our investigation to a synchronic look at these broad areas, creating a snapshot of each unit. Using this synchronic approach, we may compare the archaeological patterns with those observed among modern social systems described through ethnographic studies.

For example, Hitchcock and Bartram (1998) conducted ethnographic studies in the Western Sandveld Region of the Central District of Botswana on several occasions from 1975 to 1987. Their study area encompassed about 28,000 km^2 (or about 10,800 square miles). An area of approximately equivalent size if superimposed on the North Carolina Coastal Plain would encompass the 14 counties south of the Neuse River (Figure 9.1). Hitchcock and Bartram (1998:16) estimated the population in this region during the period from 1978 to 1979 to be about 4,000 individuals belonging to 22 distinct ethnic groups. Although in terms of subsistence technology the inhabitants were characterized as "part-time hunter-gatherers," due to the importance of agro-pastoralism in the economy, information on ethnic diversity, community size, and technological organization are in-

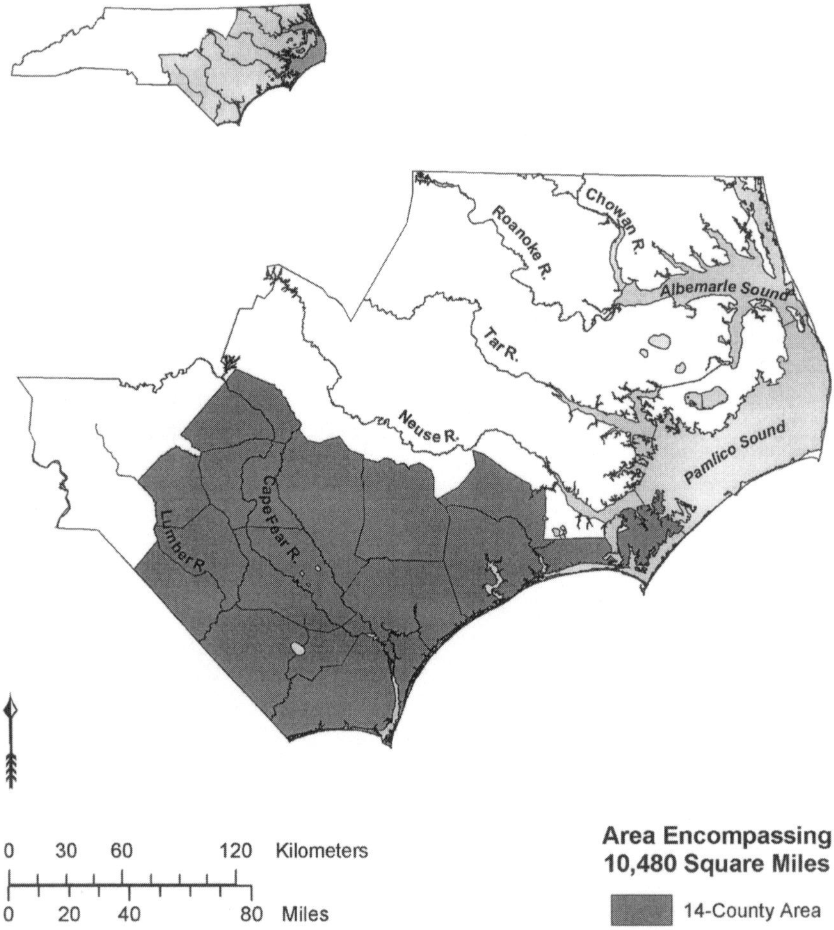

Figure 9.1. Fourteen-county area of the coast, approximately the same size as the area studied by Hitchcock and Bartram (1998).

structive. Within this region there existed seven territorial ranges clustered around water sources to which rights were restricted. Although there are many obvious differences between the modern hunter-gatherers of the central Kalahari Desert and the prehistoric inhabitants of the coast of North Carolina, the analogy is made on this general level simply to suggest the potential degree of social and ethnic complexity that may have obtained in this region during any of the three periods of Woodland prehistory.

In a study of the distribution of material culture items among groups living along the Sepik coast of New Guinea, Welsch and Terrell (1998) found similar patterns of complexity. Their study region included a 300-km (195-mile) section of the coastline. For comparison, the coastline of the 14-county area lying between South Carolina and the Neuse River is about 180 miles long (Figure 9.1). In the New Guinea case, social processes involving the exchange of objects led to a distribution of material culture that was considerably larger and more extensive than the villages and "face-to-face communities" (Welsch and Terrell 1998:50). Along this stretch of the coast were found "more than 60 mutually unintelligible languages belonging to perhaps 24 different language families and at least 6 unrelated phyla" (Welsch and Terrell 1998:68). A cluster of from 1 to 10 hamlets or villages made up a named community, each with its own identity and character that differed from others. Historically, each named community acted as a separate polity, having its own rituals, economy, leadership, and ways of doing things (Welsch and Terrell 1998:57). Social ties within each community tended to be organized around kinship and marriage, but outside the community, nearly every individual and family was linked to many other communities through historical ties of friendship. In this way, each adult had an extensive network of social relations along the coast linking him or her to as many as 25 other communities. The authors traced the distribution of several types of items including earthenware pots, outrigger canoes, shell rings, black palm bows, and sedge baskets. In none of these cases did the observable distribution coincide with the boundaries of a single ethnic or ethnolinguistic group, nor did shared material culture delineate a single society, culture, or culture area. Three distinctive pottery-making traditions were observed: (1) paddle-and-anvil shaping from a lump, (2) coiling and smoothing, and (3) slab building. None of these were found to be associated exclusively with a single language family.

Gosselain (1998) describes a somewhat different picture among potters inhabiting southern Cameroon between 1990 and 1992. Gosselain studied potters in an area roughly five and one-half times larger than that shown in Figure 9.1, an area more nearly equivalent to the size of the prehistoric pottery-style zones, or series regions, described above for the Atlantic coast. His informants consisted of 100 potters from 21 linguistic groups. In most cases, potters were members of small, politically independent, exogamous chiefdoms, but a wide variety of political and social structures and population densities were represented. In this case, "some stages of the manufacturing process, such as clay processing, firing, and post-firing, turn out to be poor cultural markers" (Gosselain 1998:92). The distribution of "fashioning" or vessel forming techniques, however, was found to generally coincide with linguistic boundaries, with some exceptions. Populations that were linguistically affiliated, and that shared a common history, tended to fashion their vessels in much the same way, or tended to use similar techniques that differed significantly from those of their nearest neighbors.

During the period from 1984 to 1995, MacEachern (1998) participated in studies of the regional archaeology and modern artifact styles in the Mandara Mountains of western Cameroon and eastern Nigeria. This study area encompassed approximately 3,600 square miles, an area about one-third the size of the 14-county region depicted in Figure 9.1. Within this region, 23 ethnic groups were identified. In MacEachern's research area, about 350 km^2 (130 square miles) in size, 11 acephalous ethnic groups divided themselves into about 70 territorial lineage groups. Illustrating the linguistic complexity of the region, MacEachern (1998:115) noted that in an area of 1,500 km^2, three language families were found. Three ceramic traditions were identified based on vessel shape, decoration such as incising, and type of handles. Within these broad types, varieties were identified based on functional categories (water jars, cooking pots, beer jars, and ceremonial vessels) and on whether vessel bottoms were molded or coil built. Although in a few instances decorative techniques or vessel shapes seemed to conform to ethnic boundaries, MacEachern (1998:122) found that "regional variation at the level of the ceramic tradition and local variation at the community level appear to be far more important than is variation at the intermediate level of the ethnic group." The spread and perpetuation of the supra-ethnic ceramic tradition is explained in large part by patrilocal exogamous marriage rules (with respect to territorial lineage) together with a high incidence of divorce (3–10 per person is common) among female potters, who are typically multilingual. With regard to the social causes of ceramic stylistic regions, MacEachern's (1998:129) archaeological and ethnographic studies led him to the conclusion that "the people responsible for these regional traditions do not speak the same language; they belong to no self-conscious corporate unit; they encompass a host of different social, cultural, and political relationships."

Obviously, these four ethnographic examples are not expected to serve as direct analogies for the Woodland hunter-gatherer bands or coastal villages of North Carolina. Nevertheless, they provide concrete examples that bring to our awareness the possibilities of ethnic and linguistic complexity that may have existed within any of the ceramic stylistic regions described for the Atlantic coast in any Woodland period. Ceramic stylistic regions described for the prehistoric Atlantic coast are typically quite large, almost certainly encompassing many ethnic groups and languages as well as smaller social groupings such as lineage territories. Both ethnographic and ethnohistoric sources suggest that social structures such as marriage and kinship rules and customs regarding extralocal hereditary friendships, divorce, and magic may have exhibited less variation geographically than did language and ethnic identity. Apparently, ceramic technological information and pottery-making customs were also supra-ethnic in nature. Despite the diversity in social structure and cultural custom in any prehistoric ceramic stylistic region, the technical choices made by potters can be determined through systematic analyses of the products of their craft, and the potter's mode of obtaining technical knowledge and the manner in which that knowledge was spread or diffused can be modeled through ethnographic analogy.

Independence of Temper and Surface Treatment

One of the most striking characteristics of the pottery analyzed for this study is that temporal trends and spatial distributions in tempering techniques and decorative modes of finishing vessel surfaces are independent of one another. Perhaps because of the habitual classification of these attribute categories as combinations, diagnostic of particular types, archaeologists have seldom dealt with this issue explicitly. These two techniques represent distinctive steps in the *chaîne opératoire:* procuring and processing raw materials, and fashioning that portion of the vessel that will be visible to all who use it. The independence of the attributes representing these two techniques, however, is indicative not only of differences in technical choices and knowledge but also of differences in the manner in which the practices were first learned, habituated, and, perhaps, understood.

Following Gosselain (1998:94), we could assign these two techniques to different phases in the learning process whereby pottery manufacturing knowledge is transferred and practices habituated. In the first phase, an apprentice assists his or her teacher with procuring, carrying, and processing clay and tempering materials; preparing for the firing process; and treating vessels after firing. This participation allows the learning of materials, transformation processes, and any taboos associated with the craft. A second learning phase consists of a formal relationship between teacher and student characterized by serious motivation. As the problems of manipulating the clay to form the desired shape arise, the apprentice is directed by the teacher, who works side by side, "correcting gestures, rectifying errors, and even taking her or his hands into her or his own, until the apprentice is able to work alone" (Gosselain 1998:94). At the end of the apprenticeship, which may last as little as two months or as long as a year, all gestures and postures related to what Gosselain calls the "fashioning process" have become inculcated as motor habits. As a result of this training, in the event a potter moves to a new village, she may change procedures for processing raw material and firing pots to share those of the new village's potters, but fashioning techniques (habituated as motor skills) would not be easily altered.

In fact, however, the archaeological record as represented in this analysis does not indicate radical differences in the size of tempering regions as opposed to surface treatment regions. Neither do the data indicate significant differences in the periodicity with which tempering techniques as opposed to surface treatments arise and then fall into disuse. In part, this may be due to the fact that different surface treatment styles are created primarily by differences in the nature of the paddle surfaces, not the manner in which the vessel was paddled. The constraints attending the selection of paddle surface textures represent a different stage or step in the chain of operations. This step, I believe, has to do with a potter's understanding of the crafting of a vessel's appearance as metaphorically associated with other important crafts such as basketry, netting, and textile weaving (Ortman 2000; Tilley 1999). As baskets, nets, and textiles are not only tools of survival but also symbols of affluence in hunter-gatherer societies, the transposition of this visual symbol into the craft of pottery making by stamping with paddles that create a basketlike appearance on the exterior of a pot is not so unusual. This transposition may also have influenced the manner in which vessels were made. Several sherds were found in the Haag collection that appear to be from unfinished vessels made with coils of very small diameter (1 cm or less). Several basal fragments revealed the use of similarly small coils, indicating that vessel bases were commonly formed with coils rather than being drawn from a lump or molded with a slab. This method of building the container by encircling with small coils beginning from the center of the base is not necessary: molding from a lump would be easier and less prone to drying and firing failure. So what motivated the perpetuation of this more costly, less effective trait? One possible answer is that the act of winding small coils from the center of the base is reminiscent of basket weaving, therefore reflecting the transposition of methods from one craft to another. This process represents not simply a transposition of technical practices from one medium to another but a metaphorical connection among crafts at several levels. The crafting of ceramic containers that metaphorically express textile and basket-making crafts draws these practices together into a sphere of related activities that create functional artifacts that nurture the health and well-being of family members, while also reflecting the self-assuredness, accomplishment, and participatory engagement of the makers, thus linking artisans across ethnic and linguistic boundaries into transcultural communities of practice.

One of the most interesting challenges facing anthropological archaeology is the exploration of transcultural communities of practice with the goal of explaining the nature of the linkage, or the source and mechanisms whereby the practices are held in common, among ethnic and linguistic groups that are widely dispersed across space, through time, and along the continuum of cultural variation. Although the conceptual pendulum has in recent years swung away from the nomothetic construction of formulaic prescriptions designed to expose cultural processes as derived from environmental contexts, there is an underlying foundation to this school of thought to which all modern theorists must acquiesce. Human culture is the product of biological evolution, and the mechanics of the process are manifested in cultural practices that we may observe today, as witnessed through the archaeological record. While most archaeologists would acknowledge the truth of this statement, few recognize its importance. Perhaps, as Cosmides and Tooby (1987:277) point out, this is due to "a widespread tendency to overlook a crucial link in the causal chain from evolution to behavior: the level of innate psychological mechanisms, described as information processing systems." As they explain, "it is these mechanisms that evolve over generations; within any single generation it is these mechanisms that, in interaction with environmental input, generate manifest behavior." The causal link between evolution and behavior is made through the psychological mechanism.

Nature of Boundaries

What is it then that we are witnessing when we observe the boundaries of spatial distributions of tempering or surface treatment styles, or the combinations of these traits as pottery types? Although it is possible that in the Late Woodland certain pottery series identified in this study represent distinctive ethnic and linguistic groups, the probability that this is true for all of the pottery series identified seems low. So, although it would be simple and satisfying to imagine the Hanover potters standing on the south bank of the Neuse River jeering, in an unintelligible language, at the Townsend potters on the north bank, this is a generally inaccurate representation of the archaeological record. Although such a sharp territorial boundary may have obtained in specific instances, this scenario is generally an inappropriate characterization of either the archaeological or the ethnohistoric record. Although it is likely that many ethnic and linguistic subgroups simultaneously inhabited the pottery regions represented by the distributions of ceramic series described in this study, ethnohistoric accounts clearly describe regions of allied groups in competition (often via violent warfare) with neighboring alliances. Despite the fact that the ceramic technological styles may represent polyethnic contexts, at some level, ceramic technological styles are expressed over areas with shared cultural histories. The boundaries of these areas, evident in the archaeological record, mark the limits of the region in which the tradition was practiced.

There are several factors that may have influenced distributions and boundary conditions. Clay and temper types found only in certain areas most certainly influenced distributions and boundaries to some degree. Fiber-tempered Stallings ware is not found far north of the northern limits of Spanish moss. Marl-tempered Hamp's Landing ware is not often found outside of the region in which marl formations are exposed by surface erosion. Oyster shells, on the other hand, can be found on every part of the coast and yet the shell-tempered Townsend ware exhibits a relatively abrupt boundary near the middle of the North Carolina coast. In this case, however, the southern boundary of the Townsend distribution falls very near the ecological boundary between the Sea Island and Embayed sections of the coast. To the north of this boundary lie the broad sounds with their rich estuarine resources. To the south, embayments are relatively small and the estuarine ecotone between freshwater swamps and the Atlantic coast is narrow. In this case, it would seem that the economic activities practiced by those who made shell-tempered pottery were so focused on estuarine resources that they chose to make their habitations along the sounds of the northern coast. Certainly, however, oyster shell was no less abundant on the southern coast, and yet the inhabitants did not avail themselves of this resource as a ceramic tempering agent.

Demographic factors may also have influenced distributions and boundaries. In regions where resources were scarce or widely dispersed, such as in the pine-dominated upper Coastal Plain and Sandhills, carrying capacity would likely be low. Low population density and high residential mobility would promote the diffusion of ceramic technological information and practices through a widely extended network of social alliances developed as a strategy to avoid risk. Conversely, in regions of high resource density the capacity for carrying larger or denser populations, such as that found in the Carolina Sounds region, might be expressed as smaller regions of stylistic tradition conforming to territorial boundaries. Such conditions might arise not only in regions rich in natural resources, such as the embayments on the northern coast, but also as a result of food production. The conditions appropriate for higher population expansion are manifested in the rich estuarine sounds and through the practice of corn agriculture evident at coastal sites in the central and northern areas. The data in this study do, in fact, suggest a firmer boundary for the distribution of Townsend ware than for that of earlier pottery series, with the exception of those series whose distributions appear to be dependent on the availability of tempering materials (e.g., crushed limestone or granitic rock).

Summary

As has been cogently argued elsewhere, pots as tools evidence the evolution of human adaptive behavior. Nevertheless, whereas the tendency has sometimes been to seek direct relationships between the performance of technologies and the selection of those technological styles, it is not the technology but the practice and the psychological mechanisms behind the practice that mediate the selective process. It is abundantly evident from the richly textured variegation of cultural solutions to the problem of constructing ceramic cooking vessels that there are innumerable possible solutions. It is also quite clear that among the solutions can be found significant differences in effectiveness measurable in terms of mechanical performance, e.g., between the thick-walled, flat-bottomed vessels of the Early Woodland and the thin-walled, conical-based vessels of the Middle and Late Woodland period. But much more common are variations in technological styles, the basis of pottery class definitions, that do not appear to represent significant differences in mechanical performance. This sort of variation has been called "isochrestic," referring to the apparent functional equivalency of solutions, and its source attributed to historical custom (Sackett 1977, 1982, 1985a). Although the apparent circularity of this interpretation (i.e., culture causes culture) and the inappropriateness of assuming functional isomorphism without adequate testing have been ardently argued (Binford 1989), perhaps the greatest deficit is that such an approach fails to address the problem of the source of variation. As Lemonnier (1989:160) notes, "to attribute the distribution [of technological styles] to historical factors . . . is a way of sending the technological or general social logic of the phenomena observed back to an inaccessible past."

In a similar critique, it has often been argued that Neo-Darwinists view social agency as "passive and culturally meaningless" (e.g., Gosselain 1998:81). These critics conclude that in their desire to discriminate between the source of variation and the selective processes acting on variation evolutionists have viewed social agency and innovation as essentially irrelevant to the process of selection and ultimately to the patterning we see in the archaeological record. This critique fails to take into consideration the fact that the source of technological variation (i.e., innovation) is a nonrandom product of the evolutionary process; human cognition is an evolved mechanism that is highly selective in the sense that at any given time of observation cognitive processes are prefigured or programmed in innumerable ways by millions of years of evolution.

It is important therefore to attempt to determine how an adaptive problem would have manifested itself in prehistory and to develop a theory of information processing that integrates the model of the adaptive problem with as much knowledge as possible regarding relevant prehistoric conditions. The theory may then be used to identify design features that any cognitive program capable of solving the problem must have and to develop models of cognitive programs that might have evolved to solve the adaptive problem. Alternative candidate models may be eliminated by experimentation and field observation, and ultimately models may be compared against modern behavior patterns (Cosmides and Tooby 1987:302–303).

By approximating to some degree the process prescribed by Cosmides and Tooby (1987), the problem may be framed in terms of spatial and temporal patterning in ceramic technological styles in the context of the prehistoric adaptive environment, both ecological and social, on the coast of North Carolina. Models of learning, practice, and the transmission of technological styles have been proposed and evaluated by exploring cognitive issues and examining steps in the production process. Ethnographic observations have allowed some refinement of the models. On balance, given the scale at which we view the manifest results of evolutionary processes, we can be reasonably confident that the ceramic types, composed of independently varying traits, reflect communities of practice encompassing multiple ethnic and linguistic groups but somehow sharing common cultural histories. Replicating technological styles that metaphorically express the relatedness of crafts and of artisans has the effect of drawing practitioners together into a sphere of common culture that encourages engagement of participants. In the concluding chapter, I review the contributions of this volume to the study of coastal ceramics with regard to taxonomy, chronology, geography, and meaning.

10
Conclusion

Technological styles of material culture are the language of practice, shaped by shared understandings of what is effective, or proper, or pleasing, formed in the context of family and peers, kin groups, and community networks of every description. Understanding the linkage between archaeological patterns of material culture and the dynamics of practice requires (1) an appropriate artifact taxonomy, (2) a reasonably well-established chronology, (3) knowledge of the spatial distribution of the technologies in question, and (4) some idea of the social and environmental factors that constrained and impelled behavioral expressions. In exploring the variation present in the Woodland pottery of North Carolina's Coastal Plain, several compelling conclusions have been reached in each of these domains, and these are summarized below.

Taxonomy

This study has proceeded under the assumption that the ceramic classes are defined by traits that reflect variation in two behavior sets: (1) the selection and preparation of the materials, including clay and tempering agents, and (2) forming the vessel (Rye 1981). Relying on temper and surface treatment is not unique to this study, but the strictness or rigor with which temper and surface treatment variations have been used in assigning pottery specimens to mutually exclusive classes is an essential feature of this study. Archaeologists often seem to feel that assigning specimens to typological classes is a matter of getting a "sense" of where an assemblage fits in the local sequence. As a result of using this approach, it is not unusual to find type definitions becoming more inclusive as additional variations in temper and surface treatment are found in assemblages that seem to fit into some time and place in the local sequence. Under these conditions types tend to expand to the point that they are no longer mutually exclusive, whereupon the assignment of specimens to the proper place in the system becomes more a matter of understanding where the assemblage fits in time and space, rather than the other way around.

Of course, understanding the provenience of assemblages is an essential archaeological goal and, certainly, assemblages are often composed of pottery exhibiting a wide array of traits.

The potential down side to insisting on mutual exclusivity is that although logically coherent, classes may have questionable anthropological or technological relevance. This study has sent up several such logically coherent, as yet untested, typological trial balloons. For example, the trait used to segregate the Mount Pleasant and Deep Creek series in the northern region is the presence or absence of granule-sized, subrounded quartz inclusions as opposed to quartz inclusions varying in size from very coarse to fine. A pottery specimen having granule-sized inclusions is classified as Mount Pleasant and one lacking granules is classified as New River, although the presence of granule particle sizes of quartz, often mixed in their natural state, may not reflect any particular technological behavior. Although this typological construction may in fact obscure tempering variation in some assemblages, were it not to be applied, previous definitions for Mount Pleasant and Deep Creek classes would not be exclusive.

In other examples, restricting the definition of the Yadkin series to only specimens containing angular quartz inclusions (presumably crushed) is essential if this series is to be distinguished from the sand-tempered types from the same time period. Restricting the New River series to specimens with very sandy paste and parallel cord marking is necessary to separate the long continuum of sand tempering on the southern coast. Admittedly, such typological boundaries are imposed on a gradient of more–less continuous variation, but as these cut points have proven to be somewhat specific, both temporally and geographically, there is ample reason to propose cultural correlates. Moreover, the approach taken is not assemblage based but designed to provide the tools for interpreting assemblage composition across large geographic regions.

Although the current taxonomy defines pottery type boundaries that restrict class inclusion, it simultaneously requires synthesis of some preexisting types. For instance, if the only difference between a Deep Creek sherd and a New River sherd is that one is found in the northern part of the coast and the other in the southern part, then archaeologists whose sites are situated in the central coast are likely to find themselves in the midst of an existential crisis. The reaction of many archaeologists to this problem seems to have been to simply define a new type, which eliminates the immediate problem but increases the difficulty of appreciating regional patterns. The premise of this study, therefore, has been that the justification for creating new types must be compelling. It is hoped the modifications to the regional sequences that are suggested here not only refine series and type definitions but also lay the foundation upon which a more nuanced classification system can be built as the complexities of additional well-dated assemblages are described in detail.

Chronology

It is fair to say that the section on chronology, presented in Chapter 7, offers no major changes to the existing ceramic sequences that were in place when this study began. The fact that there were no big surprises is a testament to the thoroughness of earlier researchers. This study has, however, added a great deal of new chronological data to the southern coast and Sandhills regions, where existing sequences were based on very limited collections associated with almost no dates at all.

Chronological data were added primarily through thermoluminescence (TL) dating. The principal advantage of TL dating is that it targets the pottery itself. Given this advantage, TL dating is fast becoming an essential tool for sorting out multiple assemblages on sites situated in sandy terrain—a common circumstance on Coastal Plain sites.

Aside from contributing to the refinement of regional pottery sequences and possible assistance to those exploring methods for acquiring chronological data on coastal sites, the chronology section of this study draws attention to two features of prehistoric pottery making that, although well known, are seldom discussed. The first is the longevity of trait-producing traditions and the second is that the forces influencing change in tempering practices appear to be unconnected to those producing different surface treatment styles.

Geography

Early Woodland traditions on the southern coast of North Carolina resonate with those found on the South Carolina coast, suggesting social interaction with groups in this region producing Stallings, Thom's Creek, and Refuge pottery.

It appears that social alliances in the latter part of the Archaic and Early Woodland periods focused on the cultures of coastal South Carolina and during this time there occurred a shift from male-centered trade networking to female-centered craft production at the household level. Pottery-making technology evolved as an integral part of local economies, with Hamp's Landing and New River being fully developed, indigenous technologies based in southern North Carolina and characterized by stamping traditions that produced pottery vessels whose surfaces appear as metaphors for perishable fiber arts—a distinctly female craft.

The practice of tempering with crushed limestone exhibited in the Hamp's Landing material seems to reflect an indigenous expression, but this interpretation is clouded by the possibility that Hamp's Landing may represent a multiplicity of traditions that happened to use marly clay. The distribution of Hamp's Landing appears to conform to the geographic region in which marl deposits occur and were mined for commercial purposes in the twentieth century. The four dates associated with Hamp's Landing do not yet appear to be adequate for determining the chronological position of this series.

With the New River series we see the first indigenous, truly pan-coastal tradition. Net-impressed and parallel or oblique cord-marked wares made with paste tempered with sand in high proportion are found at coastal sites from Virginia to South Carolina. The earliest dates for New River series sherds are TL assays with very large error terms. The youngest date in this cluster also appears to be an outlier. A conservative estimate of the chronological position of the New River series would be 1200–400 B.C. The distribution of the next oldest series, Cape Fear, looks very much like that of New River, as we might expect, given the subtle distinctions in tempering and surface treatment techniques that distinguish these two series. One very interesting feature of the distribution is the high frequency of Cape Fear sherds along the central coast in Carteret, Pamlico, and Beaufort counties. It has long been suspected by those most familiar with the pottery of the North Carolina coast that a Late Woodland sand-tempering tradition was in place prior to the southward migration of Algonquians and that this tradition persisted alongside the shell-tempering technique so characteristic of the Late Woodland of the central and northern coast.

Among the Cape Fear series TL dates, the oldest and youngest assays appear to be outliers; consequently, a reasonable age estimate for this series is 400 B.C.–A.D. 400. Together, the New River and Cape Fear series compose a technological continuum characterized by sand-and-grit tempering that lasted at least 1,600 years. Throughout this period, subtle shifts in tempering and surface treatment styles are apparent. An attempt has been made in this study to segment this continuum by proposing possible temporal shifts in the popularity of cord-marking techniques (parallel earlier and perpendicular later) and by noting a tendency for the earlier New River material to include slightly more sand than the later Cape Fear material. But although these tentative partitions appear to exhibit some time-space distinctions, it must be admitted that the overall appearance is one of a very long tradition (almost 2,000 years) of stamping sand-tempered vessels with cord-wrapped paddles—unquestionably, a very effective technological solution to an enduring economic need.

Following Cape Fear, the tradition of tempering with crushed pottery or grog emerged in the Middle Woodland, and Hanover series pottery appears to be ubiquitous on the Coastal Plain for many centuries. The continuous sequence of dates for Hanover suggests an age range of about 1,100 years from A.D. 400 to A.D.

1500. Originally thought to be a Middle Woodland series, the accumulation over the past few years of assays for grog-tempered sherds or contexts that postdate A.D. 900 has required some adjustments to our thinking.

Current evidence suggests that cord marking was the more popular surface treatment style early in the Hanover tradition, with fabric impressing gaining dominance as the technology evolved. The northernmost extent of the tempering practice appears to have been on the northern coast. Very little grog-tempered pottery is found along the Virginia coast, but the Wilmington series on the South Carolina coast parallels, or is part of, the Hanover tradition.

Ceramic technological styles of the Early and Middle Woodland were shared with cultures to the south, but the direction of influence reversed during the Late Woodland. Shell-tempered pottery on the North Carolina coast is clearly part of the Townsend-Rappahannock tradition found throughout the Chesapeake and Tidewater Virginia. This geographic distribution suggests the sort of zero-sum relationship that might be expected in two competing cultural traditions, with the southern boundary of the Townsend series appearing just south of the New River Valley and the northern boundary for the Hanover series found near the North Carolina–Virginia line. Evidence indicates that as Algonquian-speaking groups moved south into northern North Carolina they displaced people making grog-tempered ware, moving the northern boundary for Hanover further south. Shell-tempered Water Lily, Currituck, and Mockley series, however, may well represent an indigenous Middle Woodland shell-tempering tradition.

Cultural Causes

It is assumed that pottery types express the behaviors of potters who learned to prepare paste, construct, decorate, and fire vessels in the context of extended, exogamous matrilineal families. It follows that the diachronic variation and spatial distribution of types maps the geographic range of intermarrying or interacting groups.

On the Carolina coast, as elsewhere in the Southeast, by Middle Woodland times (about 400 B.C.) the practice of building conical-based cooking and storage pots by the coil-built, paddle-and-anvil system was fully developed. Perhaps because of its commonness, coil building is often taken for granted. In fact, coil building in the manner in which it was practiced in coastal Carolina, using coils about 1 cm in diameter, marked a radical departure from the foregoing slab-building technique that is assumed to have been the preferred method for making pots in the earliest part of the Early Woodland period (ca. 1500–1000 B.C.). Laying up coils horizontally and annealing them with vertical paddle strokes imitates the "weaving" of clay, much in the manner of basketry. The fact that many surface treatments reproduce a basketlike appearance is another expression of the kindred nature of these crafts.

In contrast, were we able to travel back in time to the earliest Stallings Island villages, it would not surprise me to find men making the clumsy slab-built vessels that so closely resemble soapstone bowls. Trade in soapstone was almost certainly driven by prestige, as well as any technological advantage it might have represented. The mortuary practices of the preceramic Wade phase culture of central Tennessee (Amick et al. 1986) provide an interesting snapshot of a culture engrossed in the soapstone trade. At the Ol' Roy site, several males were buried with soapstone vessels inverted over their heads, perhaps an odd symbol of prestige to us, but one no doubt signifying the importance of the bowls in the psychology of economic prestige. Weaponry was very evident in the tool assemblage found with this culture and skeletal remains with embedded stone projectiles testified to the level of violence sustained, perhaps in the business of acquiring and maintaining prestige.

Coil-built pots, on the other hand, are locally made domestic cooking and storage tools. They are built like baskets, decorated to look like baskets, and used in household context to nurture and sustain family members. Just at the time coil-built pottery making begins to emerge as a domestic technological practice, we find the first evidence for experimentation in the domestication of seed-bearing food plants.

The sequence of surface treatment styles represented among the TL-dated sherds on the North Carolina coast begins with net impressing, simple stamping, and parallel cord marking, followed by perpendicular cord marking and fabric impressing, then, in the very late period, by the reemergence of simple stamping and finally burnishing. It may be concluded that the regions in which specific pottery types are distributed represent areas where technological styles, consisting of both knowledge and practice, were passed down from one generation of women potters to the next. In essence, then, what are being mapped are enormous matrilineages, the breadths of which have been shaped by social practices that encouraged the faithful replication of crafted objects and by exogamy that served to export technological styles to neighboring communities. Along the boundaries of these regions where women married into communities of potters whose technological styles were different from the ones of their native communities, the opportunity for variation increased. What is certain is that a history of the learning process, the negotiation of cultural standards of performance and style, and the constraints that materials imposed on a potter's decisions are all encoded in the subtle differences in traits exhibited by the Woodland pottery of coastal North Carolina.

References Cited

Abbott, Lawrence E., Jr.

1993 *Spring Lake Bypass, NCDOT TIP No. R-2629, Archaeological, Historical and Architectural Historical Consulting Services/Cultural Resources Survey: Spring Lake Bypass, Cumberland County, North Carolina.* New South Associates, Inc., Stone Mountain, Georgia, Technical Report No. 209. Submitted to McGuire and Associates, Raleigh, North Carolina.

Abbott, Lawrence E., Jr., Erica E. Sanborn, Leslie E. Raymer, Lisa D. O'Steen, William J. Cleary, and G. Craig Turner

1999 *Data Recovery at 31CB114, Columbus County, North Carolina: Prehistoric Settlement and Subsistence Practices within the Lower Cape Fear River Valley.* New South Associates, Inc., Stone Mountain, Georgia, Technical Report No. 618. Submitted to the International Paper Company, Inc., Riegelwood Operations, Riegelwood, North Carolina.

Adamiec, G., and M. J. Aitken

1986 Dose Rate Conversion Factors: Update. *Ancient TL* 16:37–50.

Adams, Natalie, and Michael Trinkley

1993 *Archaeological Survey of the Seaside Farms Tract, Charleston County, South Carolina.* Research Series 35. Chicora Foundation, Inc., Columbia, South Carolina.

Aitken, M. J.

1990 *Science-Based Dating in Archaeology.* Longman, London.

Aitken, M. J., M. S. Tite, and J. Reid

1964 Thermoluminescence Dating of Ancient Pottery. *Nature* 202:1032–1033.

Amick, Daniel S., Mary Ellen Fogarty, and Joseph M. Herbert

1986 *Cultural Adaptations in the Shelby Bend Archaeological District.* Department of Anthropology, University of Tennessee, Knoxville. Submitted to the National Park Service Southeastern Archaeological Center, Tallahassee, Florida.

Anderson, David G., John S. Cable, Niels Taylor, and Christopher Judge

1996 *Indian Pottery of the Carolinas: Observations from the March 1995 Ceramic Workshop at Hobcaw Barony.* Council of South Carolina Professional Archaeologists, South Carolina Department of Archives and History, Columbia.

Anderson, David G., Charles E. Cantley, and A. Lee Novick
1982 *The Mattassee Lake Sites: Archaeological Investigation along the Lower Santee River in the Coastal Plain of South Carolina.* Commonwealth Associates, Inc., Jackson, Michigan. Submitted to the National Park Service, Interagency Archaeological Services-Atlanta, Contract No. C54030(80).

Artusy, Richard E.
1976 An Overview of the Proposed Ceramic Sequence for Southern Delaware. *Maryland Archaeology* 12(2):1–15.

Barka, Norman F., and Ben C. McCary
1977 *Early Shell Tempered Pottery in the James River Valley, Virginia.* Eastern States Archaeological Federation, Bulletin 36.

Barnett, S. M.
1999 Date List 6: Luminescence Dates for Late Bronze Age and Iron Age Pottery Assemblages in Eastern and Northern Britain. *Ancient TL* 17:23–40.
2000 Luminescence Dating of Pottery from Later Prehistoric Britain. *Archaeometry* 42:431–457.

Barth, Frederick (editor)
1969 *Ethnic Groups and Boundaries: The Social Organization of Culture Difference.* Little Brown, Boston.

Binford, Lewis
1965 Colonial Period Ceramics of the Nottoway and Weanock Indians of Southeastern Virginia. *Archaeology Society of Virginia Quarterly Bulletin* 19(4):78–87.
1989 Styles of Style. *Journal of Anthropological Archaeology* 8:51–67.
1992 *In Pursuit of the Past: Decoding the Archaeological Record.* University of California Press, Berkeley.

Bishop, Ronald L., Robert L. Rands, and George R. Holley
1982 Ceramic Compositional Analysis in Archaeological Perspective. In *Advances in Archaeological Method and Theory,* Vol. 5, edited by M. B. Schiffer, pp. 275–330. Academic Press, New York.

Blanton, Dennis B., Christopher T. Espenshade, and Paul E. Brockington Jr.
1986 *An Archaeological Study of 38Su83: A Yadkin Phase Site in the Upper Coastal Plain of South Carolina.* Garrow and Associates, Inc., Atlanta. Submitted to the South Carolina Department of Transportation, Columbia.

Boyd, Robert, and Peter J. Richerson
1985 *Culture and the Evolutionary Process.* University of Chicago Press, Chicago.

Braun, David P.
1982 Radiographic Analysis of Temper in Ceramic Vessels: Goal and Initial Methods. *Journal of Field Archaeology* 9(2):183–192.
1983 Pots as Tools. In *Archaeological Hammers and Theories,* edited by J. A. Moore and A. S. Keene, pp. 107–134. Academic Press, New York.
1987 Coevolution of Sedentism, Pottery Technology, and Horticulture in the Central Midwest, 200 B.C.–A.D. 600. In *Emergent Horticultural Economies of the Eastern Woodlands,* edited by W. F. Keegan, pp. 153–181. Occasional Paper

No. 7. Center for Archaeological Investigations, Southern Illinois University, Carbondale.

1995 Style, Selection, and Historicity. In *Style, Society, and Person: Archaeological and Ethnological Perspectives,* edited by C. Carr and J. E. Neitzel, pp. 123–141. Plenum Press, New York.

Braun, David P., and Stephen Plog

1982 Evolution of "Tribal" Social Networks: Theory and Prehistoric North American Evidence. *American Antiquity* 47:504–525.

Bronitsky, Gordon

1986 The Use of Materials Science Techniques in the Study of Pottery Construction and Use. In *Advances in Archaeological Method and Theory,* Vol. 9, edited by M. B. Schiffer, pp. 209–276. Academic Press, San Diego.

Bronitsky, Gordon, and Robert Hamer

1986 Experiments in Ceramic Technology: The Effects of Various Tempering Materials on Impact and Thermal-Shock Resistance. *American Antiquity* 51(1):89–101.

Byrd, John E.

1996 Preliminary Report of the Archaeological Survey of the Contentnea Creek Drainage. Ms. on file, David S. Phelps Archaeology Laboratory, East Carolina University, Greenville, North Carolina.

1999 Ceramic Types and Typology in Northeastern North Carolina: The View from the Davenport Site (31BR39). *North Carolina Archaeology* 48:95–106.

Byrd, John E., and Charles L. Heath

1997 *The Rediscovery of the Tuscarora Homeland: A Final Report of the Archaeological Survey of the Contentnea Creek Drainage.* David S. Phelps Archaeology Laboratory, East Carolina University, Greenville, North Carolina. Report submitted to the Office of State Archaeology, Raleigh, North Carolina.

Cable, John S., Kenneth F. Styer, and Charles E. Cantley

1998 *Data Recovery Excavations at the Maple Swamp (38HR309) and Big Jones (38HR315) Sites on the Conway Bypass, Horry County, South Carolina.* New South Associates, Inc., Stone Mountain, Georgia. Submitted to South Carolina Department of Transportation, Columbia.

Caldwell, Joseph R.

1952 The Archaeology of Eastern Georgia and South Carolina. In *Archeology of Eastern United States,* edited by J. B. Griffin, pp. 312–321. University of Chicago Press, Chicago.

Caldwell, Joseph R., and Antonio J. Waring Jr.

1939 Some Chatham County Pottery Types and Their Sequence. *Southeastern Archaeological Conference Newsletter* 2:6–7.

Cashdan, Elizabeth

1992 Spatial Organization and Habitat Use. In *Evolutionary Ecology and Human Behavior,* edited by E. A. Smith and B. Winterhalder, pp. 237–266. Aldine de Gruyter, New York.

Chilton, S. Elizabeth
1996 *Embodiments of Choice: Native American Ceramic Diversity in the New England Interior.* Ph.D. dissertation, Department of Anthropology, University of Massachusetts, Amherst. University Microfilms, Ann Arbor, Michigan.
1998 The Cultural Origins of Technical Choice: Unraveling Algonquin and Iroquoian Ceramic Traditions. In *The Archaeology of Social Boundaries,* edited by M. T. Stark, pp. 132–160. Smithsonian Institution Press, Washington, D.C.
Claggett, Stephen R., and John S. Cable
1982 *The Haw River Sites: Archeological Investigation at Two Stratified Sites in the North Carolina Piedmont,* Vols. 1–3. Commonwealth Associates, Inc., Jackson, Michigan. Submitted to the Wilmington District, U.S. Army Corps of Engineers, Contract No. DACW54-79-C-0052.
Coe, Joffre L.
1952 The Cultural Sequence of the Carolina Piedmont. In *Archeology of Eastern United States,* edited by J. B. Griffin, pp. 301–311. University of Chicago Press, Chicago.
1964 *The Formative Cultures of the Carolina Piedmont.* Transactions of the American Philosophical Society, n.s. 54(5). American Philosophical Society, Philadelphia.
1995 *Town Creek Indian Mound: A Native American Legacy.* University of North Carolina Press, Chapel Hill.
Coe, Joffre L., H. Trawick Ward, Martha Graham, Liane Navey, S. Homes Hogue, and Jack H. Wilson Jr.
1982 *Archaeological and Paleo-osteological Investigations at the Cold Morning Site, New Hanover County, North Carolina.* Research Laboratories of Anthropology, University of North Carolina, Chapel Hill. Submitted to the National Park Service, Interagency Archaeological Services-Atlanta, Contract No. C55082(79).
Conkey, Margaret W.
1978 Style and Information in Cultural Evolution: Toward a Predictive Model for the Paleolithic. In *Social Archaeology beyond Subsistence and Dating,* edited by C. L. Redman, M. J. Berman, E. V. Curtin, W. T. Langhorne Jr., N. M. Versaggi, and J. C. Wanser, pp. 61–85. Academic Press, New York.
Conkey, Margaret W., and Christine A. Hastorf (editors)
1990 *The Uses of Style in Archaeology.* Cambridge University Press, Cambridge.
Cordell, Ann S.
1983 Patterns of Resource Selection in the Manufacture of North Florida Weeden Island Pottery. *Southeastern Archaeology* 2(2):84–97.
1984 *Ceramic Technology at a Weeden Island Period Archaeological Site in North Florida.* Ceramic Notes No. 2, Occasional Publications of the Ceramic Technology Laboratory. Florida State Museum, University of Florida, Gainesville.
1993 Chronological Variability in Ceramic Paste: A Comparison of Deptford and Savannah Period Pottery in the St. Marys River Region of Northeast Florida and Southeast Georgia. *Southeastern Archaeology* 12(1):33–58.
Cosmides, Leda, and John Tooby
1987 From Evolution to Behavior: Evolutionary Psychology as the Missing Link. In

The Latest on the Best: Essays on Evolution and Optimality, edited by J. Dupre, pp. 277–306. Massachusetts Institute of Technology Press, Cambridge.

Crawford, Robert Guy Hodges
1966 An Archaeological Survey of Lenoir County, North Carolina. Unpublished Master's thesis, Department of Anthropology, University of Florida, Gainesville.

Culpepper, Stacy, Charles L. Heath, Jeffrey D. Irwin, and Joseph M. Herbert
1999 *From Drowning Creek to Sicily: Archaeological Investigations at Fort Bragg.* Cultural Resources Management Series, Research Report No. 2. Fort Bragg Cultural Resources Program, Fort Bragg, North Carolina.

Cuomo di Caprio, Ninina, and Sarah Vaughan
1993 An Experimental Study in Distinguishing Grog (Chamotte) from Argillaceous Inclusions in Ceramic Thin Sections. *Archaeomaterials* 7:21–40.

Daniel, I. Randolf, Jr.
1999 *Archaeological Excavations at Hammocks Beach West (31On665): A Woodland Shell Midden on the North Carolina Coast.* Occasional Papers of the Phelps Archaeology Laboratory, No. 1. East Carolina University, Greenville, North Carolina.

Deal, Michael, and Melissa B. Hagstrum
1995 Ceramic Reuse Behavior among the Maya and Wanka: Implications for Archaeology. In *Expanding Archaeology,* edited by J. M. Skibo, W. H. Walker, and A. E. Nielsen, pp. 11–125. University of Utah Press, Salt Lake City.

DeBoer, Warren R.
1991 The Decorative Burden: Design, Medium, and Change. In *Ceramic Ethnoarchaeology,* edited by W. A. Longacre, pp. 144–161. University of Arizona Press, Tucson.

DeBoer, Warren R., and Donald W. Lathrap
1979 The Making and Breaking of Shipibo-Conibo Ceramics. In *Ethnoarchaeology: Implications of Ethnography for Archaeology,* edited by C. Kramer, pp. 102–138. Columbia University Press, New York.

DeBoer, Warren R., and James A. Moore
1982 The Measurement and Meaning of Stylistic Diversity. *Nawpa Pacha* 20:147–162.

DePratter, Chester B.
1979 Ceramics. In *The Anthropology of St. Catherines Island,* Vol. 2, *The Refuge-Deptford Mortuary Complex,* edited by D. H. Thomas and C. S. Larsen, pp. 109–132. Anthropological Papers, No. 56(1). American Museum of Natural History, New York.

Dietler, M., and I. Herbich
1994 Ceramics and Ethnic Identity: Ethnoarchaeological Observations on the Distribution of Pottery Styles and the Relationship between the Social Context of Production and Consumption. In *Terre Cuite et Société: La Ceramique, Document Technique, Economique, Culturel,* edited by D. Binder and J. Courtin, pp. 459–472. Editions APDCA, Juan-les-Pins, France.

Dobres, Marcia-Ann, and John E. Robb (editors)
2000 *Agency in Archaeology.* Routledge, London.

Drooker, Penelope B.
1992 *Mississippian Village Textiles at Wickliffe.* The University of Alabama Press, Tuscaloosa.

Dunnell, Robert C.
1978 Style and Function: A Fundamental Dichotomy. *American Antiquity* 43(2):192–202.
1980 Evolutionary Theory and Archaeology. In *Advances in Archaeological Method and Theory,* Vol. 3, edited by M. B. Schiffer, pp. 35–99. Academic Press, New York.
1989 Aspects of the Application of Evolutionary Theory in Archaeology. In *Archaeological Thought in America,* edited by C. C. Lamberg-Karlovsky, pp. 35–49. Cambridge University Press, Cambridge.
1995a What Is It That Actually Evolves? In *Evolutionary Archaeology: Methodological Issues,* edited by P. A. Teltser, pp. 33–50. University of Arizona Press, Tucson.
1995b Style: Concepts and Practice. Paper presented at the 52nd Annual Meeting of the Southeastern Archaeological Conference, Knoxville, Tennessee.

Dunnell, Robert C., and James K. Feathers
1991 Late Woodland Manifestations of the Malden Plain, Southeast Missouri. In *Stability, Transformation, and Variation: The Late Woodland Southeast,* edited by M. S. Nassaney and C. R. Cobb, pp. 21–45. Plenum Press, New York.
1994 Thermoluminescence Dating of Surficial Archaeological Material. In *Dating Exposed and Surface Contexts,* edited by C. Beck, pp. 115–138. University of New Mexico Press, Albuquerque.

Dykeman, Douglas D.
2000 Accuracy and Precision in Archaeological Dating: A Correlation of Tree-Ring, Thermoluminescence, and Radiocarbon Techniques. Paper presented at the 65th Annual Meeting of Society for American Archaeology, Philadelphia.

Dykeman, Douglas D., Ronald H. Towner, and James K. Feathers
2002 Correspondence in Tree-Ring Dating and Thermoluminescence Dating: A Protohistoric Navajo Pilot Study. *American Antiquity* 67(1):145–164.

Eastman, Jane M.
1994a The North Carolina Radiocarbon Date Study (Part 2). *Southern Indian Studies* 43. Research Laboratories of Anthropology, University of North Carolina, Chapel Hill.
1994b The North Carolina Radiocarbon Date Study (Part 1). *Southern Indian Studies* 42. Research Laboratories of Anthropology, University of North Carolina, Chapel Hill.

Eastman, Jane M., Loretta Lautzenheiser, and Mary Ann Holm
1997 A Re-evaluation of Ceramics from the Tower Hill Site. *North Carolina Archaeology* 46:109–120.

Egloff, Keith T.
1985 Spheres of Cultural Interaction across the Coastal Plain of Virginia in the

Woodland Period. In *Structure and Process in Southeastern Archaeology,* edited by R. S. Dickens Jr., and H. T. Ward, pp. 229–242. University of Alabama Press, University, Alabama.

Egloff, Keith T., Mary Ellen N. Hodges, Jay F. Custer, Keith R. Doms, and Leslie D. McFaden

1988 *Archaeological Investigations at Croaker Landing 44JC70 and 44JC71.* Research Report Series 4. Commonwealth of Virginia, Department of Conservation and Historic Resources, Division of Historic Landmarks, Richmond.

Egloff, Keith T., and Stephen R. Potter

1982 Indian Ceramics from Coastal Plain Virginia. *Archaeology of Eastern North America* 10:95–117.

Espenshade, Christopher T.

1996 South Carolina Prehistoric Pottery: Reflections on the 1995 Conference at Georgetown, S.C. In *Indian Pottery of the Carolinas: Observations from the March 1995 Ceramic Workshop at Hobcaw Barony,* edited by D. G. Anderson, J. S. Cable, N. Taylor, and C. Judge, pp. 42–52. Council of South Carolina Professional Archaeologists, Columbia.

Evans, Clifford

1955 *A Ceramic Study of Virginia Archaeology.* Bulletin 160. Bureau of American Ethnology, Washington, D.C.

Feathers, James K.

1989 Effects of Temper on Strength of Ceramics: Response to Bronitsky and Hamer. *American Antiquity* 54(3):579–588.

1993 Thermoluminescence Dating of Pottery from Southeastern Missouri and the Problem of Radioactive Disequilibrium. *Archaeomaterials* 7:3–20.

1997a The Application of Luminescence Dating in American Archaeology. *Journal of Archaeological Method and Theory* 4:1–66.

1997b Luminescence Dating of Sediment Samples from White Paintings Rockshelter, Botswana. *Quaternary Science Reviews (Quaternary Geochronology)* 16:121–131.

1997c Luminescence Dating of Early Mounds in Northeast Louisiana. *Quaternary Science Reviews (Quaternary Geochronology)* 16:333–340.

2000 Why Luminescence Dating Deserves Wider Application in American Archaeology. In *It's About Time,* edited by S. Nash, pp. 152–166. University of Utah Press, Salt Lake City.

2001 Date List 7: Luminescence Dates for Prehistoric and Proto-historic Pottery from the American Southwest. *Ancient TL* 18:51–61.

Feathers, James K., and D. Rhode

1998 Luminescence Dating of Protohistoric Pottery from the Great Basin. *Geoarchaeology* 13:287–318.

Fleming, S. J., and D. Stoneham

1973 The Subtraction Technique of Thermoluminescent Dating. *Archaeometry* 15(2):229–238.

Fritz, Gayle J.

1993 Early and Middle Woodland Period Paleoethnobotany. In *Foraging and Farm-*

ing in the Eastern Woodlands, edited by C. M. Scarry, pp. 39–56. University Press of Florida, Gainesville.

Gardner, William M., and Charles W. McNett

1971 Early Pottery in the Potomac. In *Proceedings of the Middle Atlantic Archaeological Conference,* edited by W. M. Gardner and C. W. McNett, pp. 42–53. Catholic University of America, Washington, D.C.

Godfrey-Smith, D. I., M. Deal, and I. Kunelius

1997 Thermoluminescence Dating of St. Croix Ceramics: Chronology Building in Southwestern Nova Scotia. *Geoarchaeology: An International Journal* 12(3): 251–273.

Gosselain, Olivier P.

1998 Social and Technical Identity in a Clay Crystal Ball. In *The Archaeology of Social Boundaries,* edited by M. T. Stark, pp. 78–106. Smithsonian Institution Press, Washington, D.C.

Griffin, James B.

1943 *An Analysis and Interpretation of the Ceramic Remains from Two Sites near Beaufort, South Carolina.* Anthropological Papers, No. 22, Bulletin 133, pp. 155–168. Bureau of American Ethnology, Washington, D.C.

1945 Ceramic Collections from Two South Carolina Sites. *Papers of the Michigan Academy of Science, Arts, and Letters* 30:465–478.

Griffith, Daniel R.

1980 Townsend Ceramics and the Late Woodland of Southern Delaware. *Maryland Historical Magazine* 75(1):23–41.

Gunn, Joel D., and Kathy J. Wilson

1993 *Archaeological Data Recovery Investigations at Sites 38CT54 and 38CT58 along the SC-151 Jefferson Bypass, Chesterfield County, South Carolina.* Garrow and Associates, Inc., Raleigh, North Carolina. Submitted to the South Carolina Department of Highways and Public Transportation, Columbia.

Haag, William G.

1958 *The Archaeology of Coastal North Carolina.* Louisiana State University Press, Baton Rouge.

Hargrove, Thomas H.

1993 *Archaeological Excavations at 31NH142, Hamp's Landing, River Road Park, New Hanover County, North Carolina.* Archaeological Research Consultants, Inc., Raleigh, North Carolina. Submitted to the New Hanover County Department of Parks and Recreation, Wilmington, North Carolina, Contract Nos. ER 93-8840 and ER 92-7821. Copies available from the North Carolina Office of State Archaeology, Raleigh.

Hargrove, Thomas H., and Jane M. Eastman

1997 Limestone- or Marl-Tempered Ceramics from the Lower Cape Fear River Region, New Hanover County, North Carolina. *North Carolina Archaeology* 46:91–108.

1998 Limestone- or Marl-Tempered Ceramics from the Lower Cape Fear River Region, New Hanover County, North Carolina. Paper presented at the 55th

Annual Meeting of the Southeastern Archaeological Conference, Greenville, North Carolina.

Herbert, Joseph M.

1995 *The Thomas Point Site (18ST570): Emerging Late Woodland Traditions in Southern Maryland.* Jefferson Patterson Park and Museum Occasional Papers No. 5. Maryland Historical Trust, Annapolis.

1997 Refining Prehistoric Culture Chronology in Southern North Coastal Carolina: Pottery from the Papanow and Pond Trail Sites. Ms. on file, State of North Carolina, Department of Cultural Resources, Division of Archives and History, Office of State Archaeology, Raleigh.

1999a Practical Experiments to Determine the Nature of Perpendicular Over-stamped Surface Treatment. Paper contributed to the Working Group on Perishables: Cordage, Netting, Fabric and Textiles Impressed on Prehistoric Pottery, 64th Annual Meeting of the Society for American Archaeology, Chicago.

1999b Prehistoric Pottery Taxonomy and Sequence on the Southern Coast of North Carolina. *North Carolina Archaeology* 48:37–58.

2000 Luminescence Dating of Pottery from Coastal North Carolina. Paper presented at the 65th Annual Meeting of the Society for American Archaeology, Philadelphia.

Herbert, Joseph M., James K. Feathers, and Ann S. Cordell

2002 Building Ceramic Chronologies with Thermoluminescence Dating: A Case Study from the Carolina Sandhills. *Southeastern Archaeology* 21(1):92–108.

Herbert, Joseph M., and Mark A. Mathis

1996 An Appraisal and Re-evaluation of the Prehistoric Pottery Sequence of Southern Coastal North Carolina. In *Indian Pottery of the Carolinas: Observations from the March 1995 Ceramic Workshop at Hobcaw Barony,* edited by D. G. Anderson, J. S. Cable, N. Taylor, and C. Judge, pp. 136–189. Council of South Carolina Professional Archaeologists, Columbia.

Herbert, Joseph M., Theresa E. McReynolds, Michael S. Smith, Michael D. Glascock, and Robert J. Speakman

2005 *Clay Sources, Pottery Production, and Circulation in the Carolina Sandhills.* Paper presented at the 62nd Annual Meeting of the Southeastern Archaeological Conference, Columbia, South Carolina.

Hitchcock, Robert K., and Laurence E. Bartram Jr.

1998 Social Boundaries, Technical Systems, and the Use of Space and Technology in the Kalahari. In *The Archaeology of Social Boundaries,* edited by M. T. Stark, pp. 12–49. Smithsonian Institution Press, Washington, D.C.

Hodder, Ian

1982 *Symbols in Action: Ethnoarchaeological Studies of Material Culture.* Cambridge University Press, Cambridge.

1990 Style as Historical Quality. In *The Uses of Style in Archaeology,* edited by M. Conkey and C. Hastorf, pp. 44–51. Cambridge University Press, Cambridge.

Holmes, J. A.

1916 Indian Mounds of the Cape Fear. In *Chronicles of the Cape Fear River: Be-*

ing Some Account of Historic Events on the Cape Fear River, edited by J. Sprunt. Edwards and Broughton, Raleigh, North Carolina.

Huntley, D. J., J. T. Hutton, and J. R. Prescott

1993 The Stranded Beach-Dune Sequence of South-East South Australia: A Test of Thermoluminescence Dating, 0–800ka. *Quaternary Science Reviews* 12:1–20.

Hutchinson, Dale L.

2002 *Foraging, Farming, and Coastal Biocultural Adaptation in Late Prehistoric North Carolina.* University of Florida Press, Gainesville.

Ichikawa, Y., T. Nagatomo, and N. Hagihara

1978 Thermoluminescent Dating of Jomon Pattern Pottery from Taishaku Valley. *Archaeometry* 20(2):171–176.

Irwin, Jeffrey D., Wayne C. J. Boyko, Joseph M. Herbert, and Chad Braley

1999 Woodland Period Burial Mounds in the North Carolina Sandhills. *North Carolina Archaeology* 48:59–86.

Johnson, William C.

1996 A New Twist to an Old Tale: Analysis of Cordage Impressions on Late Woodland Ceramics from the Potomac River Valley. In *A Most Indispensable Art: Native Fiber Industries from Eastern North America,* edited by J. B. Petersen, pp. 144–159. University of Tennessee Press, Knoxville.

Johnson, William C., and Scott Speedy

1992 Cultural Continuity and Change in the Middle and Late Woodland Periods in the Upper James Estuary, Prince George County, Virginia. *Journal of Middle Atlantic Archaeology* 8:91–106.

Jones, David C., Christopher T. Espenshade, and Linda Kennedy

1997 *Archaeological Investigation at 31ON190, Cape Island, Onslow County, North Carolina.* Garrow and Associates, Inc., Atlanta. Submitted to The Island Development Group, Inc., Ringgold, Virginia. Copies available from the Office of State Archaeology, Raleigh, North Carolina.

Jones, George T., Robert D. Leonard, and Alysia L. Abbott

1995 The Structure of Selectionist Explanations in Archaeology. In *Evolutionary Archaeology: Methodological Issues,* edited by P. A. Teltser, pp. 13–33. University of Arizona Press, Tucson.

Jones, Lea D.

1986 *Lowland Maya Pottery: The Place of Petrological Analysis.* BAR International Series 288. British Archaeological Reports, Oxford.

Keel, Bennie C.

1970 Excavations at the Red Springs Mound RB°4, Robeson County 1971. *Southern Indian Studies* 22:16–22.

Klein, Terry H., Joseph M. Herbert, and Suzanne S. Pickens

1994 *Phase I Archaeological Survey: Wilmington Bypass New Hanover and Brunswick Counties.* Greiner Engineering, Raleigh, North Carolina. Submitted to Planning and Environmental Branch, North Carolina Department of Transportation, Raleigh. State Project No. 8u25091, TIP No. R-2633.

Larick, Roy

1985 Spears, Style, and Time among Maa-Speaking Pastoralists. *Journal of Anthropological Archaeology* 4:206–220.

Lautzenheiser, Loretta, Thomas Hargrove, Jane M. Eastman, Patricia Samford, J. Darter, and Mary Ann Holm

1997 *Archaeological Testing at the Neils Eddy Tract, International Paper, Riegelwood Operations, Riegelwood, Columbus County, North Carolina.* Coastal Carolina Research, Inc., Tarboro, North Carolina, and Archaeological Research Consultants, Raleigh, North Carolina. Submitted to International Paper, Riegelwood Operations, Riegelwood, North Carolina.

Lautzenheiser, Loretta, Mary Ann Holm, Jane M. Eastman, and D. O'Brien

1995 *Archaeological Survey, Proposed Treated Wastewater Holding Ponds, Federal Paper Board, Riegelwood Operations, Riegelwood, Columbus County, North Carolina.* Coastal Carolina Research, Inc., Tarboro, North Carolina. Submitted to International Paper, Riegelwood Operations, Riegelwood, North Carolina. Copies available from the Office of State Archaeology, Raleigh, North Carolina.

Lave, Jean, and Etienne Wenger

1991 *Situated Learning: Legitimate Peripheral Participation.* University of Cambridge Press, Cambridge.

Leach, Edmund R.

1954 *Political Systems in Highland Burma: A Study of Kachin Social Structure.* Harvard University Press, Cambridge, Massachusetts.

Leigh, David S.

1998a Evaluating Artifact Burial by Eolian versus Bioturbation Processes, South Carolina Sandhills, USA. *Geoarchaeology: An International Journal* 13(3):309–330.

1998b *Geomorphic Reconnaissance of the Overhills Tract at Fort Bragg with Special Emphasis on Bioturbation and Burial of Artifacts in Upland Sites.* Southeastern Archaeological Services, Athens, Georgia. Submitted to Fort Bragg Cultural Resources Program, Fort Bragg, North Carolina.

Lemonnier, Pierre

1989 Bark Capes, Arrowheads and Concorde: On Social Representations of Technology. In *The Meaning of Things: Material Culture and Symbolic Expression,* edited by I. Hodder, pp. 156–171. Unwin Hyman, London.

Leonard, Robert D., and G. T. Jones

1987 Elements of an Inclusive Evolutionary Model for Archaeology. *Journal of Anthropological Archaeology* 6:199–219.

Lipo, Carl P., Mark E. Madsen, Robert C. Dunnell, and Tim Hunt

1997 Population Structure, Cultural Transmission, and Frequency Seriation. *Journal of Anthropological Archaeology* 16(4):301–333.

Loftfield, Thomas C.

1976 A Brief and True Report . . .: An Archaeological Interpretation of the Southern North Carolina Coast. Unpublished Ph.D. dissertation, Department of Anthropology, University of North Carolina, Chapel Hill.

1979 *Excavations at 31On33, A Late Woodland Seasonal Village.* Department of Anthropology, University of North Carolina-Wilmington. Submitted to Interagency Archaeological Services, Contract No. C-5558(78).

1990 Ossuary Interments and Algonquian Expansion on the North Carolina Coast. *Southeastern Archaeology* 9(2):116–123.

Loftfield, Thomas C., and David C. Jones

1995 Late Woodland Architecture on the Coast of North Carolina: Structural Meaning and Environmental Adaptation. *Southeastern Archaeology* 14(2): 20–35.

Longacre, William A.

1985 Pottery Use-Life among the Kalinga, Northern Luzon, the Philippines. In *Decoding Prehistoric Ceramics,* edited by B. Nelson, pp. 334–346. Southern Illinois University Press, Carbondale.

MacCauley, Charles

1966 Appendix I: Notes on the Cameron Mound, Harnett County. *Southern Indian Studies* 18:46–47.

MacCord, Howard A., Sr.

1966 The McLean Mound, Cumberland County, North Carolina. *Southern Indian Studies* 18:3–45.

MacEachern, Scott

1998 Scale, Style, and Cultural Variation: Technological Traditions in the Northern Mandara Mountains. In *The Archaeology of Social Boundaries,* edited by M. T. Stark, pp. 107–131. Smithsonian Institution Press, Washington, D.C.

Manson, Carl

1948 Marcey Creek Site: An Early Manifestation in the Potomac Valley. *American Antiquity* 13(3):223–227.

Marshall, Adam

1999 Interior Rim Impressions as an Indicator of Typological Relationships. *North Carolina Archaeology* 48:87–94.

Maslowski, Robert F.

1984 The Significance of Cordage Attributes in the Analysis of Woodland Pottery. *Pennsylvania Archeologist* 54(1-2):51–60.

Mathis, Mark A.

1998 Oak Island: A Retiring Type. Paper presented at the 55th Annual Meeting of the Southeastern Archaeological Conference, Greenville, North Carolina.

1999 Oak Island: A Retiring Type. *North Carolina Archaeology* 48:18–36.

McCormick, Olin F.

1969 Archaeological Resources of the New Hope Reservoir Area, North Carolina. Unpublished Master's thesis, Department of Anthropology, University of North Carolina, Chapel Hill.

McReynolds, Theresa, and Joseph M. Herbert

2004 An Evaluation of the Utility of Carolina Clays for Woodland Potters. Paper presented at the 2004 joint meeting of the Southeastern Archaeological Conference and the Midwestern Archaeological Conference, St. Louis.

Mejdahl, V., and L. Bøtter-Jensen
1994 Luminescence Dating of Archaeological Materials Using a New Technique Based on Single Aliquot Measurements. *Quaternary Geochronology* 13:552–554.

Michie, James
1990 Bioturbation and Gravity as a Potential Site Formation Process: The Open Area Site, 38GE261, Georgetown County, South Carolina. *South Carolina Antiquities* 22(1-2):27–46.

Minar, Jill
2001 Motor Skills and the Learning Process: The Conservation of Cordage Final Twist Direction in Communities of Practice. *Journal of Anthropological Research* 57(4):381–405.

Neff, Hector
1992 Ceramics and Evolution. In *Archaeological Method and Theory,* Vol. 4, edited by M. B. Schiffer, pp. 141–193. University of Arizona Press, Tucson.
1993 Theory, Sampling, and Analytical Techniques in the Archaeological Study of Prehistoric Ceramics. *American Antiquity* 58(1):23–44.

Neff, Hector, Ronald L. Bishop, and Edward V. Sayre
1989 More Observations on the Problem of Tempering in Compositional Studies of Archaeological Ceramics. *Journal of Archaeological Science* 16:57–69.

Neiman, F.
1995 Stylistic Variation in Evolutionary Perspective: Inferences from Decorative Diversity and Interassemblage Distance in Illinois Woodland Ceramic Assemblages. *American Antiquity* 60(1):7–36.

North Carolina Geological Survey
1988 *Preliminary Explanatory Text for the 1985 Geologic Map of North Carolina.* Contractual Report 88-1. North Carolina Geological Survey, Raleigh.

O'Brien, Michael J., and G. L. Fox
1994 Assemblage Similarities and Dissimilarities. In *Cat Monsters and Head Pots: The Archaeology of Missouri's Pemiscot Bayou,* edited by M. J. O'Brien, pp. 61–93. University of Missouri Press, Columbia.

O'Brien, Michael J., and Thomas D. Holland
1990 Variation, Selection, and the Archaeological Record. In *Archaeological Method and Theory,* Vol. 2, edited by M. B. Schiffer, pp. 31–80. Academic Press, New York.
1992 The Role of Adaptation in Archaeological Explanation. *American Antiquity* 57(1):36–59.
1995a The Nature and Premise of a Selection-Based Archaeology. In *Evolutionary Archaeology: Methodological Issues,* edited by P. A. Teltser, pp. 149–200. University of Arizona Press, Tucson.
1995b Behavioral Archaeology and the Extended Phenotype. In, *Expanding Archaeology,* edited by J. M. Skibo, W. H. Walker, and A. E. Nielsen, pp. 143–161. University of Utah Press, Salt Lake City.

O'Brien, Michael J., Thomas D. Holland, Robert J. Hoard, and Gregory L. Fox
1994 Evolutionary Implications of Design and Performance Characteristics of Prehistoric Pottery. *Journal of Archaeological Method and Theory* 1(3):259–304.

Opperman, Anthony F.
1980 A Study of the Prehistoric Ceramics from Maycocks Point, Prince George County, Virginia. Unpublished Bachelor's thesis, Department of Anthropology, College of William and Mary, Williamsburg, Virginia.

Ortman, Scott G.
2000 Conceptual Metaphor in the Archaeological Record: Methods and an Example from the American Southwest. *American Antiquity* 65(4):613–645.

O'Steen, Lisa D.
1994 *The Bear Creek Site (38FA204/205): PaleoIndian and Archaic Occupation in the Lower Piedmont of South Carolina.* Southeastern Archaeological Consultants, Inc., Athens, Georgia. Submitted to the Kennecott-Ridgeway Mining Company, Ridgeway, South Carolina.

Painter, Floyd
1977 The Beaker Makers of Currituck Sound. *Archaeology of Eastern North America* 5:43–61.

Peabody, Charles
1910 The Exploration of Mounds in North Carolina. *American Anthropologist* 12(3): 425–433.

Petersen, James B.
1996 Fiber Industries from Northern New England: Ethnicity and Technological Traditions during the Woodland Period. In *A Most Indispensable Art: Native Fiber Industries from Eastern North America,* edited by J. B. Petersen, pp. 100–119. University of Tennessee Press, Knoxville.
1999 Prehistoric Textile Remnants and Other Evidence of Native Fiber Industries from the Whitehurst Freeway Project, Washington, D.C. Paper presented at the 64th Annual Meeting of the Society for American Archaeology, Chicago.

Petersen, James B., and Nathan D. Hamilton
1984 Early Woodland Ceramic and Perishable Fiber Industries from the Northeast: A Summary and Interpretation. *Annals of Carnegie Museum, Carnegie Museum of Natural History* 53(14):413–445.

Pfaffenberger, Bryan
1992 Social Anthropology of Technology. *Annual Review of Anthropology* 21:491–516.

Phelps, David S.
1968 Thom's Creek Ceramics in the Central Savannah River Locality. *The Florida Anthropologist* 21(1):17–30.
1975 *Test Excavation of the Parker Site (31ED29) at Speed, Edgecombe County, North Carolina.* Archaeology Laboratory, East Carolina University, Greenville, North Carolina.
1976 *An Archaeological Survey of First Flight Village, Kill Devil Hills, North Carolina.* Archaeological Impact Studies No. 13. Archaeology Laboratory, East Carolina University, Greenville, North Carolina.
1981a *The Archaeology of Colington Island.* Archaeological Research Report No. 3. Archaeology Laboratory, Department of Sociology and Anthropology, East Carolina University, Greenville, North Carolina.

1981b Test Excavation of the Parker Site (31ED29) at Speed, Edgecombe County, North Carolina. In *Archaeological Surveys of Four Watersheds in the North Carolina Coastal Plain,* edited by D. S. Phelps, pp. 57–105. North Carolina Archaeological Council Publication 16, North Carolina Archaeological Council and the Archaeology Branch, Division of Archives and History, North Carolina Department of Cultural Resources, Raleigh.

1981c Archaeological Survey of the Stoney Creek Watershed, Wayne County, North Carolina. In *Archaeological Surveys of Four Watersheds in the North Carolina Coastal Plain,* edited by D. S. Phelps, pp. 107–138. North Carolina Archaeological Council Publication 16, North Carolina Archaeological Council and the Archaeology Branch, Division of Archives and History, North Carolina Department of Cultural Resources, Raleigh.

1983 Archaeology of the North Carolina Coast and Coastal Plain: Problems and Hypotheses. In *The Prehistory of North Carolina: An Archaeological Symposium,* edited by M. A. Mathis and J. J. Crow, pp. 1–51. Division of Archives and History, North Carolina Department of Cultural Resources, Raleigh.

Phelps, David S., and Charles L. Heath

1998 Cashie Series Ceramics from the Interior Coastal Plain of North Carolina. Paper presented at the 55th Annual Meeting of the Southeastern Archaeological Conference, Greenville, South Carolina.

Poplin, Eric C., Christopher T. Espenshade, and David C. Jones

1993 *Archaeological Investigations at the Buck Hall Site (38CH644), Francis Marion National Forest, South Carolina.* Brockington and Associates, Inc., Atlanta and Charleston, South Carolina. Submitted to the USDA Forest Service, Francis Marion National Forest, McClellandville, South Carolina, Contract No. 53-4670-1-27.

Potter, Stephen R.

1982 An Analysis of Chicacoan Settlement Patterns. Unpublished Ph.D. dissertation, Department of Anthropology, University of North Carolina, Chapel Hill.

1993 *Commoners, Tribute, and Chiefs: The Development of Algonquian Culture in the Potomac Valley.* University of Virginia Press, Charlottesville.

Prescott, J. R., D. J. Huntley, and J. T. Hutton

1993 Estimation of Equivalent Dose in Thermoluminescence Dating: The Australian Slide Method. *Ancient TL* 11:1–5.

Prescott, J. R., and J. T. Hutton

1988 Cosmic Ray and Gamma Ray Dosimetry for TL and ESR. *Nuclear Tracks and Radiation Measurements* 14:223–227.

Prezzano, Susan C.

1985 Physical Properties of Ceramic Sherds from Five Middle and Late Woodland Stage Components in the Susquehanna Drainage. Unpublished Master's thesis, Department of Anthropology, State University of New York, Binghamton.

Pullins, Stevan C., James B. Stoltman, Veronica L. Deitrick, Denis B. Blanton, and Anna L. Gray

1996 *Ceramic Technology, Early Woodland Settlement, and Enfield Plantation Phase III*

Archaeological Data Recovery for Mitigation of Effects to Site 44KW81 Associated with the Route 629 Bridge Replacement, King William County, Virginia. Technical Report Series No. 21. William and Mary Center for Archaeological Research, Department of Anthropology, College of William and Mary, Williamsburg, Virginia.

Reid, William H., and Kay Simpson

1996 *Phase II Investigation of Nine Prehistoric Sites and Phase I Survey of the P-028 Range Area, Greater Sandy Run Acquisition Area, Marine Corps Base, Camp Lejeune, Onslow County, North Carolina.* The Cultural Resources Group, Louis Berger and Associates, Inc., Richmond, Virginia. Submitted to the Marine Corps Base, Camp Lejeune, Contract No. DACW 54-93-D-0003. Copies available from the Department of Historic Resources, Richmond, Virginia.

Rice, Prudence M.

1987 *Pottery Analysis: A Sourcebook.* University of Chicago Press, Chicago.

Rye, Owen S.

1976 Keeping Your Temper Under Control. *Archaeology and Physical Anthropology in Oceania* 11(2).

1981 *Pottery Technology: Principles and Reconstruction.* Taraxacum, Washington, D.C.

Sackett, James R.

1973 Style, Function, and Artifact Variability in Paleolithic Assemblages. In *The Explanation of Culture Change,* edited by C. Renfrew, pp. 317–325. Duckworth, London.

1977 The Meaning of Style in Archaeology: A General Model. *American Antiquity* 42:369–380.

1982 Approaches to Style in Lithic Technology. *Journal of Anthropological Archaeology* 1:59–112.

1985a Style, Ethnicity and Stone Tools. In *Status, Structure, and Stratification: Current Archaeological Reconstructions,* edited by M. Thompson, M. T. Garcia, and F. J. Kense, pp. 277–282. Proceedings of the 16th Annual Chacmool Conference, University of Calgary, Calgary, Alberta, Canada.

1985b Style and Ethnicity in the Kalahari: A Reply to Wiessner. *American Antiquity* 50:154–159.

1990 Style and Ethnicity in Archaeology: The Case for Isochrestism. In *The Uses of Style in Archaeology,* edited by M. Conkey and C. Hastorf, pp. 32–43. Cambridge University Press, Cambridge.

Sampson, C. Garth

1988 *Stylistic Boundaries among Mobile Hunter-Foragers.* Smithsonian Institution Press, Washington, D.C.

Sampson, E. H., S. J. Fleming, and W. Bray

1972 Thermoluminescent Dating of Colombian Pottery in the Yotoco Style. *Archaeometry* 14(1):119–126.

Sanborn, Erica E., and Lawrence E. Abbott Jr.

1999 Early Ceramic Traditions on the Southern Coastal Plain of North Carolina: Radiocarbon Data from 31CCB114. *North Carolina Archaeology* 48:3–17.

Sassaman, Kenneth E.
1993 *Early Pottery in the Southeast.* The University of Alabama Press, Tuscaloosa.

Sassaman, Kenneth E., and Wictoria Rudolphi
2001 Communities of Practice in the Early Pottery Traditions of the American Southeast. *Journal of Anthropological Research* 57(4):407–425.

Schiffer, Michael B.
1990 The Influence of Surface Treatment on Heating Effectiveness of Ceramic Vessels. *Journal of Archaeological Science* 17(4):373–381.
1999 *The Material Life of Human Beings: Artifacts, Behavior, and Communication.* Routledge, London.

Schiffer, Michael B., and James M. Skibo
1987 Theory and Experiment in the Study of Technological Change. *Current Anthropology* 28(5):595–622.

Schiffer, Michael B., James M. Skibo, Tamara C. Boelke, Mark A. Neupert, and Meredith Aronson
1994 New Perspectives on Experimental Archaeology: Surface Treatments and Thermal Response of the Clay Cooking Pot. *American Antiquity* 59:197–217.

Shepard, Anna O.
1956 *Ceramics for the Archaeologist.* Carnegie Institution of Washington, Washington, D.C.

Shumate, Scott M., and Patti Evans-Shumate
2000 *Archaeological Investigations at Long Point (31JN2) and Haywood Landing (31JN3) on the Croatan National Forest, Jones County, North Carolina.* Appalachian State University Laboratories of Archaeological Science and Blue Ridge Cultural Resources, Boone, North Carolina. Submitted to National Forest Service, National Forests in North Carolina, Asheville.

Sinopoli, Carla M.
1991 *Approaches to Archaeological Ceramics.* Plenum Press, New York.

Skibo, James M., and Michael B. Schiffer
1995 The Clay Cooking Pot: An Exploration of Women's Technology. In *Expanding Archaeology,* edited by J. M. Skibo, W. H. Walker, and A. E. Nielsen, pp. 80–91. University of Utah Press, Salt Lake City.

Skibo, James M., Michael B. Schiffer, and Kenneth C. Reid
1989 Organic-Tempered Pottery: An Experimental Study. *American Antiquity* 54:122–146.

Smith, Gerald P.
1971 Protohistoric Sociopolitical Organization of the Nottoway in the Chesapeake Bay-Carolina Sounds Region. Unpublished Ph.D. dissertation, Department of Anthropology, University of Missouri, Columbia.

South, Stanley A.
1960 An Archaeological Survey of Southeastern Coastal North Carolina. Ms. on file, North Carolina Office of State Archaeology, Raleigh.
1966 Exploratory Excavation of the McFayden Mound, Brunswick County, N.C. *Southern Indian Studies* 18:59–61.

1976 An Archaeological Survey of Southeastern Coastal North Carolina. *The Institute of Archaeology and Anthropology Notebook,* Vol. 8. The Institute of Archaeology and Anthropology, University of South Carolina, Columbia.

Steen, Carl

2000 *Archaeological Investigations at Heron Pond/Diamond Back Development, Horry County, South Carolina.* Diachronic Research Foundation, Columbia, South Carolina. Submitted to the State Historical Preservation Office, Columbia, South Carolina.

Stephenson, Robert L., Alice L. L. Ferguson, and H. G. Ferguson

1963 *The Accokeek Creek Site: A Middle Atlantic Seaboard Culture Sequence.* Anthropological Papers, No. 20. Museum of Anthropology, University of Michigan, Ann Arbor.

Steponaitis, Vincas P.

1983 *Ceramics, Chronology, and Community Patterns: An Archaeological Study at Moundville.* Academic Press, New York.

1984 Technological Studies of Prehistoric Pottery from Alabama: Physical Properties and Vessel Function. In *The Many Dimensions of Pottery: Ceramics in Archaeology and Anthropology,* edited by S. E. Van der Leeuw and A. C. Pritchard, pp. 81–122. CINGULA 7. Institute for Pre- and Proto-history, University of Amsterdam, Amsterdam, The Netherlands.

Stoltman, James B.

1972 The Late Archaic in the Savannah River Region. In *Fiber-Tempered Pottery in Southeastern United States and Northern Columbia: Its Origins, Context and Significance,* edited by R. P. Bullen and J. B. Stoltman, pp. 37–62. Florida Anthropological Society Publications 6, Tallahassee.

1974 *Groton Plantation: An Archaeological Study of a South Carolina Locality.* Monographs No. 1. Peabody Museum of Archaeology and Ethnography, Harvard University, Cambridge, Massachusetts.

Stuiver, Minze, and Thomas F. Braziunas

1993 Modeling Atmospheric ^{14}C Influences and ^{14}C Ages of Marin Samples to 10,000 BC. *Radiocarbon* 35(1):137–189.

Stuiver, Minze, and Paula J. Reimer

1993 Extended ^{14}C Database and Revised CALIB Radiocarbon Calibration Program. *Radiocarbon* 35:215–230.

Teltser, Patrice A.

1995 The Methodological Challenge of Evolutionary Theory in Archaeology. In *Evolutionary Archaeology: Methodological Issues,* edited by P. A. Teltser, pp. 51–68. University of Arizona Press, Tucson.

Terrell, William, Kenneth W. Robinson, Kristin Hill, and J. Ned Woodall

2000 *Archaeological Data Recovery: Testing Phase Investigations at Site 31NH707, Wilmington Bypass, New Hanover County, North Carolina.* Wake Forest Archaeological Laboratories, Wake Forest University, Winston Salem, North Carolina. Submitted to Project Development and Environmental Analysis Branch, Division of Highways, North Carolina Department of Transportation, Raleigh, TIP No. R-2633-C, Federal-Aid No. STPNHF-17[1].

Tilley, Christopher Y.

1999 *Metaphor and Material Culture.* Blackwell, London.

Trinkley, Michael B.

1980 Investigation of the Woodland Period along the South Carolina Coast. Unpublished Ph.D. dissertation, Department of Anthropology, University of North Carolina, Chapel Hill.

1989 An Archaeological Overview of the South Carolina Woodland Period: It's the Same Old Riddle. In *Studies in South Carolina Archaeology: Essays in Honor of Robert L. Stephenson,* edited by A. C. Goodyear III and G. T. Hanson, pp. 73–90. Anthropological Studies 9. Occasional Papers of the South Carolina Institute of Archaeology and Anthropology, University of South Carolina, Columbia.

1990 *An Archaeological Context for the South Carolina Woodland Period.* Research Series 22. Chicora Foundation, Inc. Submitted to the South Carolina Department of Archives and History, Columbia.

Ward, H. Trawick, and R. P. Stephen Davis

1999 *A Time before History: The Archaeology of North Carolina.* University of North Carolina Press, Chapel Hill.

Ward, H. Trawick, and Jack H. Wilson Jr.

1980 Archaeological Investigations at the Cold Morning Site. *Southern Indian Studies* 32:5–40.

Waring, Antonio J., Jr., and Preston Holder

1968 The Deptford Ceramic Complex. In *The Waring Papers: The Collected Works of Antonio J. Waring, Jr.,* edited by S. Williams, pp. 135–151. Papers of the Peabody Museum of Archaeology and Ethnology, 58. Harvard University, Cambridge, Massachusetts.

Waselkov, Gregory A.

1982 Shellfish Gathering and Shell Midden Archaeology. Unpublished Ph.D. dissertation, Department of Anthropology, University of North Carolina, Chapel Hill.

Welsch, Robert L., and John Edward Terrell

1998 Material Culture, Social Fields, and Social Boundaries on the Sepik Coast of New Guinea. In *The Archaeology of Social Boundaries,* edited by M. T. Stark, pp. 50–77. Smithsonian Institution Press, Washington, D.C.

Wetmore, Ruth Y.

1978 Report on Excavations at the Buie Mound, Robeson County, North Carolina. In *The Institute of Archaeology and Anthropology Notebook,* vol. 10, edited by R. L. Stephenson and K. Pinson, pp. 30–71. The Institute of Archaeology and Anthropology, University of South Carolina, Columbia.

Whallon, Robert

1972 A New Approach to Pottery Typology. *American Antiquity* 37(1):13–33.

Whitbread, I. K.

1986 The Characterization of Argillaceous Inclusions in Ceramic Thin Sections. *Archaeometry* 28:79–88.

1989 A Proposal for the Systematic Description of Thin Sections towards the Study of Ancient Ceramic Technology. In *Archaeometry. Proceedings of the 25th Inter national Symposium,* edited by Y. Maniatis, pp. 127–138. Elsevier, Amsterdam, The Netherlands.

Whittle, E. H., and J. M. Arnaud

1975 Thermoluminescent Dating of Neolithic and Chalcolithic Pottery from Sites in Central Portugal. *Archaeometry* 17(1):5–24.

Wiessner, Polly

1983 Style and Social Information in Kalahari San Projectile Points. *American Antiquity* 48:253–276.

1984 Reconsidering the Behavioral Basis for Style: A Case Study among the Kalahari San. *Journal of Anthropological Archaeology* 3:190–234.

1985 Style or Isochrestic Variation? A Reply to Sackett. *American Antiquity* 50:160–166.

1989 Style and Changing Relations between the Individual and Society. In *The Meaning of Things: Material Culture and Symbolic Expression,* edited by I. Hodder, pp. 56–63. Unwin Hyman, London.

Wilde-Ramsing, Mark

1978 A Report on the New Hanover County Archaeological Survey: A C.E.T.A. Project. Ms. on file, North Carolina Office of State Archaeology, Raleigh.

Wobst, H. Martin

1977 Stylistic Behavior and Information Exchange. In *For the Director: Research Essays in Honor of James B. Griffin,* edited by C. Clelend, pp. 317–342. Anthropological Papers, No. 61. Museum of Anthropology, University of Michigan, Ann Arbor.

Wright, Henry T.

1973 *Archaeological Sequences in the Middle Chesapeake Region of Maryland.* Johns Hopkins University Press, Baltimore, Maryland.

Yarnell, Richard A.

1993 The Importance of Native Crops during the Late Archaic and Woodland Periods. In *Foraging and Farming in the Eastern Woodlands,* edited by C. M. Scarry, pp. 13–26. University Press of Florida, Gainesville.

Yarnell, Richard A., and M. Jean Black

1985 Temporal Trends Indicated by a Survey of Archaic and Woodland Plant Food Remains from Southeastern North America. *Southeastern Archaeology* 4:93–106.

Zimmerman, D. W., and J. Huxtable

1969 Recent Applications and Developments in Thermoluminescent Dating. *Archaeometry* 11:105–108.

1971 Thermoluminescent Dating of Upper Palaeolithic Fired Clay from Dolni Vestonice. *Archaeometry* 13:53–57.

Index